nil me poenitet

DUGDALL

ODNB

ex libris

Jan Broadway Ph. D

Early Modern Literature in History

General Editors: **Cedric C. Brown**, Professor of English and Dean of the Faculty of Arts and Humanities, University of Reading; **Andrew Hadfield**, Professor of English, University of Sussex, Brighton

Advisory Board: **Donna Hamilton**, University of Maryland; **Jean Howard**, University of Columbia; **John Kerrigan**, University of Cambridge; **Richard McCoy**, CUNY; **Sharon Achinstein**, University of Oxford

Within the period 1520–1740 this series discusses many kinds of writing, both within and outside the established canon. The volumes may employ different theoretical perspectives, but they share a historical awareness and an interest in seeing their texts in lively negotiation with their own and successive cultures.

Titles include:

John M. Adrian
LOCAL NEGOTIATIONS OF ENGLISH NATIONHOOD, 1570–1680

Robyn Adams and Rosanna Cox
DIPLOMACY AND EARLY MODERN CULTURE

Andrea Brady
ENGLISH FUNERARY ELEGY IN THE SEVENTEENTH CENTURY
Laws in Mourning

Jocelyn Catty
WRITING RAPE, WRITING WOMEN IN EARLY MODERN ENGLAND
Unbridled Speech

Dermot Cavanagh
LANGUAGE AND POLITICS IN THE SIXTEENTH-CENTURY HISTORY PLAY

Patrick Cheney
MARLOWE'S REPUBLICAN AUTHORSHIP
Lucan, Liberty, and the Sublime

David Coleman
DRAMA AND THE SACRAMENTS IN SIXTEENTH-CENTURY ENGLAND
Indelible Characters

Katharine A. Craik
READING SENSATIONS IN EARLY MODERN ENGLAND

James Daybell (*editor*)
EARLY MODERN WOMEN'S LETTER-WRITING, 1450–1700

James Daybell and Peter Hinds (*editors*)
MATERIAL READINGS OF EARLY MODERN CULTURE
Texts and Social Practices, 1580–1730

Matthew Dimmock and Andrew Hadfield (*editors*)
THE RELIGIONS OF THE BOOK
Christian Perceptions, 1400–1660

Tobias Döring
PERFORMANCES OF MOURNING IN SHAKESPEAREAN THEATRE AND EARLY MODERN CULTURE

Sarah M. Dunnigan
EROS AND POETRY AT THE COURTS OF MARY QUEEN OF SCOTS AND JAMES VI

Mary Floyd-Wilson and Garrett A. Sullivan Jr. (*editors*)
ENVIRONMENT AND EMBODIMENT IN EARLY MODERN ENGLAND

Kenneth J. E. Graham and Philip D. Collington (*editors*)
SHAKESPEARE AND RELIGIOUS CHANGE

Teresa Grant and Barbara Ravelhofer
ENGLISH HISTORICAL DRAMA, 1500–1660
Forms Outside the Canon

Andrew Hadfield
SHAKESPEARE, SPENSER AND THE MATTER OF BRITAIN

William M. Hamlin
TRAGEDY AND SCEPTICISM IN SHAKESPEARE'S ENGLAND

Johanna Harris and Elizabeth Scott-Baumann (*editors*)
THE INTELLECTUAL CULTURE OF PURITAN WOMEN, 1558–1680

Constance Jordan and Karen Cunningham (*editors*)
THE LAW IN SHAKESPEARE

Claire Jowitt (*editor*)
PIRATES? THE POLITICS OF PLUNDER, 1550–1650

Gregory Kneidel
RETHINKING THE TURN TO RELIGION IN EARLY MODERN ENGLISH LITERATURE

Edel Lamb
PERFORMING CHILDHOOD IN THE EARLY MODERN THEATRE
The Children's Playing Companies (1599–1613)

Jean-Christopher Mayer
SHAKESPEARE'S HYBRID FAITH
History, Religion and the Stage

Scott L.Newstok
QUOTING DEATH IN EARLY MODERN ENGLAND
The Poetics of Epitaphs Beyond the Tomb

Jane Pettegree
FOREIGN AND NATIVE ON THE ENGLISH STAGE, 1588–1611
Metaphor and National Identity

Jennifer Richards (*editor*)
EARLY MODERN CIVIL DISCOURSES

Marion Wynne-Davies
WOMEN WRITERS AND FAMILIAL DISCOURSE IN THE ENGLISH RENAISSANCE
Relative Values

The series Early Modern Literature in History is published in
association with the Renaissance
Texts Research Centre at the University of Reading.

Early Modern Literature in History
Series Standing Order ISBN 978–0–333–71472–0 (Hardback)
978–0–333–80321–9 (Paperback)
(outside North America only)

You can receive future titles in this series as they are published by placing a standing order. Please contact your bookseller or, in case of difficulty, write to us at the address below with your name and address, the title of the series and the ISBN quoted above.

Customer Services Department, Macmillan Distribution Ltd, Houndmills, Basingstoke, Hampshire RG21 6XS, England

Local Negotiations of English Nationhood, 1570–1680

John M. Adrian

First published 2011 by
PALGRAVE MACMILLAN

Palgrave Macmillan in the UK is an imprint of Macmillan Publishers Limited,
registered in England, company number 785998, of Houndmills, Basingstoke,
Hampshire RG21 6XS.

Palgrave Macmillan in the US is a division of St Martin's Press LLC,
175 Fifth Avenue, New York, NY 10010.

Palgrave Macmillan is the global academic imprint of the above companies
and has companies and representatives throughout the world.

Palgrave® and Macmillan® are registered trademarks in the United States,
the United Kingdom, Europe and other countries.

ISBN 978–0–230–27771–7   hardback

This book is printed on paper suitable for recycling and made from fully
managed and sustained forest sources. Logging, pulping and manufacturing
processes are expected to conform to the environmental regulations of the
country of origin.

A catalogue record for this book is available from the British Library.

Library of Congress Cataloging-in-Publication Data

Adrian, John M., 1975–
    Local negotiations of english nationhood, 1570–1680/ John M. Adrian.
        p. cm.
    Includes index.
        ISBN 978–0–230–27771–7 (hardback)
1. English prose literature—Early modern, 1500–1700—History and
    criticism.   2. Regionalism in literature.   3. Local history in literature.
    4. National characteristics, English, in literature.   5. Literature and
    society—England—History—16th century.   6. Literature and
    society—England—History—17th century.   I. Title.
PR767.A37 2011
820.9'35841—dc22   2011004878

10   9   8   7   6   5   4   3   2   1
20 19 18 17 16 15 14 13 12 11

Printed and bound in the United States of America

For Wendy

Contents

List of Illustrations and Maps

Acknowledgments

For a book that revolves around the importance of local places, it seems only natural to proceed with my acknowledgments via the locations that had a role in its making. The early work for this book occurred during my graduate school years in Chapel Hill, North Carolina. There I was privileged to work with a dissertation committee – Jessica Wolfe, Reid Barbour, Mary Floyd-Wilson, Ritchie Kendall, and Barbara Harris – that both engaged my ideas and asked the difficult questions needed to refine them. I am particularly grateful to Jessica Wolfe and Reid Barbour for their continued feedback and advice. I would also like to thank Chris Hill and Alice Espinosa for reading and commenting on early versions of my work. The Department of English provided an atmosphere of scholarly collaboration and funding for conference travel, while the Graduate School supported me with an Off-Campus Dissertation Award that allowed for a semester of archival work in England. Finally, the helpful staff at the Walter Royal Davis Library – especially Glenn Hayslett and Joe Mitchem – offered resource assistance at every turn.

For the past five years, I have called the University of Virginia's College at Wise home. Here, my work has benefited from a generous administration, thoughtful colleagues, and enthusiastic students. Gil Blackburn, Amelia Harris, and the Faculty Development Committee have provided conference and research travel grants, a summer stipend, and a semester's leave in the fall of 2009 that was crucial in completing the book manuscript. My department chair, Ken Tiller, has offered encouragement, advice, and practical assistance in carving out time for research amidst a busy teaching schedule. Tom Goyens, Chris Scalia, Mark Clark, and Don Leech have all read sections of the manuscript and provided insightful comments. Finally, the congenial staff at the John Cook Wyllie Library – especially Robin Benke, Bill Statzer, Kris Pottenger, and Kim Marshall – have tracked down resources (often from beyond Wise) and provided a quiet but friendly space in which to complete this book.

Local Negotiations has also been shaped by its contact with places further afield. A Folger Institute seminar, 'Genealogies of Britishness,' helped broaden my perspective on the complexities of early modern nationhood. The patient and helpful staffs at the Folger Shakespeare Library, Norfolk Record Office, Bodleian Library, British Library, and

Bristol Record Office have all supported the research phase of this book. I would also like to thank my editors at Palgrave Macmillan: Paula Kennedy for her initial interest in the manuscript, Catherine Mitchell for her tireless fielding of my many queries, Andrew Hadfield and Cedric Brown for their insightful suggestions for revision, and Jo North for her careful reading of the manuscript at the copy-editing stage. An earlier version of Chapter 2 appeared in *English Literary Renaissance* 36:3 (Autumn 2006), and of Chapter 4 in *The Seventeenth Century* 24:1 (Spring 2009), and I am grateful to *English Literary Renaissance* and Manchester University Press, respectively, for permission to reproduce this material.

Finally, my wife Wendy has filled all of these places with her enthusiasm, encouragement, and love. She has accompanied me on research trips, listened to half-baked ideas, jotted down notes, and shared in the inevitable highs and lows that come with a project of this scope. She is the *genius loci* of this text.

Introduction

It is not surprising that many early copies of William Camden's *Britannia* (1586) contain handwritten annotations.[1] After all, the text features hundreds of densely packed place names and antiquities. What *is* surprising is the uneven distribution of these notes. In one first edition copy, an anonymous early modern reader's marginal jottings are strictly confined to the Midlands section.[2] In a volume published fourteen years later, a vigilant hand has written notes in the chapters on Leicestershire, Lincolnshire, and Rutlandshire to ensure that obliquely mentioned Nottinghamshire places are not wrongly ascribed to these other counties.[3] A 1610 *Britannia* contains manuscript notes in several hands.[4] One reader contributes copious marginalia, but only for the adjoining counties of Essex and Hertfordshire. The flowery brown calligraphy seems especially concerned with keeping up with the prominent gentry families of the neighborhood. Meanwhile, a scratchy black script appears for only a ten-page stretch in the section on the West Riding of Yorkshire. This reader turned writer provides a running list of the prominent place names mentioned in the text. A third hand, made orange by age, seems to have been particularly engaged by Camden's description of a minor river in Surrey: 'Not farre from hence the cleere riveret Wandle in Latin Vandalis, so full of the best trouts, issueth forth from his head . . . where by a tuft of trees upon an hil-top there are to be seene manifest signes of a pretty towne, and diverse wels built of flint stone' (299). In the adjacent margin, the reader has drawn a diminutive hand with index finger extended towards the passage, as if to quaintly underscore its importance. Then, on the fold-out map of Surrey, tucked neatly into the text five pages earlier, the same orange ink has been employed to write the label 'Wandle flu' next to the appropriate river, once at its source and then again a few inches away along the main channel. This gesture is made all the more extraordinary because Camden has not labeled any of the rivers on the map – not even the Thames. Clearly, the River Wandle meant something to this reader. Maybe he was from the pretty town on the lush hilltop at the source of the Wandle, or maybe he had once enjoyed a memorable day of trout fishing in this same 'cleere riveret.' Whatever the cause, the surviving marginalia testifies to the importance of this local place for this anonymous person.

The late sixteenth century has been frequently described as a time of burgeoning nationhood. Fueled by expansive texts like Camden's *Britannia*, English men and women were beginning to imagine and take pride in the nation. But even if such a lofty goal was Camden's intention, it is hard to say what the *Britannia's* actual effect was. The evidence above suggests that at least some people read Camden 'locally.' That is, they read the *Britannia* for what it had to say about their own particular region, county, or neighborhood rather than for the nationalistic picture that it provided. At times, they even augmented Camden's text (and maps) by adding emphasis to the things that mattered to them most. These local responses are not incompatible with nationhood, but they do remind us of the continued importance of the local sphere in the early modern period.

It was the Victorians who first associated the Tudor age with the birth of the nation.[5] They saw the formation of the Protestant church, the colonization of the New World, the defeat of the Spanish Armada, and the forceful personalities of monarchs like Henry VIII and Elizabeth I as catalysts for the formation of the English nation. In our own day, this perception has persisted. Richard Helgerson's seminal *Forms of Nationhood: The Elizabethan Writing of England* (1992) argued that the generation of English writers working in the late sixteenth century 'engendered . . . a national cultural formation.'[6] Subsequent literary critics have been eager to demonstrate how the new English nation was 'imagined' and constructed by writers like Sidney, Spenser, Drayton, Camden, Hakluyt, Coke, Shakespeare, and Jonson.[7] Rather than focusing on particular writers, other scholars have sought to isolate and examine particular factors that promoted the emergence of nationhood, like maps, historiography, biblical rhetoric, language standardization, the Protestant calendar, and even the wool cloth industry.[8] More recently, scholars have begun to further complicate constructions of nationhood by looking at how it was affected by the growth of empire and the question of Britishness.[9]

While insightful, these studies have tended to overlook the importance of local identity in the period, suggesting that it was either swept away by or absorbed into the forces of nationhood.[10] This book will explore the vitality of early modern local consciousness. Even in an age of emerging nationhood, English men and women were still profoundly influenced by – and even drew their primary identity from – the parish, the town, and the county. This book examines how early modern writers invoke local places, traditions, and ways of thinking to respond to the larger political, religious, and cultural changes of the sixteenth and seventeenth centuries. Far from functioning merely as a retreat from nationhood, local consciousness emerges as a dynamic site of negotiation where broader changes are interrogated, modified, and adapted to the needs of smaller communities. The first chapter will discuss the historical basis of local identity and describe the ways in which it was transformed in the second half of the sixteenth century. Each of the succeeding five chapters then focuses on a specific author and historical moment, and explores how local habits of thought are invoked to respond to a particular national initiative (political centralization, religious uniformity, court culture, civil war, and empire). Together, these chapters illustrate both the pervasiveness of local discourse and the range of possible responses to nationhood that it engendered.

1
Local Consciousness in Renaissance England

In the past fifty years, the main proponents of early modern local identity have been, not surprisingly, local historians. In following H. P. R. Finberg's famous charge to portray the 'origin, growth, decline, and fall of a local community,' local historians have produced numerous studies of particular villages, parishes, and hundreds.[1] These studies have been invaluable in revealing what provincial life was like in a variety of places. While some historians have been content to focus solely on a few square miles, others – like Eamon Duffy and David Underdown – have endeavored to show how national events like the Reformation and Civil War played out in particular local communities.[2] More recently, scholars have begun to rethink some of the basic terminology – like 'identity' and 'community' – on which Local Studies has been built. One point of emphasis has been to attempt to identify the boundaries of the local community. Suggestions range from the relatively large (county) to the medium-sized (hundred) to the small (parish or village).[3] Others have eschewed 'artificial' administrative units in favor of more natural divisions like landscape or agricultural regions.[4] Christopher Lewis, however, has argued that the single-community approach ignores the complexity of individual identity, which is actually best imagined as a series of 'concentric circles' that radiate outward.[5] Such a formulation would seem to better allow for the multiple identities that we find in early modern people. For instance, we might expect Elizabeth's chief advisor, of all people, to have a decidedly national outlook. Yet in 1584 we find Lord Burghley specifically requesting the antiquarian William Lambarde to write a description of Lincoln, the most prominent city in Burghley's native region.[6] This does not suggest that Burghley secretly discounted the nation, but rather, as Charles Phythian-Adams puts it: 'A sense of belonging more or less simultaneously to a variety of societal levels does not diminish the significance of any one of them.'[7] Such formulations help explain how local identity could remain important even in era of increasing nationhood. But why *did* it? Why was local identity – that innermost of concentric circles – so tenacious? We will now turn to two historical factors that were especially important in creating and sustaining local identity in England: diversity and insularity.

Diversity and insularity

'England is . . . a varied country, one of the most varied in the world in relation to its size,' says Alan Everitt.[8] What is true today was even more apparent in the sixteenth century. One factor that contributed to this diversity was the variation in local topography. First, there was the traditional distinction between the cool, wet Highland Zone and the warmer and drier Lowland Zone. These zones formed a general division between the north and west of England and the south and east, and affected landscape features as diverse as climate, soil, flora and fauna, and economic activities. There were also a variety of distinct landscapes within those zones – including forest, vale, downland, heath, moor, fenland, marsh, plains, hills, sandy beaches, and coastal cliffs – which occurred in complex patterns and in close proximity to one another. These diverse landscapes did more than just create diverse scenery. Historians have posited a number of correlations between landscape and the settlement patterns and types of communities to which they gave rise. Joan Thirsk has argued that the Highland/Lowland division helped create two distinct types of farming communities: 'open pasture' and 'mixed farming.'[9] These communities also exhibit markedly different settlement patterns: 'Communities in "fielden" [mixed farming] areas were usually physically-compact villages with only a few outlying farms; whereas settlements in "forest-pasture" [open farming] regions were in hamlets and farms scattered throughout large parishes.'[10] Alan Everitt moves beyond this basic Highland/Lowland dichotomy to argue for a complex range of landscape/settlement relationships. In *Landscape and Community in England*, he explores the effects of no fewer than eight types of English landscape – field, forest, fell, fen, marsh, heath, down, and wald – on the formation of local communities.[11] Nevertheless, both Coward and Everitt agree that one of the distinguishing features of these different communities was their close proximity to one another: 'contrasting communities . . . were not always separated by long distances. Indeed, they could be next door to one another and this proved to be the case in many different counties in all parts of the country.'[12]

Along with topography, another natural factor in the diversity of early modern England was geology. According to Paul Coones and John Patten, 'It would be difficult to find a region of the globe of comparable extent that presents such a bewildering variety of rocks of different types and ages as does Britain. Whereas one may travel for hundreds of miles in the continental heartland of Eurasia without observing a fundamental change in geology or structure, it is sometimes difficult to progress more than a few hundred yards, or at most a few miles, in Britain without encountering a new rock type.'[13] Chalk, granite, limestone, flint, iron, lead, clay, marl, greensand, coal, and slate are but a few of the rocks that dramatically diversify the physical makeup of England. Like landscape variety, geological diversity could also profoundly affect local communities. Natural deposits of tin in Cornwall, iron in Sussex, coal in Nottinghamshire, lead in Derbyshire, and zinc in Somerset all gave rise to specialized local industries.[14] Furthermore, the nature and quality of local stone also affected building practices. In the *Survey of Cornwall* (1602), for instance, Richard Carew reports that the hard, gray 'Pentuan digged out of the sea cliffs' is commonly used to dress local houses and that 'the sea strand . . . affordeth pebble stones' that 'serve very handsomely for paving of streets and courts.'[15] T. D. Atkinson has even argued that local building materials helped create distinctive local architectural styles that flourished in the fourteenth through the seventeenth centuries.[16] Kentish ragstone, London clay, Portland (lime)stone, Purbeck marble, the red sandstone of the Midlands and the west, and the granite of Devon and Cornwall all 'had a marked effect on building and on architectural form' in their respective areas.[17]

Other types of local diversity were not the product of natural causes like landscape or geology, but a result of local cultural traditions. Charles Kightly has detailed the staggering range of customs and ceremonies found in the British Isles, claiming that it is 'local particularism which lends British festivals and ceremonies so much of their variety and interest.'[18] Many of these customs predate the seventeenth century, including the Abbots Bromley (Staffordshire) Horn Dance, the Dunmow (Essex) Flitch, and the Burrator (Devon) Reservoir Ceremony.[19] Other, less extraordinary local customs centered around the 'church ales' that were traditionally held in each parish.[20] These communal gatherings originally coincided with the feast date of the patron saint to whom the parish church was dedicated, and even after the Reformation many communities 'obstinately stuck as close as possible to the proper saint's day, even (or indeed especially) if the saint commemorated was an obscure and local one.'[21] And even though most church ales had similar components (feasting, games, beautifying the church), they also had particular local features. For instance, 'many places served their own special feast dish – like the famous "Eccles cakes" of Eccles in Lancashire, the baked warden pears of Bedford, the "Puppy-dog pies" of Painswick or eponymous delicacies eaten at Cow Head Wakes [Lancashire] and on Pig Face Sunday [Gloucestershire].'[22] Even national customs (like May Day, morris dances, mumming plays, and wassailing) which might otherwise forge a shared cultural heritage were not without regional variations.[23] Finally, even when Stuart monarchs went out of their way to create an English Protestant calendar (centered on royal anniversaries and national political culture), David Cressy has shown how it could become 'contentious, politicized, and divisive' depending on how local communities chose to observe (or not observe) specific dates.[24] Local customs and ceremonies thus reinforced regional diversity.

And although the vast majority of English men and women were tied to agriculture and husbandry, even that widespread occupation was subject to local variations. Farming was marked by 'regionally differentiated field systems' and 'forms of land use.'[25] The timetables for planting and harvesting also varied slightly by location, as can be seen in Thomas Tusser's *Five Hundred Points of Good Husbandry* (1573). Of course, many regions of England specialized in a particular agricultural product (Herefordshire cider, Cheshire cheese, Essex saffron, Suffolk carrots) or type of livestock (pig-keeping on the Welsh borders, dairying in east Somerset and west Dorset, and the breeding of horses and oxen around Newcastle).[26] Even a quintessential English activity like wool production admitted of considerable local variation. Since the Middle Ages, breeds of sheep had been named after the localities in which they first developed (Border Cheviot, Cotswold, Derbyshire Gritstone, Norfolk Horn), types of cloth reflected the towns in which they were pioneered (Kerseys, Worsteds, Lincolns), and color names (Coventry blue, Kendal green, Bristol red) derived from the tendency of particular towns to dye their cloths a trademark color.

Even something that has been held up as a great unifier and force for nationalism in the sixteenth century – the English vernacular language – exhibits a surprising degree of local variety. In the first place, not everyone spoke English. In the sixteenth century, a considerable number of people in England's westernmost county still spoke Cornish, 'a Celtic dialect coming somewhere between Welsh and Breton.'[27] In other parts of the realm, some 15–20 English dialects prevailed. Variations in speaking and pronunciation and vocabulary could be significant, as anyone who has ever heard or read Edgar's West Country dialect in *King Lear* can attest. What is most striking about early modern dialects is not just differences in elocution, but the development of separate vocabularies. In his *Complete Herbal* (1653), Nicholas Culpeper prefaces his descriptive entries of English herbs with the consideration that since 'divers shires in this nation give divers names to one and the same herb, and the common name which it bears in one county, is not known in another; I shall take the pains to set down all the names that I know of each herb.'[28] Although early modern writers were aware of such local variations, it was really left to the nineteenth century to fully collect and record these separate linguistic traditions.[29] Works like the *Vocabulary of East Anglia* (1830), *Northamptonshire Glossary* (1851), *The Folk-Speech of South Cheshire* (1887), and *Ancient Words of the West Riding of Yorkshire* (1814) attest to just how inventive and fruitful local vocabularies could be. As we shall see, many counties, towns, and hundreds also boasted their own proverbs and local sayings. Some parishes could even be said to have developed their own separate literary traditions.[30]

As the preceding paragraphs have tried to display, English local diversity was created by a number of factors, both natural and man-made. Differences in landscape, settlement patterns, geology, architecture, customs, agriculture, economic activities, and language all combined to create local distinctions. The ultimate testament to such diversity can be found in the difficulty that local historians have had in identifying a 'typical' early modern community. The tendency, says Margaret Spufford, is to extrapolate from one's work on a particular settlement and say, '"So this is what 'the English village' was like before industrialization." But, of course, it isn't. It is what one type of English village was like, perhaps.'[31] Spufford goes on to observe that factors such as economic and geographic patterns play such a formative role that each community is ultimately 'unique.'[32]

One reason that English diversity was so pronounced in the early modern period was the relative insularity of most communities. In 1520, 'almost 95% of the English population [of 2.4 million] lived in villages and smaller settlements across the nation.'[33] Even with the phenomenal growth of London in the period, a relatively small number of people actually lived in the capital.[34] The vast majority of early modern English men and women lived in scattered settlements that were made even more isolated by poor roads and slow communication. In his *Chorographical Description, or, Survey of the County of Devon* (c. 1633), Tristram Risdon observes that the 'Ways . . . are cumbersome and uneven, amongst Rocks and Stones, painful for Man and Horse . . . For be they never so well mounted upon Horses out of other Countries, when they have travelled on Journey in these Parts, they can, in respect of Ease of Travel, forbear a second.'[35] Risdon doesn't just blame the roads; he also notes that 'the Inhabitants [are] very laborious, rough, and unpleasant to Strangers travelling these Ways' (2). The implication is that not only is Devonshire remote, its native inhabitants are perhaps eager to keep it that way.

But for most, insularity was not so much a choice as a reality. 'For the majority of the population,' says Alan Everitt, 'contacts with other parts of the kingdom . . . were still spasmodic and occasional rather than normal.'[36] As a result, many people had only a dim knowledge of the world beyond their local sphere. Indeed, very few people even knew what the reigning monarch looked like.[37] Everitt relates an anecdote of how an impostor landed at Sandwich in 1648 and claimed to be the Prince of Wales. The townsmen, not knowing what the future Charles II looked like, were easily deceived; they flocked to his side, kissed his hand, brought him fine clothes, and threw him an elaborate banquet.[38] Even a town in the county of Kent – that actually bordered London – was still far removed from the center in some ways.

Civil War historians, in particular, have played up the insularity that Everitt describes. The inwardness of gentry kinship webs and social interactions has been seen as a driving force in the formation of county communities prior to the Civil War. Insularity, says John Morrill, also helped ensure lukewarm local reactions to the national conflict. According to Morrill, bands of 'Club Men' in the 1640s zealously asserted their disinterest in the Civil War and were determined to stay free of entanglements that did not (as they saw them) relate to their own local existences.[39]

In recent years, however, there has been a reaction against the idea that England was composed primarily of self-contained and inward-looking local units.[40] Clive Holmes has challenged the county community assumption that provincial gentry moved in narrow circles; he points to the broadening effects of university education and extended social networks that made them participants in a larger, national culture.[41] Meanwhile, Keith Wrightson has argued that between 1580 and 1680, 'local communities were penetrated more deeply than had been the case previously by forces of economic, administrative and cultural integration which bound them more closely together into a national society and economy.'[42] A number of factors helped bring about this 'intensified interaction between the locality and the larger society.'[43] It is now accepted that population mobility was greater than previously thought and included both 'subsistence' migrants and 'betterment' migrants.[44] Informal news networks were also springing up to keep people apprised of distant happenings.[45] 'Communications between London, and therefore the printing trade of which it was the centre, and the rest of the kingdom were much more regular than has been supposed,' asserts Margaret Spufford.[46] As a result, the growth of cheap print literature (especially ballads and chapbooks) and its widespread distribution by pedlars to most parts of the realm created common reading material for literate laborers.[47] All of these developments seemingly lessened the insularity of local communities and made them more aware of the larger nation.

But increased contact with the nation need not lead to the abdication or absorption of the local. In fact, the penetration of the national could actually serve to intensify local awareness. In *The Shaping of a Community: The Rise and Reformation of the English Parish c. 1400–1560*, Beat Kumin locates the rise of the parish – that fundamental unit of English local community – in the same period as the growth of Tudor centralization. As the Tudors 'appropriated the existing parochial framework to tackle . . . social and administrative problems,' they made the parish less autonomous and more responsive to central government.[48] But as a result of this national investment, the parish also came into its own as both a local government unit and a locus of social community.[49] Robert Tittler has noted a similar dynamic in the rise of many sixteenth-century towns.[50] After the Dissolution, the Crown looked to towns to fill the voids left by ecclesiastical institutions and so incorporated 44 new boroughs. Meanwhile, urban elites used the situation to consolidate their own power and strengthen the position of the town. Ultimately, these developments stimulated civic identities and led to flourishing civic cultures.[51]

As both Kumin and Tittler demonstrate, the national and the local are not mutually exclusive. Although sixteenth-century parishes and towns were strengthening their contact with and accountability to Westminster, this did not necessarily erode local identity. On the contrary, national penetration may have served to stimulate local self-definition. At the very least, Tudor encroachment ultimately gave local identity clearer units (parish and town) around which it could cohere.

In fact, I would argue that the conditions I have just described made the late sixteenth century the perfect moment for the emergence of local consciousness. As we have seen, England possessed a native diversity, and local communities were still insular enough to preserve and maintain that diversity. At the same time, mobility, news networks, print culture, and central incursions were beginning to broaden local horizons and impart a heightened sense of the wider world. Whereas previous local identity derived primarily from insularity (i.e. a lack of interaction with the world beyond the village), people were now becoming more knowledgeable about other places and beginning to recognize and appreciate how their own locale was different from others.

A perfect example of this dynamic can be seen in the 'lottery poesies' submitted by individuals and groups to identify their entries in the first national lottery of 1567–1569. David Dean has shown how many people turned to 'local knowledge and local particularities for inspiration,' suggesting 'that for some Elizabethans, their place of residence was the first, or at least the definitive, form of identification that came to mind as they stood in the marketplace before the collector's table.'[52] A typical poesy is: 'Drawe Brightempston a good lot, or else return them a turbot.' This rhyme names the town of the man submitting the lot (Brighton) and also makes a humorous reference to a common type of fish (turbot) caught off the Sussex coast. In addition to local economic specialties, other poesies revolve around prominent local landmarks, historical events, topographical features, and even patron saints.[53] The lottery was sponsored by the Elizabethan government and the proceeds were meant to address the national problem of decaying harbors and havens.[54] As such, it seems to fit nicely with other sixteenth-century initiatives that effectively drew local communities into the larger life of the nation. Yet the lottery's effect, far from fostering national solidarity, was to encourage people to take stock of and articulate their local identity. Some poesy writers even mention the plight of their own particular harbor or otherwise promise to use any winnings to benefit the local situation.[55] Ultimately, these lottery poesies demonstrate the strength of existing local identities and also show how encounters with the nation could further sharpen them.

Geographical works

Another catalyst for the heightened awareness of local places was the explosion of geographical works that occurred in the second half of the sixteenth century. Overseas exploration, English involvement in European affairs, increased travel, cartographic advances, and antiquarianism are just some of the factors that led to the production of print and manuscript works that focus on or are organized around geographic units. Such works describe (*Diary of a Voyage to Jerusalem*), depict (*Map of Cambridge*), and discuss (*Of the Russe Commonwealth*) a range of places in England, Europe, and throughout the known world. From 1500–1549, only 84 such works were composed. In the next five decades, that number jumped by a factor of seven to 644![56] A look at particular decades is also revealing:

Decade	Number of geographical works
1520s	8
1530s	18
1540s	42
1550s	56
1560s	45
1570s	123
1580s	193
1590s	226

The 1540s represented a marked increase, as that decade matched the overall number (42) of the four previous decades combined. That number held steady in the 1550s and 1560s before increasing dramatically in the 1570s (123). The 1580s and 1590s saw similar jumps (193, 226). The proliferation of such works, I will argue, transformed the English imagination and created a heightened awareness of place in general and local places in particular.

Maps were among the most important geographical works in this regard. As is now widely acknowledged, the sixteenth century experienced nothing less than a cartographic revolution. As a result of technical and mathematical advancements, geographical space came to be represented more accurately than ever before. On the continent, these efforts culminated in Mercator's *Europe* (1554) and Ortelius's *Theatrum* (1570), but in England the key work was Christopher Saxton's *Atlas* (1579). For the first time, English men and women could gaze upon an accurate representation of their nation and its constituent counties. 'In the late sixteenth century,' writes D. K. Smith, 'the new introduction of cartographic representation to a widespread, literate public, brought about a shift in the way terrestrial space could be represented and manipulated, ushering in a whole new way of thinking about the world.'[57] The 'cartographic imagination' that Smith goes on to describe has often been seen as something that facilitated the emergence of nationhood (i.e. it allowed people to better imagine the nation of which they were a part). But cartographic advances affected local consciousness as well. If, as Rhonda Lemke Stanford has argued, maps were integral in transforming 'space' to 'a sense of place,' then mapping also allowed people to think about their own corner of England both more concretely and more imaginatively.[58] This was true not only on the county level,[59] but also the city/town level. In the second half of the sixteenth century, maps, panoramas, and bird's eye views were created for King's Lynn, Bristol, Dunwich, Cambridge, Exeter, Manchester, and of course London. The new land-measuring techniques were also being applied to the mapping and surveying of private estates.[60] Together, maps and surveys enabled people to think about their local spheres not just as their physical reality (where they were born, worked, had families, and attended church), but as particular, discrete place that could be defined and imagined in relation to other places.

Another prominent category of geographical works are those that describe foreign places. Jerusalem, India, China, Africa, Turkey, Russia, and Syria are but a few of the 'exotic' places that were featured in individual works of the 1570s, 1580s, and 1590s. These works range from topographical descriptions to historical geographies to traveler's accounts. Some, like *A Discourse . . . to know the Situation and Customes of forraine Cities* (1600) limit themselves to cities. Others, like *A brief description of the whole worlde* (1599) are more ambitious in scope. A few are composed in verse, like George Turbeville's *Description of Moscovia* (1568). Still others capitalize on contemporary interest in classical culture, as *A Summarie . . . touching the topography of Rome in ancient time* (1599). Not surprisingly, quite a few reflect English interest in the New World. Familiar works by John White, Thomas Hariot, and John Smith that describe contemporary English ventures in Virginia are supplemented by others that report on developments in Florida, Peru, Mexico, Brazil, Guiana, and the West Indies. Other foreign descriptions are much closer to home. According to E. G. R. Taylor, two dozen 'books dealing with different European countries [were] published between 1583 and 1625' – including works on Scandinavia, Italy, France, the Low Countries, Germany, and Portugal – and Ireland alone was the focus of no fewer than six works.[61] Together, these foreign descriptions both reflect and helped create an intense interest in place. As English readers began to look beyond their island, they developed a heightened sensitivity to particular places and the ways in which they differed from one another.

Foreign travel accounts seem particularly relevant to this dynamic. Whereas the topographical writer frequently adopts an objective voice as he parcels out and describes his subject place, the travel writer is more likely to gravitate towards what is distinctive or unusual about the foreign places he visits. This motive is particularly clear in a work like Edward Webbe's *The Rare and Wonderful things which Edward Webbe hath seen* (1590).[62] The traveler, moreover, also retains his English identity and is only a temporary visitor to the foreign land he is describing; thus, he tends to be more conscious of (or at least more likely to indulge in) cultural comparisons. When reading *A Book of the travaile and lief of me Thomas Hoby, 1547–1555*, we experience Italy through the eyes of an Englishman and are frequently invited to reflect on the differences between the two countries. One comes away with a clear sense of the essential and defining characteristics of not only Italy, but England as well. While sixteenth-century travel accounts expose English readers to far-flung and exotic places, they also invite them to make comparisons to their own, more familiar scope. In doing so, they help bring English national and local characteristics into sharper relief. Descriptions of foreign lands *were* making England – and the local communities within it – less insular, but this need not translate into a decline of local consciousness.

In fact, many travelers returned even more attached to the local places from which they originated. Thomas Coryat, one of the most prolific travelers in Renaissance England, went by the self-designated nicknames of 'The Peregrine of Odcombe' and 'The Odcombian Leg Stretcher' to show the affection that he retained for his native village of Odcombe, Somerset. His most famous work is *Coryat's Crudities* (1611), the full title of which is actually: *Coryat's Crudities: hastily gobled up in five moneths travels in France, Savoy, Italy, Rhetia commonly called the Grisons country, Helvetia alias Switzerland, some parts of high Germany and the Netherlands: newly digested in the hungry aire of Odcombe in the county of Somerset, and now dispersed to the nourishment of the travelling members of this kingdome.* This title not only goes into exhaustive detail about the scope and duration of Coryat's travels, it also suggests that what was 'hastily gobled up' while he was abroad can only be properly 'digested in the hungry aire of Odcombe.' In other words, only in returning to his native locale can Coryat truly reflect on and make sense of his journey. The experience of travel may have broadened Coryat's horizons, but it has not severed his connection to the local. If anything, travel may even have intensified it. The frontispiece of *Coryat's Crudities* provides another way of thinking about the impact of international travel on local identity. Amidst several images that capture key moments from the travels is a depiction of Coryat's travel clothes and shoes displayed in the village green on the author's return to Odcombe. The gesture could be seen as boastful – a visual emblem of where he has been and what he has seen, directed at his more sedentary village-dwellers. But this public display may also suggest that Coryat's travels have become a sort of ornament for his native place, a curiosity or mark of distinction that now characterizes this tiny Somerset village.[63]

Along with the rise in foreign travel, there was also increased move-ment *within* England in the sixteenth century. Andrew McRae's *Literature and Domestic Travel in Early Modern England* details the motives and experiences of those who traveled internally, including migrant labor-ers, domestic merchants, and pleasure-seeking gentry.[64] Domestic travel was making English communities less insular, as it brought people face to face with the variety and diversity outside of their own native villages and counties. A messenger's arrival at the royal Court 'Stained with the variation of each soil / Betwixt that Holmedon [Northumberland] and this seat of ours' in the opening scene of *1 Henry IV* registers this grow-ing awareness of and fascination with England's native diversity.

However – as with foreign travel – the effect of domestic travel could heighten rather than decrease the sense of local consciousness. Cheshire native Daniel King published *The Vale-Royall of England. Or, The County Palatine of Chester Illustrated* (1656) only *after* he moved away to London to pursue business opportunities.[65] In a prefatory commendation of the work, Thomas Brown (another Cheshire native) praises it as 'so emi-nently Beneficiall to your Country-men' and says that 'though you had your beginning in this Countrey, yet like a plant removed, you have elsewhere grown up to a more compleat Man, and to that perfection which speaks itself in this work. Had you still kept home, its more than probable you had not prospered so well in your own soyl, nor born such pleasant fruit, as herein your Countrey-men may Taste and refresh themselves withall.'[66] Brown seems to be anticipating an objection that some Cheshire natives might have: King's emigration to London makes him less of a 'county man.' Brown counters this objection by asserting that King's departure has made him a 'more compleat Man' who is now better able to bring 'perfection' and 'pleasant fruit' back to his native county. Brown doesn't explain why this is the case – has King become better educated? gained a sense of perspective? or simply had more lei-sure time to devote to writing? – but the application back to the county is what ultimately matters. Far from having his local consciousness stripped away, King's sojourn in London has seemingly made it more valuable.

If increased mapping and travel brought about a more general aware-ness of place (one's own and others), other geographical works signal some of the channels along which this awareness was proceeding. A number of sixteenth-century works connect specific agricultural and commercial activities with particular places. For instance, Reginald Scot's *Perfite Platforme for a Hoppe Garden* (1574) details the art of culti-vating hops that was just emerging in Kent, and Thomas Churchyard provided . . . *a description and commendation of a Paper-mill now of late set up at Dartford* (1588). Both publications served to identify particular places by their economic specializations. Other locales were rendered distinct by their natural resources. Works like *The Laws and Statutes of the Stannaries of Devon* (1575) and . . . *Of the Baths of Bathe* (1587) helped cement the long-standing association of Devon with tin mining and Bath with medicinal waters. The knowledge of local economic activities was also augmented by English almanacs and other miscellaneous works of the 1560s and 1570s, which for the first time began to list the principal fairs and markets in towns and cities across the realm.[67] Economic specialization, it seemed, was becoming a defining feature of local places.

Another category of geographical works helped bring attention to the distinct histories of local places throughout the realm. The anonymous *Declaracion howe . . . to know what compass . . . the towne of Donwiche hath been of in olde tyme past, &c.* (1573 m.s.) reflected the aspirations of a small Suffolk village to know more about its proud Saxon past.[68] Another intriguing work of local history is W. Vallans's *A tale of two Swannes: wherein is comprehended the Original and Encrease of the River Lea, commonly called Ware River, together with the Antiquities of sundries Places and Townes seated upon the same* (1590). The author is atypical in focusing on the antiquities of a river basin (rather than a county or city), though not, as we have seen, in suggesting that such natural landscape divisions often give rise to their own organic units of identity. This sort of topographical history writing found its fullest expression in the chorographies that I will discuss shortly, but it is worth noting here that history was one of the key channels along which the awakening of local awareness was proceeding.

But not all evocations of local places in the sixteenth century were serious and scholarly. Just as many foreign travelers gravitated towards the unusual and the extraordinary abroad, the English presses issued frequent reports (usually in pamphlet or broadside form) of anything noteworthy or fantastic that occurred in the provinces. Natural disasters such as fires, floods, and earthquakes were particularly well-covered, as in *A very lamentable and woful discourse of the fierce floods in Bedfordshire* (1570) and *A most true report of the moving and sinking of the ground at Westram in Kent* (1596).[69] Other reports concentrate on the miraculous – *A wonderful and strange news which happened in . . . Suffolk and Essex, where it raigned wheat the space of VI or VII miles compas* (1583) – and the monstrous – *The true reporte of the forme and shape of a monstrous chylde borne at . . . Colchester, in the county of Essex* (1562).[70] Although the focus of such reports is clearly on the extraordinary *event* that has occurred, in almost every case the *place* in which it occurs is specified in the title. This tendency may be a function of the authors' desire to create verisimilitude (i.e. a story seems more authentic when it can be located in a particular place). But regardless of the authors' intentions, the effect is to associate marvelous events with particular places. To most sixteenth-century English men and women, Westram, Kent would have been little more than a name. But in 1596, it became the place where the ground 'moves and sinks.'[71] I am not trying to oversimplify how the public responded to such news reports or make definitive claims about Westram's reputation in the 1590s. Rather, I am only making the point that these reports, because they insist on the primacy of the location of marvelous events, added to the growing awareness of place and place distinctions. Whereas other geographical works prompted an awareness of *existing* distinctions (like economic specialization or historical importance), these reports actually participate in the formation of *new* distinctions. Thus, a work like W.G.'s *Newes out of Cheshire of the new founde well* (1600) both reflects and helps contribute to the late sixteenth-century fascination with local distinctiveness.

A final category of geographical works combines the emphasis on the strange and unusual that we have just noted with the dynamics of travel. To this category belongs Richard Ferris's *The most dangerous and memorable adventure of Richard Ferris . . . who departed from Tower Wharfe . . . who undertook in a small wherry boate to row by sea to the City of Bristowe* (1590). As with the popular news reports above, Ferris's point is not so much to edify as to describe something unusual and 'memorable.' The emphasis is again on particular places, but here the appeal is to the reader's sense of geographical space. What makes the journey remarkable is the great distance between London and Bristol and the even more circuitous coastal route that connects them. Ferris assumes an existing knowledge of English geography, but he also endeavors to enhance the reader's awareness via description of this 'dangerous and memorable adventure.' There are many other sixteenth-century travel narratives of this kind. John Chandler notes 'a new appetite for travel literature, especially the exotic and unusual' including '[j]ourneys and adventures by "ordinary" people . . . published by the popular presses from the 1580s.'[72] William Kemp's *Nine Daies Wonder* (1600) is among the most famous. Kemp morris-danced from London to Norwich (a distance of some 100 miles) in only nine days. John Taylor, 'the water poet,' is probably the most well-known seventeenth-century traveler in this vein. Beginning in 1618, Taylor's twelve major journeys took him throughout

England and even into Scotland and Wales. Taylor published accounts (generally a mixture of prose and verse) of all twelve journeys and even took subscriptions prior to some of them. Many of Taylor's voyages featured calculated attempts to make them unusual, as when he and Roger Bird floated from London to Queenborough (Kent) in a boat made entirely of brown paper.[73] Nevertheless, 'travelers' like Ferris, Kemp, and Taylor contribute to the heightened awareness of local places that I have been describing. They rely on and add to a sense of geographical space and also give detailed accounts of the places that they visit.[74] On at least one occasion, a place actually gains notoriety *because* the traveler has visited it. At the conclusion of Taylor and Bird's paper-boat voyage to Queenborough, Taylor boasts: 'We to the Mayor gave our adventurous boat; / The which (to glorifie that towne of Kent) / He meant to hang up for a monument.'[75] In Taylor's mind at least, these travel accounts not only report but also help create local distinctiveness.

In the past few pages, I have argued that the marked increase in geographical works in the second half of the sixteenth century both reflected and led to a heightened awareness of places both within and beyond England. I have also tried to show how this 'opening up of the world' could lead not an erosion but to an intensification of local consciousness. Travel and foreign descriptions do make the reader look beyond their own local scope, but they also serve as a catalyst for examining one's own locale and bringing its distinctions into sharper relief. If, as Claire McEachern says, the formation of nationhood relies on distinguishing your nation from other nations – 'there is no such thing as a single nation' – the same dynamic would seem to apply to local identity.[76] Only in defining other locals (cities, town, parishes, regions, etc.) could the distinctiveness of one's own local sphere truly take shape. For those whose local identity is only the product of insularity, there is a tendency to define it as typical or normative. But the explosion of geographical works in the sixteenth century meant that even for the most provincial person, there could no longer be any such thing as a single local.

I have also looked closely at the types of geographical works and tried to suggest the channels along which this emerging awareness of local places proceeded. Different locales began to be associated with distinctions such as economic specialization, topography, history and antiquities, and the strange and wondrous contemporary events that they were witness to.

Finally, this brief survey of geographical works has suggested that a range of people – including travelers, estate owners, merchants,

antiquarians, and soldiers – took part in this awakening of local consciousness. Indeed, E. G. R. Taylor suggests that on the whole these
geographical works are 'indicative of what was actually read by the
general public.'[77] The geographical 'movement' was not then just an
elitist phenomenon; it was experienced on multiple levels of society.
Although the particular genre of geographical works that I will discuss
next – chorography – was typically written by and for the gentry, it
belongs to the wider context of geographical works that I have just
described.

Chorography

As we have just seen, chorography was not the only geographical work
that emerged in the second half of the sixteenth century. It was, however, among the most important in both facilitating the emergence of
local consciousness and determining how this consciousness developed
moving forward into the seventeenth century. Chorography has been
described as a 'verbal map' of a particular geographical unit that moves
beyond the cartographer's representation of the physical landscape to
include 'invisible' details about the people, history, and customs of
particular places.[78] As such, the genre participates in the same emphasis
on local places that we have noted elsewhere, but it also represents a
much more formal, lengthy, and systematic attempt to capture local
distinctiveness. One reason that chorographies can go into such detail
is because the writer is typically a native or 'countryman' of the area
in question and has intimate, first-hand knowledge of his subject. The
intended audience is likewise a local one, eager to read about the places
and people with which they are already familiar. Chorographies – works
by native writers focusing on local places for native audiences – would
seem to be among the purest expressions of local consciousness. What
then, do they suggest about the nature and form of local consciousness
in the sixteenth century?

It is first necessary to get a sense of the range and scope of the
works themselves. The first county chorography, William Lambarde's
Perambulation of Kent, was written in 1570 and published in 1576. It
was followed by similar works that described other counties: William
Smith's *Vale-Royall of England, or Countie Palatine of Chester* (1584),
Sampson Erdeswicke's *Survey of Staffordshire* (1593), and Richard Carew's
Survey of Cornwall (1602). Particular descriptions of Middlesex, Surrey,
Essex, Sussex, Hampshire, Hertfordshire, Cumberland, Northumberland,
Westmorland, Durham, Suffolk, Leicestershire, and Devonshire were all

either begun or completed by around the turn of the century.[79] Other chorographers were eager to describe English cities. The most famous is John Stow's *Survey of London* (1598), but his account was actually preceded by sixteenth-century descriptions of Exeter (1575), Norwich (1575), and Lincoln (1584), and closely followed by two accounts of Great Yarmouth in 1599.[80] This catalogue of works locates the rise of chorography in the same few decades (1570s, 1580s, and 1590s) that saw the proliferation of other geographic works, suggesting that the genre both responded to and helped create the sixteenth-century fascination with place.

Despite the peculiarities of individual works, most county chorographies follow a standard format. They begin by broadly defining the features of their chosen area, including its name, situation, topography, soil, air, minerals, and chief commodities. They then provide a much more detailed description – usually in the form of a 'guided tour' – of the particular places to be found within the county or city. This secondary, particularized description is usually much longer than the initial overview. William Burton is typical: his 'Generall Description of Leicester-Shire' takes only seven pages while the 'Particular Description of Leicester-Shire' comprises 309 pages.[81] Although topography continues to feature prominently as the writer minutely inspects the county on the 'ground' level, other important topics emerge: primary towns, the seats of the local gentry, commercial activities, history and antiquities, past and present worthies, prominent bridges and other structures, as well as local customs, pastimes, and traditions. Individual writers add their own idiosyncratic categories – Carew's *Cornwall* includes sections on coinage, edible and non-edible fowl, and popular recreations, while John Smyth is particularly interested in describing 'certaine words proverbs and phrases' that are 'native' to the hundred of Berkeley in Gloucestershire (23). But whatever the writer's predilection, the discourse is always subjected to the strictures of place. In fact, sometimes place is the only thing that could possibly yoke the otherwise disparate pieces together. Consider the full title of Robert Reyce's chorography: *The Breviary of Suffolk: OR a plaine and familiar description of the Country, the fruits, the buildings, the people, and inhabitants, the customs, the division politicall and ecclesiasticall, houses of Religion, with all their severall valuations, the chiefest men of learning, as of Divines privy Councellours, martiall men, and Navigators of former times, with severall other things of memorable note, and observation within the County of Suffolk.*[82] What seems like a disorganized and indiscriminate list is ultimately unified by the county of Suffolk. In fact, it is this very diversity of information that allows Reyce to paint the most complete picture of the county that he possibly can. Reyce's use of the term 'breviary' (as in 'epitome') is significant in so much as it implies that these disparate categories don't stray from the primary subject so much as constitute it.[83] For Reyce, Suffolk is not simply its county boundaries or position in space, but all of those items enumerated above. In some ways, it seems self-evident to modern readers that you come to know a place by asking questions like what does it look like? who lives there? what historical and human factors have shaped it? But it is only in the sixteenth century that these questions were beginning to be pursued in a systematic way. And it is chorography that plays the most important role in creating and formalizing the categories of definition by which local places were beginning to be known. Whereas other geographical works helped to create an awareness of place according to one or possibly two methods of inquiry (like economic specialization or antiquities or natural disaster), it is chorography that brings all these approaches together and even creates further categories by which to define and know places.

Chorography also amplifies another tendency that we have noted in other geographic works: the inclination to focus on what is *distinctive* about local places. Travel accounts and news reports, as we have seen, often focus on the 'wonders' and 'marvels' that have occurred in their subject locales. But there, the focus is typically on the unusual event itself rather than the place. Chorography inverts this relationship so that place is the operative factor. The writers themselves use different phrases to characterize this practice. For instance, Thomas Gerard promises to describe 'places of note,' Tristram Risdon prefers 'Things, worthy observation' (i) and 'memorable matter' (35), and John Smyth simply searches for what is 'remarkeable' (33).[84] But their goals are similar: to include anything that is unique, strange, atypical, curious, extraordinary, or rare and that therefore helps to distinguish the subject place from other places.[85] Thus, Smyth points to the linguistic peculiarities of Berkeley hundred – like pronouncing 'ff' for the letter 'v' (23) – while Carew's *Cornwall* notes how 'the shire varieth, not only from others, but also in itself' in its system of weights and measurements.[86] Both Smyth and Carew also note the distinctive games and recreations that are found within their shires.[87] These sorts of observations are 'remarkable' and 'memorable' mainly in the sense that they are specific to Berkeley and Cornwall and not found elsewhere. No doubt these sorts of singularities had long existed – as part of the native diversity of England that we have already noted – but for the first time they were being appreciated as such. A big reason for this appreciation is simply that such characteristics came to be *recognized* as distinctive. In his 1584 description of the city of Chester, William Smith is particularly impressed with the Chester Rows, a timbered shopping storefront with ingeniously covered walkways: 'which manner of building, I have not heard of in any place of Christendome.'[88] Smith's appreciation of The Rows is contingent on the knowledge of other building styles throughout 'Christendome' – knowledge that may not have been readily apparent when The Rows were first constructed in 1278. But with the heightened awareness of other places and other building styles (facilitated, in part, by sixteenth-century geographical works), Chester's native glory could be more fully appreciated.[89] By drawing attention to the distinguishing traits of local places, chorography emerges as a key vehicle for awakening writers and readers alike to the native diversity of the realm.

Of course, I am not the first person to note the tendency of chorographers to invest in the distinctions of particular places. However, this tendency has traditionally been seen as serving the larger cause of nationhood. Some chorographical works were indeed national in scope, including William Harrison's *Description of England* (1577), William Camden's *Britannia* (1586), John Speed's *Theatre of the Empire of Great Britain* (1610), and Michael Drayton's *Poly-Olbion* (1613). Not surprisingly, such works have been identified by Helgerson and others as playing a crucial role in the 'national cultural formation' of the Elizabethan Age.[90] But what of the numerous 'sub-national' chorographies that focus on the various counties, cities, towns, and hundreds of the realm? These too have been seen mostly as symptoms of an emerging nationhood. Helgerson argues that the focus on local distinctions only serves to ratify the nation – 'the particularities . . . constantly remind us of the whole' and 'Nationalism is what ultimately justifies a project as particular as Dugdale's.'[91] More recently, Norman Jones and Daniel Woolf have echoed this conclusion by asserting that 'antiquaries and "chorographers" . . . even when they characterized single shires only, did so within the context of that broader Britain described by the most influential of their number, William Camden in his *Britannia*.'[92] Such assessments of county and city chorographies seem overly tidy. Were they really just further symptoms of an emerging nationhood?

When we begin to look at what chorographers themselves made of place distinctions, a different picture emerges. In the first place, chorographers don't merely note, but boast of these distinctions. Robert Reyce says that Suffolk is known to 'excel in growing corne,' asserting that 'no country, butt hath improved to the uttermost the enclination of their soil thereunto' (28). William Burton praises the sheep of his native

Leicestershire, noting that many attain a 'height and goodnesse, so that . . . neither Lemster nor Cotswould can exceed them, if one respect either largnesse of the body, finenesse of the wooll, or goodnesse of the breed' (2).[93] In both cases, the distinctions arise from comparisons to the soil and livestock of other counties. Both authors also convey a palpable sense of pride in this distinctiveness. Similarly, William Gray's satisfaction in reporting his city's reputation for producing grindstones is apparent in his repeating of a local proverb: 'A Scot, a rat, and a New-Castle grindstone, you may find all the world over.'[94] The proverb seems to celebrate the ubiquitousness of this Newcastle export and also suggest something about the indefatigable toughness of its quality. The awareness of agricultural and economic specialization noted in other geographical works has here become a source of pride and identity. The positive effects of such perceived differences also inform chorographers' assessments of the people of the county or city as a whole. 'The Scots their neighbouring enemies, hath made the inhabitants of Northumberland fierce and hardy' and skilled in the arts of war, says William Gray (24). The enthusiasm of chorographers for their native places can sometimes cross over into obvious bias, as when Robert Reyce tries to put a positive spin on the flatness of Suffolk by creating a special section on 'The evennes of the Country.' The landscape is not tedious and repetitive but 'delight[s] in a continuall evenes' (25). In the chorographies of the sixteenth and seventeenth centuries, almost any difference can become a valued distinction.

In many works, this dynamic actually takes on the tone of rivalry and competition with other English places. A number of chorographers argue for the preeminence of their subject locales in particular areas. William Lambarde boasts that the 'Diocese of Lincolne . . . conteineth yet more shires in number, then ani other Bishoprick doth.'[95] Tristram Risdon claims that 'no shire in England exceeds [Devonshire] for Bridges' (6) and that the city of Exeter is the 'principal Ornament of the West' (9). John Smyth asserts that Berkeley hundred is 'better stored with deere' than any other hundred in Gloucester – and possibly in all of England (4). Daniel King proudly proclaims that 'no County in this nation doth exceed [Cheshire] for a Succession of Ancient Gentry' (ii) – and adds that those who don't believe him are invited to check the 'publique Records . . . carefully preserved in the Castle at Chester' (vii). Sometimes chorographers are interested not so much in claiming preeminence in a particular matter as seeking to aggrandize the county in general. The frontispiece of *The Description of Leicestershire* features an allegorical representation of Leicestershire crowned by Fame, and the Dedication promises to 'give light to the Countie of Leicester, whose beauty hath long beene shadowed and obscured.' In Daniel King's *Vale-Royall*, a prefatory poem actually addresses the county and implores it to:

> Rise noble CHESIRE, rise again from th'dead,
> And from thine Urne, erect thy royall Head:
> CHESIRE, Palatinates most noble pile,
> CHESIRE the glory of the Brithish Isle![96]

Such effusions don't seem intended to 'remind us of the whole' in the unifying way that Helgerson has in mind. Instead, other English places are really only invoked so that the writer can assert how his locality surpasses them or deserves pride of place.

Other works simply refrain from putting their subject place 'within the context of that broader Britain,' preferring instead to think of them as their own little worlds. Thomas Gerard plays up the self-sufficiency of Dorsetshire, noting that 'Manie are the Commodities of this Countrie, according to the severall Places' so that 'if there bee not a Competencie in everie Place, yet it is sufficientlie furnished from other Partes of the Countie by their Superaboundance' (4). Similarly, William Gray goes out of his way to depict Newcastle's economic autonomy from its southern rival, London: its merchant adventurers 'are ancient, their priviledges and immunities great' and 'they have no dependance upon London' (14, 18). Still other chorographers employ language to suggest the circumscribed nature of their subject. A number of writers refer to their counties as their 'countries.' In the *Description of Exeter*, John Hooker frequently calls Exeter a 'commonwealth.'[97] William Lambarde speaks of the main body of Kent as a 'continent' and those parts of the shire that lie near other counties as 'frontiers.'[98] Such practices suggest that, at least for their writers, chorographies tend to be more interested in examining their subjects in isolation than in integrating them into the nation of which they are a part.

The tensions of these two competing claims can be detected in John Smyth's treatment of the linguistic peculiarities of Berkeley hundred. At the beginning of a detailed section on 'Proverbs and Phrases,' Smyth writes:

> In this hundred of Berkeley are frequently used certaine words proverbs and phrases of speach, which wee hundreders conceive, (as we doe of certain market moneyes,) to bee not only native but confined to the soile bounds and territory thereof; which if found in

the mouthes of any forraigners, wee deeme them as leapt over our wall, or as strayed from their proper pasture and dwelling place. And doubtles, in the handsome mouthing of them, the dialect seemes borne of our owne bodies and naturall unto us from the breasts of our nurses. (23)

This passage aptly captures some of the defining features of chorography that we have already noted. It focuses on a particular place (Berkeley hundred) and draws attention to something that makes it distinctive (local proverbs). In fact, Smyth goes on to list some 100 proverbs that he claims are peculiar to this hundred – which is especially remarkable considering that Berkeley is only one of thirty hundreds in the county of Gloucestershire.[99] Furthermore, Smyth's sense of pride in both the hundred and its proverbs is evident in his use of the first person and the phrase 'handsome mouthing.' The passage also asserts the intimate role of place in bringing forth these linguistic distinctions, imagining the proverbs to be as native, organic, and natural to residents as soil and breast milk. In fact, many of the 100 proverbs do stem quite literally from place associations (e.g. #27: 'When Westridge wood is motley, then its time to sowe barley'). Significantly, though, John Smyth is not interested in exporting this treasury of local proverbs to other places. It is not just that someone from a different area may not understand the reference to 'Westridge wood'; for Smyth, it is that these proverbs are properly 'confined to the soile bounds and territory' of Berkeley hundred. Like escaped deer or stray sheep, they are still private property and should be duly returned to 'their proper pasture and dwellinge place.' Thus, the hundreders' claim on these phrases takes the form of a jealous assertion of local prerogative against 'forraigners' (in this case, the residents of bordering hundreds!). Here, there is no desire that Berkeley's linguistic specialization should contribute to a larger vision of England; rather Smyth insists on Berkeley's distinctiveness being 'enclosed' in local hands.

Of course, such tendencies towards local exclusivity need not be incompatible with nationhood. I'm not suggesting, for instance, that Smyth's emphasis on Berkeley's proverbs amounts to a proposal that the hundred secede from either Gloucestershire or England. I am, however, suggesting that works like the *Description of the Hundred of Berkeley* are not primarily directed towards national synthesis.

In fact, the county/city focus on local exclusivity is not inconsistent with what we find in the more expansive national chorographies of the period. Camden, Speed, and Drayton all use the county unit as the organizing principle of their descriptions. While this seems natural enough, it is also a somewhat decentralized way of proceeding. The implication is that in order to properly describe England, one must describe its counties. In the 1610 edition of *Britannia*, the England section devotes 639 of 822 pages to particular descriptions of the counties.[100] In other words, the nation is quite clearly shown to be a product of its component parts. Furthermore, as Camden and his contemporaries move through each county, they focus on the particular characteristics that define the county and distinguish it from others. Camden's etymological discussion of the name 'Rutlandshire' is revealing. Some county inhabitants claim that a past king said he would give someone named Rut as much land as he could ride around in one day. For Camden, this doubles as an explanation for how Rutlandshire came to be the smallest county in the realm, and indeed 'in compasse so farre about, as a light horseman will ride in one day' (525). Another etymological explanation is rooted in the county's soil: 'the earth in this shire is every where red' and 'the English-Saxons called Red in their tongue Roet and Rud' (525). Although ostensibly concerned with etymology, Camden ends up revealing two things that make Rutlandshire distinctive: its small size and red soil. Once he gets into the main description for each county, Camden continues to gravitate towards the unusual and noteworthy. In a five-page (folio) tour of Westmorland, Camden discusses the cloth-making fame of Kendal, describes two waterfalls along the River Can that locals use to predict the weather, notes the prevalence of 'hollow caves' in the Lonsdale area, marvels at a fountain near Brougham that ebbs and flows many times a day, and points out some 'huge stones in forme of pyramides' erected 'for to continue the memorial of some act there atchieved' but now forgotten (759–763). Such details not only emphasize Westmorland's wonders, they also parallel many of the same categories of distinction (topography, commodities, antiquities, etc.) that we have already noted in more localized chorographies.

Speed's use of these categories of distinction is even more apparent. He condenses Camden's text into a single folio page for each county and adds numbered headings for each paragraph. Thus, the ten areas of detail for 'Darbyshire' are: (1) bounds; (2) forme (including length, breadth, and circumference); (3) aire and soyle; (4) ancient people; (5) commodities; (6) Darby (the principal town); (7) other towns (and their historical significance); (8) things of strange note (including Buxton wells, Elden-hole, and the Devils Arse in the Peake); (9) religious houses; (10) divisions (lists and/ or numbers of hundreds, castles, market towns, and parish churches).[101] Each section is brief, as the overall goal is to offer a quick snapshot of what defines Derbyshire and makes it distinct. The accompanying two-page map further condenses and packages this information (Fig. 1). The center

27

Figure 1 John Speed, *The Theatre of the empire of Great Britaine*, 1616 (2nd edn.). Courtesy of the Rare Book & Manuscript Library, University of Illinois at Urbana-Champaign

is occupied by a map of the county, but clearly delineated boxes along the outside edges provide other visual stimuli. The boxes bordering the map of Derbyshire include the arms of the past earls of the county, a bird's eye view of Derby, and a drawing of Buxton wells – the famous people, principal town, and things of strange note that we have just read about.[102] But far from just being reiterated, this information has now been given a visual component. Now we can read about Derbyshire's distinctions and also imagine them in vivid detail.

Such features give Camden and Speed a decidedly local flavor. If chorography is ultimately animated by what Helgerson calls a 'nationalist impulse,'[103] then it is a particular type of nationalism: one that values local distinctions and is self-consciously constructed from its component parts. Perhaps such local consciousness could even be said to form a key feature of sixteenth-century English nationhood. If county/city chorographers did look to Camden as their model – as Jones and Woolf have maintained – perhaps their emulation of Camden had more to do with his approach to the local than with his commitment to a broader nationalistic project.

Although all geographical works of the period aided the growing aware-ness of place, chorography played a special role. Its circumscribed scope, focus on distinctiveness, and claims of preeminence both reflected and helped construct a sense of local consciousness and even local pride. Ultimately, one of chorography's most important contributions to local consciousness was that it helped create stable categories by which local places could be known and distinguished. The chorographies of the 1570s and 1580s are organized around descriptive categories like situa-tion, soil, air, topography, shape, minerals, agriculture, commerce, people, buildings, history and antiquities, political and ecclesiastical divisions, principal towns, gentry seats, proverbs, and recreations. Though such categories may have begun as convenient ways to organize a lengthy and complex description, they also served to illustrate all of the various com-ponents that went in to defining particular places. That is, such categories show the many different ways to 'know' a place as well as the many dif-ferent ways by which a place could be distinguished from other places. Chorography thus both complicates the notion of place (by increasing the number of factors that comprise it) and also makes place more approach-able (by simplifying these factors into clear categories).

As subsequent chorographers followed the likes of Camden and Lambarde in creating descriptions of their own counties and cities, these categories hardened into conventions and thus created a shared rubric for thinking about local places. Sometimes local writers invoked these categories even when they had nothing to report. In *The Breviary*

of Suffolk (1618), for instance, Robert Reyce includes separate headings for 'castles,' 'great bridges,' and 'minerals,' only to report (in each
instance) that Suffolk does not have any of note. That Reyce feels
compelled to include these headings shows the extent to which they
had become key categories of local identification. But the best way
of seeing how these local categories had hardened into conventions
can be seen in Wilhelm Bedwell's *A Briefe Description of the towne of
Tottenham Highcrosse in Middlesex* (1631). The author's attempt to apply
chorography to such a small area (his own tiny village on the outskirts
of London) is unusual and its effect is sometimes bathetic. Even though
the *Description* is only 22 quarto pages long, it is hyper-organized, containing two books of eight chapters each. Predictably, there are separate
sections on familiar categories like etymology, situation, divisions, soil,
air, antiquities, proverbs, and bridges. Some of these categories feel like
overkill for such a small area, as when the 'Divisions' section describes
four separate ways that Tottenham can be parceled up – including the
'Naturall' division that a certain brook creates as it cuts across the town.
Elsewhere, the section on antiquities tends to include anything in the
town that is of uncertain origin.[104] One of the final sections describes
the three main bridges of the parish. Even though Bedwell doesn't
seem to find them particularly memorable or important, he appeals
to the chorographic tradition to justify their inclusion in his description: 'If this [bridges] be woorth the noting in the generall: Then is it
not to be omitted in the particular.'[105] By 1631, chorographic conventions were not only well established, they were (at least for Bedwell)
their own justification. But this is not to say that such categories as
divisions, antiquities, and bridges had become merely superficial or
lost their ability to signify place; if anything, Bedwell reveals that they
are flexible enough to define and distinguish even a small village like
Tottenham High Cross. In the introductory chapter, the author confidently declares: 'Memorable things here worth the observing are many:
Yea many more, I verily believe, then in any other Village whatsoever,
amongst those many of the neighbourhood' (D2.v). In Bedwell's work,
the long-established chorographic categories that follow are the proof
for that claim.

But it would be a mistake to see these chorographic categories as either
overly dry or formulaic. In practice, they embodied a way of thinking
and an approach to local places that could be adapted to the reader.
The Introduction already noted the prevalence of handwritten annotations in copies of Camden's *Britannia*. Such marginalia suggests that
early modern readers were not content to simply read chorographical

descriptions – they needed to participate as well. Not only did *Britannia* owners add river labels to maps, they also underlined, supplied marginal notes, created their own indexes and tables of contents, offered corrections, affixed their name to the title page, and annotated tables in the appendices.[106] Readers were also compelled to contribute to the definitions of place that they were encountering in these texts. A passage in Carew's *Survey of Cornwall* mentions a particular mansion house in the parish of St. Germane and notes the current owners, 'Ro. Moyle, who married Anne daughter of M. Lock' (109). In a 1602 (first edition) copy, an early modern reader has included six lines of family history for M. Lock, and (on the facing page) 22 cramped lines of family history for Moyle along with an explanation of how the mansion house came into his possession.[107] What's more, this anonymous editor has crossed out a few of Carew's words so that the additional commentary flows seamlessly into the existing narrative. In this way, the book owner becomes a contributing writer (literally) to the *Survey of Cornwall*.

An even more dramatic instance of reader participation can be seen in a slightly later county chorography. When Thomas Gerard's manuscript *Survey of Dorsetshire* (c. 1633) was finally printed in 1732, the verso sides of its pages were actually left blank.[108] An eighteenth-century reader used this space to correct, update, and add to the text on the facing page. These additions include a grave inscription, a sketch of a particular house and church, a landscape drawing, and a depiction of a garden altar – all corresponding to the particular places that Gerard describes in that section of the *Survey*. While it is unclear if the work was printed with such an application in mind, the effect is to make the reader an active participant in describing and characterizing the county. In one section, Gerard describes the village of Blandford and the seat of St. Mary. On the facing page, the book owner has pasted in a watercolor of the Dame Mary Oake, a large (and apparently rather famous) tree in the immediate neighborhood (Fig. 2). Since Gerard makes no mention of the tree, the owner has included a short history of the tree along with his own observations: 'During the Civil War, and till after the Restoration an old person sold Ale in the hollow part of it . . . It was Sir P.T., and my opinion that 20 men might stand within side it' (105). Thus, the reader uses Gerard's otherwise conventional treatment of the shire's antiquities, natural history, and principal families as a jumping-off point for his own observations. The additions are still in the spirit of the *Survey* (in that they serve to further describe and characterize the county) and even use standard chorographic categories in their focus on buildings, landscape, and 'wonders.' Nevertheless, the reader deploys and combines these

Figure 2   Thomas Gerard, *A Survey of Dorsetshire* (London, 1732). Handwritten annotations in Gough Dorset 5, p. 105. Courtesy of The Bodleian Libraries, University of Oxford

categories in his own way. Rather than simply applying a set of static categories to a geographical area, these works invite readers to think about local places in terms of their own knowledge and experiences – and even to participate in an ongoing definition of place.

In this section we have seen some of the ways that geographical works in general and chorographical works in particular led to a growing awareness of local places. These works take the local as subject matter, seek to articulate its distinctions, and facilitate local pride. They also create specific categories for approaching the local and even invite reader participation and engagement. Collectively, they helped bring about a sense of local consciousness in late sixteenth-century England.

Ultimately, local consciousness was so pervasive that it came to influence other, non-geographical forms of writing. The London stage seems an unlikely candidate for exhibiting local particularities, but Shakespeare's *Merry Wives of Windsor* (1597) does just that.[109] As its title suggests, the play is set in the village of Windsor, some twenty miles west of London. Given its alleged composition for Queen Elizabeth and the Court and its closing focus on the Order of the Garter, this particular setting is not surprising. What is surprising is the extent to which Shakespeare creates a detailed and deliberate evocation of Windsor as a distinct place. As the characters move through the streets of Windsor, we are actually given a sense of the town's component parts and even its spatial layout. When Simple is asked where he has gone in search of Doctor Caius, he replies: 'Marry, sir, the Petty-ward, the Park-ward, every way: Old Windsor way, and every way but the town way' (3.1.5–6). In another episode, an elaborate jest involves one group of characters going through town to the outlying village of Frogmore (southeast of Windsor), while another group cuts through the surrounding fields to arrive at a farm house on the other side of Frogmore (2.3.68–80). In both instances, the play either assumes that the audience has a working knowledge of Windsor or endeavors to give it one. Shakespeare also situates Windsor in its larger 'neighborhood,' with allusions to Banbury cheese, the fat woman of Brentford, and hunting in the Cotswolds.[110] Sir Hugh Evans even complains about recent 'cozening' activities in the nearby villages of Reading, Maidenhead, and Colebrook (4.5.74).

But the real focus is on Windsor itself. The action is anchored in specific places such as the Garter Inn, Datchett Mead, Datchett Lane, the River Thames, Windsor Forest, and Windsor Castle.[111] Furthermore, it involves groups of people – like the 'whitsters' at Datchet Mead, the 'poor knights of Windsor,' and the royal Court – that wouldn't necessarily be found in other English towns.[112] Finally, the word 'Windsor' is inserted into the text seventeen different times, though it is often not strictly necessary.[113] It is almost as if Shakespeare is intent on reminding us that we are in this particular village on the banks of the Thames.

Significantly, Shakespeare creates that sense of verisimilitude by invoking those same categories of local definition that we have noted in sixteenth-century chorographies: people, buildings, roads, rivers, parks, forests, recreations, and commercial activities. Shakespeare also uses the local legend of 'Herne the hunter, / Sometime a keeper here in Windsor Forest' (4.4.26–27) in the final plot to humiliate Falstaff.[114] Even the play's basic theme has a local dimension. While 'Wives may be merry and yet honest too' (4.2.100) could apply to any woman anywhere, the play's title makes it especially true of Windsor wives. Just as chorographies tend to imbue county inhabitants with particular character traits, *The Merry Wives of Windsor* locates a particular virtue in a concrete place. 'Windsor wives' can now be held up as a byword for a certain type of witty and adventurous – but essentially honest – woman.

The Merry Wives of Windsor is striking in its use of local details to create an authentic sense of place. This is especially noteworthy when one considers that most of these details have no real bearing on the plot.[115] Why then are these place details so prevalent? Perhaps Shakespeare himself was interested in creating an accurate picture of Windsor. Perhaps he thought that a courtly audience would appreciate such details. Or maybe they are especially calibrated to appeal to a Windsor 'native' like Queen Elizabeth. Regardless of Shakespeare's particular motives, *Merry Wives* would seem to reflect the growing interest in place that I have been describing. Nor is this play inconsistent with what we find in other plays beginning in the 1590s.[116]

What David Dean calls 'local knowledge' crops up in a variety of other literary genres as well.[117] Thomas Tusser's verse *Five Hundred Points of Good Husbandry* (1573) makes careful distinctions among local agricultural practices in different counties and also notes county variations in a section devoted to 'The Ploughmans Feasting Daies.'[118] A number of the witty constructions in *The Proverbs and Epigrams of John Heywood* (1562) either rely on or play around with local knowledge. 'Of a sharpe tunge,' for instance, puns on the place names of two villages: 'Wife, I perceive thy tunge was made at Egeware. / Ye sir, and your made at Rayly, harde by thare.'[119] Longer, more nationalistic works are not without their local color, as in the spectacular 'marriage of the Thames and Medway' passage in Spenser's *Faerie Queene*, Book IV.[120] Even London writers incorporate local subjects and ties into their works. Thomas Nashe, though generally thought of as a London writer, was an East Anglian native who composed an antiquarian history of Great Yarmouth in *Lenten Stuff* (1599) and ridicules Gabriel Harvey's Essex hometown in *Have With You To Saffron Walden* (1596). When John Davies arrived in London, he took the appellation 'of Hereford' to distinguish himself from others of the same name. But Davies's works make clear that the name was more than just a matter of convenience. In *Microcosmos* (1603) he asks his native city for the use of its name – 'that one, with other, may keep both from death' – and later promises 'Thou gav'st me breath, and I will give thee fame / By writing in a double kind . . .' (*Wit's Bedlam*, 1617).

The local becomes an even bigger focus in the poetry of the seventeenth century. A number of individual poems take the local as overt subject, including Charles Cotton's 'A Journey into the Peak: to Sir Aston Cockain,' William Basse's 'Metamorphosis of the Walnut Tree of Borestall,' Henry Vaughan's 'To the River Isca,' William Strode's 'On Westwell Downs,' Robert Herrick's 'Dean-bourn, a Rude River in Devon, By Which Sometimes He Lived,' John Cleveland's 'News from Newcastle,' and Michael Drayton's 'A Hymn to his Ladies Birth-Place [Coventry].' The local also proves to be an important consideration in the poetic process. Phineas Fletcher's poems frequently celebrate the 'Kentish Nymphs' to whom he 'often pipes and often sings'[121] while Michael Drayton concludes in 'An Ode Written in the Peake [Derbyshire]' that he cannot write poetry until he first familiarizes himself with the geographical region in which he is writing. The geographical explosion of the 1570s and 1580s had done its work: the local consciousness that it fostered came to infuse a variety of non-geographical genres.

Local ideologies

As a result, local places appear with increasing frequency in the works of the period. Or rather, textual constructions of these local places. This is in fact a useful distinction, because it implies that local places don't just appear 'as themselves' but are imagined in particular ways and invoked for particular reasons. In *The Politics of Landscape*, James Turner argues that topographia-literary depictions are rarely ideologically neutral.[122] Different types of landscape – and local places, I would argue – are associated with particular values, so that to talk about a particular place is often a way of talking about those values. The next question to consider then is what values get associated with or cohere around the local? Or to put it another way: what ideological work do local places perform in early modern texts?

The answer to this question is surprisingly varied, so let us begin by surveying some of the possibilities. One dynamic that we find is the local as a site of active opposition to the national. In the early modern period, this association applies more to regions like the Marches and the North than particular counties or towns. The historical basis for such a connection is the centuries-long threat of Welsh and Scot incursions in these areas and the associated rise of powerful magnate families like the Percies, Cliffords, and Dacres. The historical tendency of such nobles to occasionally turn against their own (English) monarch was reaffirmed in the sixteenth century with the Pilgrimage of Grace in 1536 and the Northern Rebellion of 1569–1570.[123] As a result, the popular imagination associated places like the Marches and the North with opposition to central authority. When Shakespeare invokes these places as sites of rebellion in *Henry IV, Part I* he is not only being historically accurate, he is tapping into and furthering this popular association. Shakespeare plays up the Percy link to Northumberland, emphasizes Mortimer and Glendower's connection with the Marches, and sets several of the final scenes at the rebel camp in Shrewsbury.[124] Although the play reveals the destructiveness that such rebellious regions can foment, Shakespeare also makes a point of acknowledging native virtues like bravery, honor, and self-sufficiency that fuel the region's fierce independence. These 'northern' virtues may not be properly governed by someone like Hotspur, but they are ultimately validated by and incorporated into the character of Hal, England's ideal monarch. In the seventeenth century, the North's rebelliousness was more often seen in religious undertones. Since it was a region where Catholicism still resonated, the North was seen as late as the 1640s as 'one of the "dark corners of the land" . . . where popular superstitions were said to survive and to where the gospel would need to be spread.'[125] The local as a site of opposition thus invoked a range of complex values.

Even when the local wasn't invoked as a site of rebellion, it could still serve as a vessel for national critique. This function is most clearly seen in the pastoral genre. English pastoral – like all pastoral – was used to critique the Court and provide a contrast of rural simplicity. Thus, the genre implicitly privileges places away from the center and endorses rural virtues like purity, innocence, naturalness, and simplicity. Since early English pastoral is highly artificial and heavily dependent on classical models, it generally contains Greek and Roman landscape features, place names, and character names. But as English pastoral developed, it began to take on more native elements. Although it remained an idealized depiction of the landscape, it gradually became more realistic in detail, so that by the early eighteenth century it 'can be offered as . . . an idealization of actual English country life and its social and economic relations.'[126] The English names of Spenser's swains in the *Shepherd's Calendar* (1579) and the recognizably English landscapes of Drayton's pastorals were soon followed by even more authentic local details. The Cambridge landscape, for instance, is a recognizable feature in the pastorals of both Phineas Fletcher and John Milton. And William Browne's *Britannia's Pastorals* (1613, 1616), despite its expansive title, is largely a mirror of the local rivers, hills, and valleys surrounding his native Tavistock, Devonshire.[127] As the English pastoral became more localized, it not only located pastoral virtues in actual English places, it also increased the potential of the local to serve as a site of national critique.

Finally, local places frequently serve as an alternative to the nation in retreat literature. In 'Mine Own John Poyntz,' Thomas Wyatt's flight from the corruption and duplicity of Henry VIII's Court culminates in the relieved proclamation: 'But here I am in Kent and Christendom' (100). For Wyatt, 'here' is his family's ancestral home at Allington Castle, where he spends his days hawking, hunting, reading, and rhyming. As Wyatt's poem reveals, retreat literature includes something of the innocent simplicity of pastoral verse, but it is noticeably more aristocratic and more intellectual.[128] Despite its smaller scope, the Kentish countryside also offers greater personal freedom for the speaker: 'No man doth mark whereso I ride or go; / In lusty leas in liberty I walk' (84).

Of course, retreat literature is most commonly associated with royalist literary activity during the Civil War and Interregnum. The poetic productions of Robert Herrick, Mildmay Fane, Edmund Waller, Richard Lovelace, Abraham Cowley, Henry Vaughan, and Thomas Stanley feature repeated praise of retirement and country living, with an emphasis on friendship, contemplation, and the stoic centered self. As in Wyatt, these values are frequently attached to particular places. Herrick's *Hesperides* focuses on the flora, fauna, customs, and rituals of his 'western garden' of Devonshire, Vaughan writes of the Welsh countryside in and around Breconshire, Fane describes the virtues of country estates in the East Midlands, and Izaak Walton's cadre of anglers fish the River Lea just north of London. Indeed, the retirement benefits that these writers seek derive not so much from a limitless countryside as from the limited scope, quietness, and freedom from intrusion offered by a particular place. Although retirement literature is generally less critical than the rebellious and pastoral modes that we have examined, all three turn to local places to construct an idealized alternative to the administrative, political, religious, and economic spheres of the larger nation.

But the local is not only invoked to challenge or oppose the national. Many of the values that the above writers associate with the local – bravery, honor, naturalness, simplicity, friendship, contemplation, stoicism – are not necessarily incompatible with or even oppositional to national values. The local and the national are not always mutually exclusive. In fact, they frequently interact in complex ways, and at times the local can even be a way of mediating nationhood on the county, city, and parish level.

Thomas Deloney's *Jack of Newbury* (1597) is a case in point. Loosely based on an actual historical personage, this work describes the life and adventures of the clothier John Winchcomb (aka Jack of Newbury) and those associated with his household. Although Jack occasionally journeys to London, most of the action occurs in and around the Berkshire town of Newbury, which Camden says has 'become rich . . . by clothing, and [is] very well seated in a champian plaine, having the river Kenet to water it.'[129] In Deloney's account, Newbury is not just a convenient setting, but an integral element in the story. The town is represented in detailed fashion, including references to its maypole, market cross, fairs, taverns, rivers, specific streets, and surrounding villages. One also gets a sense of the human community that occupies this space through allusions to inhabitants (laborers, widows, local gentry), neighborhood gossip, behavioral norms, and social interactions. The local cloth-making industry is particularly important for Deloney, as he describes in great detail the various buildings, equipment, and people who participate in the transforming of wool into cloth. In fact, Newbury's cloth-making industry (and Jack, the man who makes it all possible) becomes, for Deloney, a model of hard work and efficiency. The community also establishes normative standards for such non-commercial values as chastity, charity, and proper merriment. What is especially striking is the extent to which Newbury's standards are frequently contrasted with more common, national norms. In Chapter VII, an Italian merchant (who is twice associated with London) is hoodwinked in his attempt to seduce two of the town women and is ultimately rebuked: 'Walk, walk, Barkshire maids will bee no Italian strumpets, nor the wives of Newbury their baudes.'[130] In Chapter IX, Jack's willingness to take the word of a bankrupt London draper who owes him money is met with skepticism: 'And wee in London (quoth they Scrivener) doe trust Bonds farre better then honestie' (77). In both cases, the simple virtue of Newbury is contrasted with more worldly behavior. The happy results that ultimately befall Jack and other residents of the town help Newbury emerge as a more chaste, neighborly, honest, and virtuous alternative to national norms.

And yet, it is not simply another case of the local being more innocent or more traditional. On the contrary, many of the values that Deloney espouses are the virtues of the new money economy like honesty, thrift, and the middle-class work ethic. Furthermore, Deloney frequently invites correspondence between Newbury and the nation. Chapter II recounts Jack's contribution of 150 troops to Queen Catherine's battle preparations against the King of Scotland, Chapter III tells about Jack hosting and sumptuously entertaining Henry VIII in his own home in Newbury during the monarch's progress in the area, and Chapters VI, IX, and XI recount various journeys that Jack made to London. Thus, the 'Newbury ideal' is not maintained through isolation or retreat, but through contact with the wider world. The town's virtues may be exemplary, but those virtues need to be able to function within a larger scope so that they can be seen, appreciated, and adapted. In the case of Jack, Deloney repeatedly emphasizes that he is not just a good townsman, but someone who maintains a reputation and has an impact beyond Newbury.

Such a move is consistent with Deloney's insistence that the clothing industry is crucial for the health of the larger commonwealth.[131] In Chapter VI, the King's wars are negatively affecting the clothing industry in towns throughout the realm (because English merchants have been prohibited from dealing with the merchants of France and the Low Countries, many poor people are suffering). Deloney thus illustrates how local economies can be harmed by national policies. But Jack's solution is one that carefully balances local and national concerns. He convinces the King that local industries matter to the overall health of the nation (thus suggesting that local and national interests are one and the same). But he makes this point in a very elaborate (and decentralized) fashion. Rather than just going to London alone and speaking his mind, Jack sends a letter to every clothing town asking that 'two honest discreete men be chosen' to meet him in London (57). Eventually 112 people join Jack for a humble complaint that they all deliver before the King. Such a large contingency is not only calibrated to impress the King, it also provides a visual record of just how many clothing towns – fifty-six – and their economies are at stake.[132] It is also a group plea in which the smaller, individual pleas are still preserved.

We might expect Jack, as the leader of this demonstration, to pursue further political influence or even come to embody some sort of alternative bourgeois nationalism. But Jack insists on returning to his Newbury sphere. When he is elsewhere offered a knighthood (that would presumably elevate him to a much wider scope), he humbly declines and asks that the King 'let me live a poore Clothier among my people' in part so that 'I may still keepe in minde from whence I came' (49). Even when Jack does eventually hold national political office, it is to represent the

'Burgesse' of Newbury in 'the Parliament house.' The story of Jack's life is that of a broad cloth weaver's ascent to fame and fortune, but it only goes so far. Unlike another character in the story, Cardinal Wolsey, Jack's ascent does not involve moving beyond or eschewing his place of origin.[133] For all of Jack's fame, influence, and royal encounters, Deloney is careful to associate him first and foremost with Newbury and its people. In doing so, Deloney is able to create a rubric of alternative values (shared by both Jack and the town of Newbury) and show how those values might interact with and even instruct the larger nation. For our purposes, *Jack of Newbury* embodies the complex discourse that was developing between the local and the national.

Another case study that captures a different type of dialogue between the local and the national is the Cotswold Games. The Games were begun in the early years of the seventeenth century by Gloucestershire native Robert Dover and were held annually during Whitsun week on 500 acres of unenclosed land atop Dover's Hill in the Cotswolds.[134] The games included 'wrestling, leaping, dancing, pitching the bar, throwing the hammer, music, leap-frog, shin-kicking, running races, horseracing, hunting the hare, coursing, singlestick fighting, handling the pike, tumbling' and were attended by a variety of revelers, including the local gentry.[135]

But what did these particular games mean to the Cotswold natives who attended and participated in them – especially as the Games' fame grew beyond their immediate area? We have a rare chance to consider this question because of the 1636 publication of *Annalia Dubrensia. Upon the yeerely celebration of Mr. Robert Dovers Olimpick Games upon Cotswold-Hills.* This slender work, put together by Dover's friend Mathew Walbancke, is comprised of thirty-four poems by various authors who praise Robert Dover and celebrate his annual games. While the contributors include the likes of Ben Jonson, Michael Drayton, and Thomas Heywood, most of the poems were written by Dover's friends who had a direct connection to the immediate area and had actually attended the Games. Of course, such a collection naturally exhibits a variety of perspectives and areas of focus, but certain themes and values predominate.

First, it is clear that the Cotswold Games are celebrated as a unique, local phenomenon. 'The Cotswold Shepheards' and the 'Ladds of the Hills, and Lasses of the Vale' (6) take tremendous pride in the event, says Drayton, and even sing about it in their daily life.[136] In other poems, the Cotswold Games are compared to and distinguished from London pleasures and from other local recreations.[137] The Games are also featured in *Poly-Olbion* as a distinguishing feature of the Cotswold region.[138] Yet despite this intense identification with their native region, the Cotswold Games are also imagined as being meaningful on a much larger level. Shackerley Marmyon, for instance, wants the praise of these Games to 'fill this Kingdomes whole circumference' (76). Such a statement helps situate the Cotswold Games in relation to other popular recreations that had long been a feature of English communal life. These recreations offered a much-needed break from the rigors of the working week and also 'did much to excite feelings of mutuality and communal identity both among particular peer groups . . . and between people of different rank in local society.'[139] According to many of the *Annalia Dubrensia* poets, the Cotswold Games provide the same sort of harmless mirth and social harmony. They depict this local gathering as a site of genuine pastoral innocence where 'honest Pastime, harmlesse Mirth' can flourish (8). Here there are no 'ill motives' (54), no 'foule excess' (50), and 'no oath's nor cursses to infect the Aire' (57). Instead, the Games help create a sense of neighborhood and social harmony by 'Augment[ing] the bond of Love and Unitie' (60).

Of course, such an emphasis on the social benefits of mirth is closely tied to how politicized sports had become by the 1630s. Traditional games and merry-making had declined steadily in previous decades because of the zeal of local Puritan reformers, despite the fact that James and then Charles came out in support of them. And although the Cotswold Games 'were a very different phenomenon from old-style rustic merry-making,' at least four of the *Annalia Dubrensia* poets make a direct connection between the two.[140] John Trussell even asserts that 'had not Joviall DOVER well invented / A meanes whereby to have the same prevented, / Love Feasts, and friendly intercourse had perrished, / Which now, are kept alive by him, and cherished' (7).[141] So in *Annalia Dubrensia*, a previously existing local tradition gets appropriated to support a national argument about the shape of religion and society. As Ben Jonson's poem puts it, the Cotswold Games 'Renew the Glories of our blessed Jeames' and also help 'advance true Love and neighbourhood / And doe both Church and Common wealth the good' (26). Just as in *Jack of Newbury*, a local model is here invoked as a standard for national values. But whereas Jack found himself working with clothiers from other towns to educate the King, Robert Dover's games already reflect the position of the monarch. Yet in both cases, what matters is that the example of a particular locale is invoked to mediate nationhood. Both Newbury and the Cotswold Games provide tangible, particularized instances of two otherwise abstract sets of values. And while those values can be transferred, the details of their exact occurrence in these particular places cannot be. That is why in both cases the locality is imagined as continuing to be distinct. Jack returns to his Newbury sphere rather than moving to London or some other clothier town. And even though some of the *Annalia Dubrensia* poets may want the spirit of the Cotswold Games to be replicated, part of what makes the Games so laudable and potent is their singularity; they cannot be (nor should they try to be) replicated elsewhere.

Jack of Newbury and *Annalia Dubrensia* also exhibit another feature that frequently shows up in early modern local discourse: a sense of nostalgia. Deloney's idealized depiction of Newbury is not a contemporary portrait, but Newbury in the reign of Henry VIII – before the late sixteenth-century collapse of the town's clothing industry.[142] As we have already seen, *Annalia Dubrensia* aligns the Cotswold Games with traditional English merry-making that was disappearing from English local communities. Thus, the local is imagined in its past heyday in one case and as the reservoir of traditional values in another. The local may be idealized, but it is also fragile. For these and other writers, the local is typically associated with values and ways of life that are either threatened, slipping away, or already gone. John Stow provides wistful comparisons of the placid London of his boyhood with the rapidly growing metropolis of the 1590s.[143] Drayton's descriptions of particular forests in *Poly-Olbion* are shot through with laments about contemporary deforestation.[144] Chorographers seem especially sensitive to the transience of time. After all, part of their objective is to sift through the 'ruine of antiquity' and try to reconstruct what once was.[145] Even the focus on etymology is an exercise in tracing how words have changed and been corrupted. In the preface to the *Survey of Cornwall*, Richard Carew complains about how much his county has altered even since he began 'these scribblings' and acknowledges what 'a wonder it were, that in the ceaseless revolution of the Universe, any parcell should retaine a stedfast constitution' (iii). This is why so many chorographers see their work as trying to arrest or reverse these changes.

On the one hand, the tendency of writers to see local (and especially rural) communities as fragile is universal. In *The Country and the City*, Raymond Williams notes the tendency of successive generations to locate the unspoiled and pristine country in the years just prior to its own era. This allows 'the country' to function as 'the idea of an ordered and happier past set against the disturbance and disorder of the present' (45). Of course, this sort of idealization is still present today, though perhaps Americans now prefer 'small town values' to the generic countryside. These values are similarly just out of reach, though they have been found as recently as 'the greatest generation' that fought World War Two. I am not trying to oversimplify early modern depictions of local places, but I am trying to point out that there are certain universal elements that may not be the production of a particular historical period. Many of the recurring elements that Williams notes in depictions of the country (virtue, simplicity, tradition, etc.) can also be found in early modern depictions of local places. Because of its small size and traditional associations, the local offers the prospect of stability in an ever-changing world; yet because it is idealized, the local's purest form is forever retreating just beyond the horizon.

On the other hand, nostalgia for the local does have a particular resonance in the sixteenth and seventeenth centuries that goes beyond Williams's generalizations. The early modern period *was* an era of burgeoning nationhood, and that development created particular anxieties for local communities. The *Breviary of Suffolk* observes, 'There bee some shires in this realme which do recken their far distance from their Court for a high commoditie, thereby misliking other parts nearer seated . . . in respect they are evermore groaning under the remedylesse burden of the oppressive purveyors and takes' (15). Although Robert Reyce doesn't overtly validate this viewpoint that *other* shires seem to have, he does go on to give examples of collecting officers who have exceeded their commission on occasion, and even reprints a local redress document from as recently as 1592. As local communities were drawn further into the life of the nation, many of them discovered that there was a price to be paid.

But this price was not primarily financial, nor was it only limited to those shires nearest the Court and capital. Rather, it revolved around the anxiety that nationhood might elide the peculiarities that made local places distinct. One reason for this was the perception that Tudor and Stuart nationhood was largely monolithic and homogeneous. Indeed, when we look at some of the key developments that fuel nationhood during this period, they seem to confirm that one of the corollaries of nationhood was moving towards a single way of doing things. The Tudor 'revolution in government' allowed the Crown to extend its influence into the provinces, but it also tended to wipe away the diverse and peculiar mechanisms of local government that had arisen organically over centuries. The formation of a state Church in the 1530s created a spiritual component for English nationhood, but it removed such local peculiarities as patron saints and monastic orders. And although many groups – Puritans, Catholics, Laudians – fought for influence within the English Church, there was never any doubt that only one of their visions could prevail at any given time. Even the strong English monarchs of the period who were necessary to bind the nation closer together also began to exercise a disproportionate influence. In the middle of the sixteenth century, the English religious landscape swung wildly between the extremes of Catholicism and Protestantism over an eleven-year period – based solely on the religious preferences of four Tudor monarchs. Moreover, such momentous reversals were openly defended as a part of the royal prerogative and the will of God.[146] Richard Helgerson has traced the sixteenth-century identification of the monarch with the nation (as well as the dissatisfaction that it could engender), while Malcolm Smuts has chronicled the rise of a Jacobean Court culture that sought to set the tone for the cultural life of the nation.[147] Thus, in politics, religion, and culture (just to name three areas), the formation of English nationhood was creating a more homogeneous landscape. Or at least that was the perception. It is hard to determine how far national initiatives like centralization and uniformity were intended to go, or even how far they could go in the sixteenth century. But, as Claire McEachern reminds us, nationhood is really more about perception than reality: 'nor is it [nationhood] produced by any practical homogeneity of social existence. It is a performative ideal of social unity founded in . . . ideological affiliation.'[148] Since nationhood is only an 'imagined community,' the question becomes: what is it imagined to be? For many contemporaries who were witnessing these political and religious changes, the emergence of the nation must have been associated with a set of common values and a single way of doing things.

Such an association was, of course, not wholly negative. The patriotism and national unity generated by the 1588 defeat of the Spanish Armada must have been exhilarating. And, indeed, the lessons of unity that it generated must have surely resonated among people throughout the realm.[149] But if a sense of nationhood 'fluctuated in intensity' and was 'governed largely by war,' as Barry Coward has suggested, perhaps people were more reluctant to embrace its monolithic message during less dramatic times.[150]

I am not arguing that early modern people were reluctant to embrace 'Englishness' on principle. Rather, it seems more likely that they were simply hesitant to trade local variety for a homogeneous national identity. If so, it is no accident that the local consciousness that emerged in the second half of the sixteenth century came to be articulated at the very moment when the forces of nationhood were getting into full swing. 'It is at the time of its dissolution,' says Kumar Krishan, 'that an entity reveals its principles in their true form and to their fullest extent.'[151] Local distinctiveness was not actually being dissolved, but it was certainly under new pressures. Contemporaries recognized that the unity and single-mindedness that underlay nationhood might be achieved at the cost of treasured local values. Resistance to this trade-off can be seen in Eamon Duffy's *Stripping of the Altars*. According to Duffy, a crucial part of the resistance to the new Protestant national Church in the 1530s to 1550s was 'the destruction of treasured objects which had been the focus of communal pride and local identity.'[152] As the sixteenth and seventeenth centuries unfolded, the emergence of nationhood came to include the discontinuation of local government structures, the constraining of parish dexterity, the movement towards a single historical narrative, the elision of regional linguistic distinctions, the building of ubiquitous prodigy houses rather than those made of the local stone, and the replacement of traditional communal revelries with a Protestant national calendar. Although it isn't always easy to determine what people thought of these developments, it seems safe to say that they were at least *aware* of the effects that emerging nationhood was having on local places. It is no wonder, then, that the local (and its values) tend to be portrayed as fragile and fleeting.

And yet there is an additional reason that early modern thinkers might have been distrustful of a monolithic nationhood. English nationhood emerged at a time when people were increasingly skeptical of overarching systems. The late sixteenth and early seventeenth centuries saw attacks on classical authority, the emergence of the new science, and the rise of Renaissance skepticism. The last two were fueled by the twin convictions that the natural world was irregular and degenerate and that human reason was an insufficient tool for knowing either the world or God.[153] The resulting epistemological crisis included a flight to smaller areas of knowledge. What Hiram Hadyn calls the 'Counter-Renaissance' was accompanied by 'an advocacy of simplification and simplicity, and of decentralized, unsynthesized particular experience – whether in the sense of direct personal contact with the object of knowledge, or the concentration upon some one aspect or department of knowledge (rather than the attempt to fit all aspects and departments together into a coherent and consistent synthesis).'[154] In religious discourse, people stepped back from sweeping generalizations and instead gravitated towards contingency and casuistry. Scientific writers like Francis Bacon are also suspicious of grand systems, recommending instead that the advancement of learning proceed via minute 'histories' of various branches of knowledge. The profusion of pithy literary genres in the early seventeenth century seems to reflect this contracted mindset as well. The epigram, essay, paradox, character sketch, emblem, resolve, letter, and meditation all deliver practical truths from a perspective that is limited in both length and scope.

In an age of emerging nationhood, there seem to be similar epistemological reasons for clinging to and valuing the local. It is the area of 'direct personal contact' and experience for most people, and its small size makes it more finite and knowable. It is much easier to describe the commodities or proclivities of a particular parish than to make a coherent statement about the English economy or the national character. Furthermore, any attempt to ascend to such large axioms (to put it in Baconian language) is bound to prove inaccurate or oversimplified. The local therefore frequently remains unsynthesized in early modern texts. Even the great national chorographies of Camden and Speed, as we have seen, describe England inductively. As they go county by county and town by town they are certainly systematic, but they don't synthesize so much as anatomize the diverse landscape that they find. The implication is that England is the sum of all of these parts, but what we are really left with is a sense of England's variety and diversity.

In some ways it is this variety and diversity that makes the local such a flexible tool for writers who are negotiating emerging nationhood. As we have seen, the local can function as an alternative to nationhood by serving as a site of critique or retreat. It can also serve as model for the larger nation (as when Newbury is shown to embody commercial values that benefit and can also instruct the commonwealth). It can be deployed in ideological conflicts (as when the Cotswold Games are invoked to support a national argument about what other local communities have lost). Sometimes the local is simply needed to serve as a concrete manifestation of otherwise abstract values (as when Shakespeare's Windsor wives are invested with a virtue that isn't necessarily the preserve of this single Berkshire town).

In its most expansive sense, local consciousness can simply be an awareness that different places have different characteristics. Part of Ben Jonson's illustration that 'metaphors far-[fetched] hinder to be understood, and affected, lose their grace' is if 'a Gentleman of Northamptonshire, Warwick-shire, or the Mid-land, should fetch all his illustrations to his country neighbors from shipping, and tell them of the maine sheat, and the [bowline].'[155] Jonson recognizes that different parts of England have different frames of reference. One is no better or worse than another, or Jonson would simply pick one type of metaphor as a normative standard and enjoin everyone to follow it. Instead, he advises the aspiring poet to be aware of this variety and let it serve as the guide of his literary choices. A number of early modern texts are equally committed not just to a necessary awareness of diversity, but to preserving and embracing the variety that England offers. The local consciousness that they embody doesn't actively resist nationhood so much as endorse a heterogeneous model in which individual distinctions are preserved.

It is clear, then, that the local becomes an adaptable tool in the hands of early modern writers. It is invoked for different reasons, directed towards different ends, and has different implications for nationhood. This chapter has tried to briefly sketch how and why local consciousness came to be such a vibrant aspect of early modern culture. The rest of the book will offer a series of detailed case studies of individual writers who invoke localism to mediate nationhood in particular historical moments.

My work will therefore depart from much of the work that local historians have heretofore done. Instead of exploring the local allegiances and mentalities of the ploughman (for whom the local sphere was really the only sphere), I will look at a previously neglected group: the literate and educated classes. My study will investigate the writers, lawyers, clergymen, estate owners, and politicians who were not only aware of the wider world but even involved in national initiatives. Richard Helgerson has asserted that the nationalistic writers of the late sixteenth century were 'uprooted' men who had left other ties behind, making it easier for them to embrace a national perspective.[156] This would seem to imply that local writers, by contrast, were more deeply rooted in a particular locale or that they tended to produce 'regional literature' that was enjoyed by a limited audience. But, as we shall see in the chapters that follow, many writers who invoke the local not only wrote for a national audience, but were themselves mobile and 'uprooted.' William Lambarde was a recent transplant to Kent; Michael Drayton spent the 1590s in London in close contact with the Elizabethan Court; George Herbert was born in Montgomery, Wales and spent two decades at Cambridge before he became a parson in rural Wiltshire; Lucy Hutchinson left her native London to accompany her new husband north to Nottingham. One of the intriguing questions I hope to answer is why such 'worldly' men and women valued the local sphere and when/how did they tend to invoke it? Or to put it in terms of the Alan Everitt anecdote mentioned earlier: why did people who *did* know what the monarch looked like (and in some cases had direct contact with him/her) still have recourse to the local?

The other major way in which my project departs from previous local studies is that it is not primarily centered on local identity or local community. Many useful studies have already grappled with the nature and depth of local allegiances as well as the local structures that consolidated that allegiance into a sense of community. This book will be more concerned with how the local is imagined, given ideological significance, and represented in textual discourses of the period. Other scholars have focused on the basic forms that early modern local identity took; I would like to present local consciousness as a way of thinking that could be applied to a variety of intellectual tasks. Ultimately, I do end up drawing from and perhaps even contributing to scholarly debates on identity and community. According to J. D. Marshall, one of the central problems of studying local communities is that 'there are few biographical or other sources which tell us what people's deeper sentiments of local and communal attachment actually were.'[157] By probing a variety of primary religious, literary, and political texts, I bring 'new' sources to bear on our understanding of early modern localism.

My first case study (Chapter 2) will look closely at the very first county chorography, William Lambarde's *Perambulation of Kent* (1576), as a calculated response to the Tudor centralization of shire government. Lambarde's use of a perambulatory mode shows his interest in projecting order onto the landscape of his adopted county (and is therefore an assertion of his fitness to join its gentry rulers). But what sort of order does Lambarde envision? In parts of the *Perambulation*, Lambarde reveals his attraction to a uniform order in which the monarch (or county magistrates) rule over a harmonious and homogeneous landscape. But other features of the *Perambulation* privilege the dispersed histories, topographies, and legal/administrative privileges of the individual components of Kent and seem to posit a decentralized political landscape. Ultimately, Lambarde seeks to fuse the strengths of each model in the gentry class, which is best able to mediate between the demands of the center and the local.

Chapter 3 investigates how Michael Drayton's poetry combines local topography with local history to fashion a corrective to Jacobean Court values. It begins by noting the tendency of Drayton's early works (in the 1590s) to feature his own native Warwickshire as both setting and subject matter. It then investigates the integral role of place in Drayton's evolving conception of heroic literature. In works like *England's Heroicall Epistles* (1597) and the *Barons Warres* (1603), Drayton continually forges links between the historical episodes that he depicts and the locations in which they occurred. Drayton invests in the local landscape, I argue, to help access, create, and sustain the heroic virtue that his poems seek to activate. I then show how the 'unheroic' Jacobean Court threatened Drayton's heroic values, spurring him to further develop the local landscapes of England and Wales in *Poly-Olbion* (1612) as a heroic alternative to courtly values. If *Poly-Olbion* is a nationalistic poem (as many critics argue), it is also one that celebrates the heterogeneity of England's landscapes and the diverse histories, legends, and traditions that they safeguard – as well as the local rivalries and claims of exclusivity to which they give rise.

Chapter 4 assesses George Herbert's depiction of parish religion in *The Country Parson* (c. 1632). I argue that Herbert's vision of the ideal parson is an implicit challenge to ongoing Laudian attempts in the 1630s to bring the parish under a more rigid uniformity. In my view, Herbert's vision of parish religion is not as concerned with revealing his personal religious tastes (as many have argued) as it is with endorsing a concept of local variety that had been a feature of the Jacobean Church. Again and again, *The Country Parson* dwells on distinctions among parishes and emphasizes the parson's need to consider these differences in ordering the religious life of the parish. Moreover, the ideal parson repeatedly consults particular circumstances and individual experience rather than broad rules for epistemology, moral judgments, and even church ritual. In my reading, it is not really that Herbert objects to the 'beauty of holiness' or other elements of the Laudian program; it is that these changes are being insisted upon across the board for all parishes. This chapter historicizes the local variety contained within the Jacobean Church, charts the impact (beginning in the 1620s) of the Laudian program on parish religion, offers an extended reading of *The Country Parson* as a response to these changes, and finally assesses the nature of Herbert's localism in terms of his larger vision of the English Church.

Chapter 5 investigates how the local sphere is used to mediate the grand, 'national' experience of the English Civil War by writers from both the royalist and parliamentary sides. The first half of the chapter examines Izaak Walton's careful evocation of a fourteen-mile stretch of the River Lea for the setting of the *Compleat Angler* (1653). Walton's investment in this locale is a way of imaginatively reclaiming a portion of the contested nation within which to inscribe his quietest values. Further, his habit of particularizing rather than synthesizing his vast knowledge of angling lore suggests not only a mind skeptical of the larger claims of authority and epistemology, but one that also finds meaning, comfort, and recourse in the finite. In *Memoirs of the Life of Colonel Hutchinson* (1671), Lucy Hutchinson defends her husband's role in the Civil War not by telling a grand narrative of the whole war or by giving an ideological defense of Puritanism. Rather, her defense is based on reporting exactly what happened in Nottingham in the 1640s and 1650s and justifying how her husband responded to those particular events. Nottingham was *his* sphere of action – and the only sphere, she implies, to which he should be held accountable. Hutchinson's repeated use of the word 'conscience' gives this claim a religious dimension and suggests that the local sphere (like the Puritan conscience) is to be the primary realm of intuition, responsibility, and accountability.

Finally, Chapter 6 argues somewhat counter-intuitively that the local was a key site for negotiating the challenges of English commercial and imperial expansion. The basis for such an assertion is a change in the depiction of the country house as a local space over the course of the seventeenth century. Early country house poets (Jonson, Lanyer, Carew, and Herrick) carefully position the estate in its surrounding neighborhood by referencing local place names and landmarks, valuing indigenous forms of nature, and depicting native plants and animals. In contrast, Interregnum and Restoration country house poets (Cotton, Lovelace, Flecknoe, and Mackenzie) depict the estate as a closed-off and private world where native sweets are eclipsed by foreign rarities, and local topography gives way to idealized landscapes. By cataloging and celebrating the far-flung objects that an estate owner has imported and assembled, these poems explode some traditional associations of the local (as native and organic) even as they reconfirm others (the local as distinctive and harmonious). The chapter closes with a discussion of Mildmay Fane's country house poems of the 1650s and 1660s, which apply continental gardening and landscape principles to the organization of local space. Moving into the Restoration, these principles both transform the local but also help ensure that it retains its vitality and continues to contribute to a heterogeneous vision of England that is ultimately complementary to an imperial mindset.

Although these case studies strive to give detailed accounts of particular ways that the local was invoked to mediate emerging nationhood, they also serve to illustrate both the pervasiveness and variety of local discourse. For instance, each chapter illustrates the viability of a different local unit, including the county (Lambarde), topographical unit (Drayton, Walton), parish (Herbert), city (Hutchinson), and estate (Fane). Each chapter also traces a local response to a particular national initiative, including political centralization, court culture, religious uniformity, civil war, and empire. Finally, each chapter also features a particular genre or mode of writing that is serviceable to local discourse, including the county chorography, topographical poem, religious treatise, biography, and country house poem. By progressing chronologically (1570–1680), the project also provides a sense of how localism itself developed in the period. Ultimately, my foregrounding of the local also comments on the formation of nationhood to which it responds; in doing so, it contributes to our understanding of the forces and factors – and limitations – within which English nationhood arose.

2
William Lambarde and Tudor Centralization

As the very first county chorography, the *Perambulation of Kent* shares in and contributes to the general formation of local consciousness with which the previous chapter has been concerned. But Lambarde's text is a fascinating social and political document in its own right that reflects the highly charged historical moment in which it came into being. William Lambarde completed the *Perambulation of Kent* in 1570, the same year the Northern Rebellion was raging. Already in the author's lifetime, England had endured major uprisings in the North, the West Country, and in East Anglia.[1] Lambarde's Kent had also seen its fair share of recent tumult. In 1548, 1549, and 1550, Kentish commoners camped in large numbers and 'threatened to follow their counterparts in East Anglia into armed rebellion' over enclosure and other local grievances.[2] And in 1554 a contingent of county men led by Sir Thomas Wyatt the younger marched on London to oppose the Queen's Spanish marriage. It is little wonder then that Lambarde's *Perambulation* – though primarily an antiquarian and chorographical work – exhibits a manifest concern with order. When Lambarde began writing in the 1560s, 'the fences [in Kent] were long since back in place, but obedience could not be taken for granted.'[3] Recent destabilizing events, coupled with Lambarde's own ambitions for joining the local governing class, prove to be formative influences on the *Perambulation of Kent*.

Lambarde's dominant literary mode – the perambulation – reflects this heightened concern with order. In the sixteenth century, a 'perambulation' was more than just a leisurely walk. According to the *OED*, it was also 'the action . . . of walking officially round a territory for the purpose of asserting and recording its boundaries.'[4] Early modern landowners periodically traversed the perimeters of their property to ensure that natural and man-made boundary markers were still standing.[5] In the process, they affirmed control over a landscape that might slip into disarray if left to the mutability of the seasons or the encroachments of neighbors. By organizing his description of Kent along the literary equivalent – a verbal circuit of the county's two dioceses – William Lambarde reveals that he too is invested in affirming and maintaining orderliness. As he describes and harmoniously arranges the various elements that comprise Kent's historical and contemporary features, Lambarde engages in a similar establishment of boundaries and projection of order onto the surrounding landscape.

The *Perambulation*'s preoccupation with order is further reflected in its author's frequent references to his own method. Lambarde regularly pauses to update his exact position within the circuit of perambulation.[6] These recitals do help orient the reader, but their primary function is to remind Lambarde himself to stick to 'the order that I have prescribed.'[7] Indeed, the intensity of Lambarde's commitment to his perambulatory method can be measured by his frequent use of the word *order*: 'order now requireth, that I shew' (1); 'I will observe this order' (87); 'to interrupt mine own order' (89); 'I have to keepe order' (100); 'for the observation of the order which I have begun' (119); 'the purpose of mine order bindeth me to prosecute them as they lye in the order of my journey' (178).[8] Phrases like these, peppered throughout the *Perambulation*, serve as reminders that Lambarde is committed to projecting a prescribed order onto the places and antiquities of Kent.[9]

Other chorographical works of the period show a similar concern with literary order. In attempting to assemble the history, customs, people, buildings, and landscape features of a given place into a digestible form, writers employ a wide array of methodological approaches: circular perambulations (Lambarde's *Kent*), river courses (Erdeswicke's *Staffordshire*), directional trajectories (Stow's *London*), alphabetical headings (Burton's *Leicestershire*), hundreds (King's *Cheshire*), and topical categories (Reyce's *Suffolk*). After rehearsing some of the possible ways that he could organize his 'traverse' across Devonshire, Tristan Risdon chooses an amalgamation of methods: 'But propounding herein an Order to myself, I purpose my beginning in the East-Part of the Country, and with the Sun to make my Gradation into the South, holding Course about by the River Tamer . . . Lastly to take notice of such remarkable Things as the North Parts afford.'[10] But whatever the approach, the goal of all of these chorographers is to create a literary frame that will accommodate the many particulars of the description and create 'a more orderly and methodicall proceeding.'[11]

But why should these chorographical works be so attentive to order? One reason may simply be the requirements of the genre: voluminous description of details spread over a large topographical area demands heightened narrative control. But the concern with literary order is also tied to the social and political function of the gentry, who were, after all, the chief writers and readers of this popular genre. Crown government was neither large enough nor centralized enough to keep a tight rein on the provinces, so it depended on the local gentry to govern. Sixteenth-century Kentish squire Thomas Wotton bluntly describes 'the good estate of England' as 'resting chiefly upon the good judgement and service of the Gentlemen of England' (x).[12] Of course, their own service as justices of the peace (JPs), sheriffs, and other local officers was beneficial to the gentry. Their offices brought local prestige and influence, and helped ensure a more general stability that was not undesirable for a landowning class. Chorographies, then, were of interest to the gentry not only because they describe familiar topography and showcase local antiquities, but because they enact the very order that was the chief political function of the gentry.[13] The careful literary ordering of these works – that contain a mass of otherwise undigested and even chaotic detail – thus serves as both a reflection and a construction of gentry control.

Indeed, it is difficult to overestimate the gentry concern with social and political order during this period. Peter Clark observes:

> More so, perhaps, than at any other time in English history, English society in the sixteenth and seventeenth centuries was deafened by a clamour of concern over the dual questions of political order and stability . . . With a recent history of internecine wars and political factionalism, English society after 1500 encountered a menacing host of new problems: the spread of religious division and debate; the massive growth of poverty; and the danger of general economic, social and demographic upheaval.[14]

Since the dual challenges of order and stability were paramount to early modern gentry, it only makes sense to see chorography – descriptions by the gentry, for the gentry, that focus on the spheres they rule – in this historical context. Doing so surely helps us understand why these works are adorned with lists of gentry and drawings of their arms, why rebellions and disorders in the historical record are often criticized or skipped over entirely, and why there is an increased emphasis on genealogy and land ownership.[15] In one sense then, chorography becomes for the gentry what the masque becomes for the Crown: an idealized enactment of order and an affirmation of one's own rule.

In Lambarde's case, chorography also becomes a bid for social belonging. The author of the *Perambulation* is in some ways an atypical chorographer; he is neither descended from an ancient gentry family nor a native of the county he is describing. His father, John Lambarde, was a wealthy London draper who decided late in life to found a line of country gentlemen in Kent.[16] In 1553, the year before he died, John purchased Westcombe Manor in East Greenwich. William legally inherited the manor in 1558, but seems to have remained in London until being called to the bar at Lincoln's Inn in 1567. At that time, Lambarde began to take conscious steps towards becoming a Kentish gentleman. He accepted a position on one of the county's Commissions of Sewers in 1568, and in 1570 he married Jane Multon, the daughter of a Kentish gentleman of ancient stock.[17]

He was also engaged in another activity that may have been designed to solidify his standing as a Kentish gentleman: the writing of the *Perambulation of Kent*. It was begun in 1568, just at the moment when Lambarde was seeking to throw in his lot with the county. Significantly, the *Perambulation* is dedicated to Thomas Wotton, a prominent gentleman, 'for the good understanding and interest that you have in this Shire' (vi). The text also contains self-conscious references to Lambarde's own position as an aspiring new gentleman. At one point, he draws attention to the regularity with which successful Londoners are engrafted into the Kentish gentry stock (6); in another place, he praises the Saxons for admitting some prosperous merchants into their gentry ranks (454).[18] The *Perambulation's* context and content, then, make it at least partially a bid for social belonging. So too does its emphasis on ordering. By demonstrating his intimate knowledge of and mastery over the topography and history of the county, Lambarde shows his fitness to join its ruling class.

Tudor centralization and local government

But to what sort of order does an aspiring gentleman like Lambarde see fit to subject the land? Over the course of the sixteenth century, the administrative ordering of England was undergoing an important shift. As the Tudor monarchs sought to consolidate their power, they turned their attention towards the provinces. They subdued regional magnates like the Percies and the Nevilles, and replaced them with regional councils that they could more easily control. They also began to reshape county and local government, so as to eclipse the various fragmentary powers of church, manor, and city that had grown up in the Middle

Ages. The English Reformation and dissolution that followed did much to eliminate the Crown's main rival: the Church. But other traditional offices, customs, and authorities remained dispersed throughout the realm. The Crown's response was to eat away at these privileges and take a more direct shaping role.[19] By increasing the responsibilities of the justices of the peace and creating lord lieutenants to oversee the militia in each county, the Crown sought to exercise a more direct role in government outside of London. This vision of political order was more centralized and uniform than any that England had seen before.

But not everyone embraced it. A. L. Rowse observes that the jobs of the newly created lord lieutenants were 'complicated by the endemic conflict of jurisdictions, claims to privilege and exemption.'[20] In Kent, Clark notes the 'continuing friction' between the evolving 'official county government' and the 'informal realities' of local power structures.[21] Nor was the centralization that *was* occurring very recognizable by modern definitions of the word; central government was simply too small and local communities too isolated for it to closely bind the provinces to the center.[22] Instead, much of the old medieval order was still in place. David Loades claims that 'the country was still living in a world of medieval pluralism' at the end of the sixteenth century 'where numerous laws and authorities interlocked, without a tidy hierarchy.'[23] While this statement may overlook some of the progress made by Tudor monarchs, it nevertheless puts a finger on a different type of order than the uniformity and integration of centralization. For this overlapping authority was not chaos, but a type of order that had arisen organically during the Middle Ages.[24] Self-governing boroughs, church liberties, franchises, and manorial courts – all of which survived at least into the late sixteenth century – are but a few of the various structures that had brought stability for centuries.[25] They were decentralized and perhaps irregular, but their strength lay in their ability to adapt themselves to particular local circumstances and situations.

Though varying degrees of both models of order had long existed in England, Tudor centralization brought their differences into sharper relief for the local officials of the sixteenth century. Those who wielded local power in formally exempt areas like liberties would certainly have been cognizant (and probably even wary) of the Crown's gradual encroachments on their localities.[26] We can also expect this tension to manifest itself in the attitudes and work of the gentry commissioners of the peace. Historians may now view the Crown's empowerment of county commissions as a deliberate extension of royal authority into the provinces, but we should be cautious about attributing acceptance of this plan to the gentry – especially in the middle decades of the sixteenth century. For one thing, '[g]overning the shire at most times of the year [merely] meant policing the parishes nearest one's residence.'[27] Most local officials were probably not focused on (or at least not regularly faced with) their formal ties to the government center. In addition, most gentry rulers were more eager for the privileges and status of office than in thinking about the larger political dynamic that the rise of the JP implied.[28] Yet the gentry governors must have been dimly aware of these competing models of order. At the very least, there would have been moments when their duties to the center came into conflict with the ancient customs and particular circumstances of their locality.[29]

While Lambarde shares this practical experience of governance with his fellow gentry, his command of English history and his special interest in English law and legal institutions equip him to better grasp the larger changes taking place in local government.[30] It is also significant that Lambarde's adopted county contained an unusual number of specialized local government mechanisms. At the beginning of Queen Elizabeth's reign, says Peter Clark, Kent had 'one of the largest groups of municipal franchises in the kingdom.'[31] Hyde and Zell note no fewer than seventeen major liberties and 'an unusual number of small towns with charters' – many of which had their own mayor and courts, and were exempt from normal county administration.[32] As Lambarde's chorography shows, its author was not only aware of but also fascinated by these specialized arrangements. Finally, we might expect the *Perambulation* to reflect a heightened awareness of these centralizing tendencies because they became prominent in Kent during the very decade that Lambarde was writing: 'by the 1560s the county was on the brink of an administrative breakthrough. The old medieval administrative order with its maze of liberties and its ineffective shrieval leadership was in decay, while the new county government centred on the commission of the peace was starting to gain momentum.'[33]

Indeed, local government was a vital concern for Lambarde throughout his life. Beginning in 1568, he served in a number of minor capacities over a 33-year period.[34] And in 1579 Lambarde became a justice of the peace, a position that he held for the greater part of two decades. Although his legal abilities and fame as an antiquary procured him national posts as well – Master in Chancery, and Keeper of the Records of the Tower of London – Lambarde remained absorbed by the challenge of local government. After finding in 1579 that there was no manual to help him learn the office of JP, Lambarde wrote the *Eirenarcha* (1582).

It is a practical, everyday guide to 'keeping the peace,' and it served as the standard handbook for JPs well into the seventeenth century.[35] Lambarde quickly followed up this work with the equally successful *Duties of Constables, Borsholders, Tithing Men, and such other low Ministers of the Peace* (1583), a manual intended to guide minor local officials serving in parish, town, or even smaller capacities.[36] As most of these offices were filled from the yeomanry, the *Duties* show the gentry's dependence on their cooperation, and Lambarde's realization that the vigilance for order must be even more localized than the JP's typical jurisdiction of a hundred.[37] Although he remained a loyal servant to the Crown throughout his life, Lambarde believed that the local unit was the key to the stability of the realm.

But how should the local unit function? Should it take its place as a distinctive unit within a distributive frame of order, or should it become integrated into a more centralized hierarchy? In a recent book, Bernhard Klein has argued that a chorographer's investment in a particular descriptive model 'was never merely an aesthetic choice' and that each 'resulting narrative entailed a moral and political outlook which shaped a specific version of national space at the cost of excluding another.'[38] Lambarde, by juggling two descriptive models, demonstrates inclinations towards competing conceptions of political order that appropriate local space differently. In parts of the *Perambulation*, Lambarde reveals his attraction to the stability and effectiveness – and beauty – of a uniform order in which the monarch (or county magistrates) rule over a harmonious and homogeneous landscape. Here, Lambarde's literary methods and direct pronouncements affirm a uniform and centralized Kent and England. But other features of the *Perambulation* privilege the dispersed histories, landscapes, and administrative arrangements of the individual components of Kent. Here, the emphasis is on the particularities of place, and the author seems to posit a decentralized political landscape. Ultimately, Lambarde seeks to fuse the strengths of each model in the gentry class. Because of their ability to mediate between the demands of the center and the local, the gentry offer the best prospect for ordering the land. In defining the local against the backdrop of the larger nation, Lambarde enlists the gentry to maintain the distinctiveness of place even as they integrate the local into a larger and stronger vision of England.

We should begin our look at the *Perambulation of Kent* by noting some of its basic organizational features. The first section of the work contains general information on Kent, including passages devoted to the county's situation, dimensions, natural resources, people, and history. The most prominent feature of this section is a series of tables and lists that divide and order the county along the lines of administrative units, taxation, and topography. A list of gentry and nobility is also included. But the bulk of the work – 405 of its 535 pages – comprises Lambarde's treatment of particular places within the county. The author perambulates around each of Kent's two ecclesiastical units, the dioceses of Rochester and Canterbury, pausing to report on anything noteworthy that he finds in his way (Fig. 3). In general, each heading is the name of a town or village, and each entry contains historical events or contemporary features relevant to that place. Thus, one of the basic ways that the *Perambulation* sets out to order the land is by moving from the general (county) to the particular (town) and by creating a stable but flexible structure to accommodate a large amount of narrative material.

Uniformity

Within this framework, two conflicting visions of order coalesce. One is embodied in the author's treatment of the ancient town of Teynham. Lambarde calls Teynham the 'parent' and 'most large' of the fruit orchards for which Kent had gained fame in the sixteenth century. His description of its origin then turns into a panegyric of its orderliness. In the time of Henry VIII, one Richard Harrys

> obtained 105. acres of good ground in Tenham, then called the Brennet, which he divided into ten parcels, and with great care, good choise, and no small labour and cost, brought plantes . . . and furnished this ground with them, so beautifully, as they not onely stand in most right line, but seeme to be of one sorte, shape, and fashion, as if they had beene drawen thorow one Mould, or wrought by one and the same patterne. (223)

Here, the vision of order is one of uniformity and regularity. Lambarde calls Teynham 'delightsome and beautifull' because it is harmoniously aligned and its individual components seem cut from the same pattern. There is no *concordia discors* here. This regularizing approach is consistent with much of the *Perambulation*, insofar as Lambarde tries to treat the places within Kent as if they too were 'of one sorte, shape, and fashion.' For each entry, he gives the place name, explores its etymology, and then moves chronologically through its noteworthy history. As a result, each place stands 'in most right line' as a topographical and historical marker in the perambulation, and together

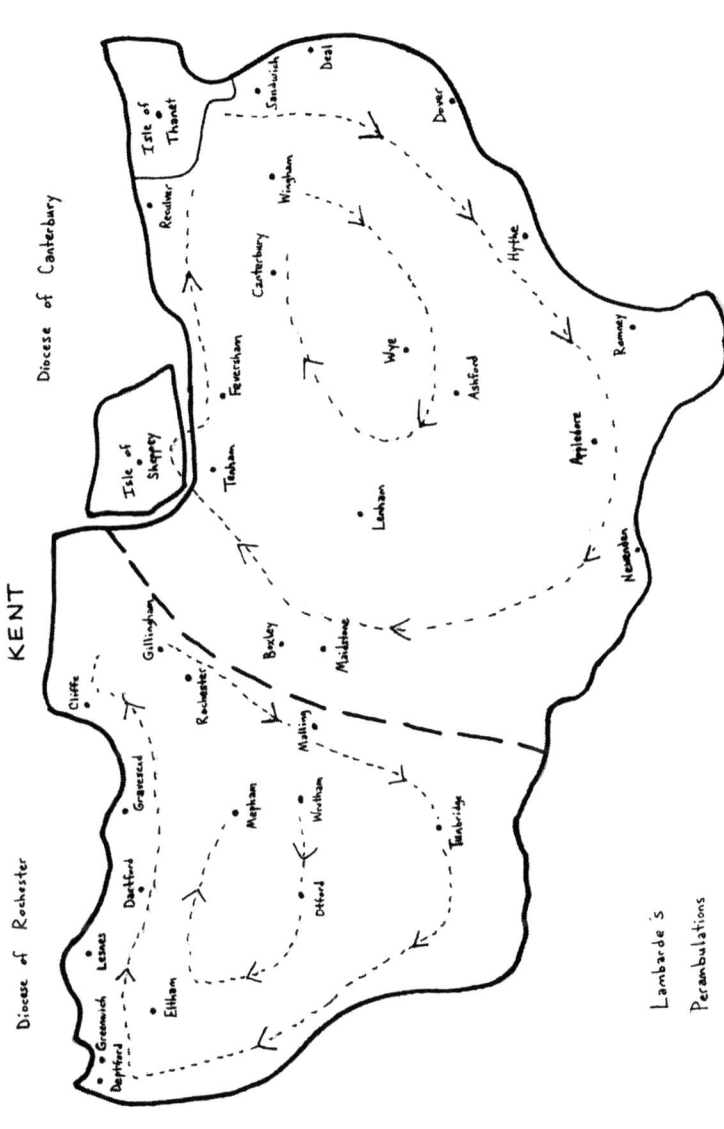

Figure 3 Map of William Lambarde's (verbal) perambulatory route through Kent

they impart a uniform vision of the county. Even when acknowledging Kent's diversity, Lambarde creates manageable categories to contain it. At different points in the text, Kent is divided into its contemporary hundreds and lathes (22–26), agricultural zones (181), ecclesiastical dioceses (70), landscape types (222), and river systems (197–198). Such generalizations are artificially simple – for example, the countryside is hardly reducible to 'three steps, or degrees, of which the first . . . offereth Wealth without health: the second, giveth both Wealth and health: and the thirde affoordeth Health onely, and little or no Wealth' (181) – but they do generate the perception of a tidy uniformity. They also show that, at times, the literary ordering of the *Perambulation* represents an attempt to bring the rest of the county to the same sort of orderly uniformity that can be seen in the Teynham orchard. But what are the political applications to be made from such a vision of order? And how do we know that Lambarde wants us to make them?

First of all, Lambarde applies the same uniform model to the governing of the county. When he comes to describe 'the people of this countrie' early in the *Perambulation*, the author discerns only two categories: the gentry and the yeomanry, 'of which the first be for the most parte . . . governors, and the other altogether . . . governed' (6).[39] Lambarde does not begin with the temperament or proclivities of Kentishmen (as later chorographers do for their county natives) but immediately foregrounds the political order and makes power the source of demarcation. But Lambarde's idealized description of the governed keeps this from seeming like an exclusionary move; because the common people are 'no where more free, and jolly, then in this shyre,' they do not seek to 'change their condition, nor desire to be apparailed with the titles of gentrie' (7–8). Lambarde concludes his account of this static social order by assuring the reader that 'no where else in all this realme, is the common people more willingly governed' (8). Here, Lambarde has created a basis for county order in which the inhabitants are a happy, homogeneous lot, and every bit as tractable as the cherry trees at Teynham.[40] Given these remarkable conditions, the gentry imposition of order is both natural and agreeable – and, presumably, as thoroughgoing and uniform as the lists of gentry families and JP jurisdictions that follow this section. By using the same mode to order the land and its people, Lambarde makes the implied connection between the two clear.

But there is another, more direct way in which the *Perambulation*'s uniformity relates to contemporary political order. Lambarde wants his gentry audience to study Kent's history for practical lessons about governance. As Thomas Wotton puts it: 'And so by these mens experience (which like the burnt childe, that then too late the fire dreadth, with much repentance they buy deerly) are we taught and brought out of danger to settle our selves, as it were, in a seat of suretie' (ix). In other words, the gentry's knowledge of past disturbances and their causes will help them keep the peace and protect their own position. The uniformity and idealization of Lambarde's method notwithstanding, a frank recognition of the fires of Kent's past will keep contemporaries from getting 'burnt' in the present.

Chief among the historical lessons offered up to the gentry is the mischief caused by a lack of uniformity in government and religion. As the historian Lambarde no doubt realizes, it is an especially apt lesson for the county of Kent.[41] Rebels of all kinds are criticized in the *Perambulation*. Lambarde dismisses the Maid of Kent as a meddlesome fool (175), graphically depicts the punishment of rebels associated with Blackheath (392), and even goes out of his way to condemn a local rebellion occurring within the larger tumult of the Wars of the Roses (431). Such passages are amply illustrated with the harms occasioned by rebellion and strife. After his narration of the Wars of the Roses, Lambarde criticizes the 'continuall wavering and inconstancie' of the common people, and warns that 'light heads (as they see here) finde heavie rappes' (433). Sometimes the admonition is directed at the people of a particular town like Maidstone: 'in the time of King Edwarde the Sixth, the towne, which before times had been governed by a Portreve, was newly incorporated and endowed with sundrie liberties, all which soone after it forfeited by ioyning in a rebellion mooved within this Shire, under the reigne of Queene Marie' (196).[42] Instead of lauding the rebels' opposition to a Catholic queen, Lambarde dwells on the liberties forfeited by the town for opposing the Crown.

Indeed, Lambarde almost always takes the English monarch's side, emphasizing the strife and disorder that frequently accompany challenges to the throne. He even defends the unpopular Edward II, asserting that too much of the fault is laid on the King for the Baron's Wars of his reign (297). That Lambarde is not a blind defender of the monarchy can be seen in his pointed criticism of Richard II for 'fierce dealing' and alienating his subjects (410). But it is also worth noting that Richard is depicted as an arbitrary ruler who ignored the judicial, parliamentary, and punitive traditions of the established order. For it is this order to which Lambarde – lawyer, antiquarian, and local official – is most committed. The king is usually the best bet to ensure this order, while rebellion is usually its biggest threat; and for these reasons Lambarde usually sympathizes with the former and eschews the latter.

But if scheming nobles and fickle commoners have at times threatened the stability of England, the Catholic Church has been an almost constant antagonist. Before the Reformation, the Catholic Church in England looked to the Pope's authority and often clashed with the King. The problem, as Lambarde sees it, is that 'in those daies, there was no Lawe in Englande to rule the proude Prelacie withall' (381). As a result, either the distant Pope or the intractable clergy was able to frustrate the royal will. The end result was a breach of political uniformity that resulted in instability and conflict for the realm. Lambarde's political attitude to the Catholic clergy is most clearly seen in the multiple place entries that relate to events in the life of Thomas à Beckett. Lambarde completely villainizes Beckett in his struggle with Henry II, but he does so for mostly political reasons. Beckett was at fault because he 'opposed himselfe against his Prince' (273); was guided by 'pride and wilfull rebellion' (276); and because he 'withstoode King Henrie in the execution of godly iustice' (395).

Although the formal presence of the Catholic Church had waned, religious uniformity in Lambarde's England was far from established. Despite the Elizabethan Settlement of 1559, the turning point of the gentry's commitment to a new English brand of Protestantism did not occur until the 1570s.[43] Thus, when Lambarde was writing the *Perambulation*, 'the most important – and often most divisive – issue of local governance' remained 'how the local political brokers would respond to the religious demands of the centre.'[44] Indeed, religious faith was not even a litmus test for serving on the county commission in the first decade of Elizabeth's reign.[45] Only in 1569 (the year before Lambarde completed the *Perambulation*) were JPs required to swear an oath to uphold the Act of Uniformity.[46] In contrast to some of the gentry's slow acceptance of the Settlement, Lambarde comes down forcefully on the side of religious uniformity. The *Perambulation* exhibits a pervasive focus on and unflinching criticism of pre-Reformation religious practices in the shire. '[I]t is . . . profitable,' affirms Lambarde, 'to the keeping under of fained and superstitious religion, to renew to mind the Priestly practices of olde time' (324). As we have seen, Lambarde's motives for 'keeping under' the old religion had as much to do with orderly uniformity as faith. Papism, for Lambarde, is 'no lesse iniurious to God, than daungerous to men' (157).

So far, I have shown how various aspects of the *Perambulation* – its literary ordering, treatment of the land, and political lessons – subscribe to a vision of order that stresses sameness and uniformity. Here, the author creates and sticks doggedly to a predetermined method, uses narrative and topographical divisions to make generalizations about the land, and maintains the danger of political and religious challenges to the dominant order. In both literary method and subject matter, then, one could connect these aspects of the *Perambulation* with the type of centralizing order that the Tudors were bringing to the provinces. The shift from medieval plurality and overlap to a more uniform hierarchy seems to be emblematized in the Teynham orchard, where disparate components are reconstituted 'as if they had beene drawen thorow one Mould, or wrought by one and the same patterne' (223). Such a model of order, I would argue, is attractive to Lambarde because it provides political and religious stability and effectively guards against rebellion.

In the *Perambulation*, the receptacle of this leveling vision of order is the county unit. Particularly in the first section, Lambarde makes generalizations about traits common to the whole county: situation, air, soil, produce, livestock, waters, people, and history. He also draws attention to the beacon network that unites the county in defense, and lists the writers who are from or have written about Kent. Finally, the author emphasizes the mutual heritage that Kentishmen share.[47] With this emphasis on commonality, Lambarde creates a sense of shared identity that seems quite serviceable to his larger vision of orderly uniformity.[48] In fact, it is noteworthy that much of the Crown's centralizing activity was also focused on the county unit (through the Commission of the Peace and the office of Lord Lieutenant).

Particularization

But if some features of the *Perambulation* envision a uniform county, others reveal the diversity of the places within its borders. Indeed, the bulk of the work is a 400-page perambulation that seems to imply the necessity of descending to the towns, villages, and variegated terrain in order to gain an accurate picture of Kent. As is typical of the chorographic genre, Lambarde's individual entries linger on what is noteworthy about each place. In Maidstone, it is an underground stream and four prominent buildings of the town (199, 196). In the Crayford entry, Lambarde's interest is piqued by the 'sundry artificiall Caves' found in the vicinity (401). The author frequently showcases some singularity that serves as a defining mark of identity for the place. '[T]he fertilitie and quantitie of the soile' of Romney Marsh, says Lambarde, 'is famous throughout the Realme' (180). In Folkestone, the local oysters are celebrated 'as well for the taste, as for the greatnes' and Lambarde repeats the legend that 'the same were they, that for Dainties were aunciently transported to Rome' (154). Indeed, Lambarde freely confesses that part of his chorographic project is to uncover 'singularities' of place (1, 131) – or as he implies in another entry: to uncover characteristics about which a place can 'vaunte it selfe' (236). In doing so, Lambarde not only commemorates what is noteworthy and distinct about the places of Kent, he also compares them to (and thus defines them against) other places in Kent, England, and even Europe. Thus, Aylesford is notable for containing the oldest antiquity in the county (369), Newenden has the distinction of 'harbour[ing] the first Carmelite Fryars that ever were in this Realme' (188), and the fine wool of Sheppey exceeds any produced not only in Kent or England, but all of Europe (226)! Clearly, Lambarde's interest in 'notable' characterization leads to a tendency to write about things that (by definition) do not parallel the attributes of other places or fit into a larger county pattern.[49] At the very least, this feature of Lambarde's writing runs counter to the uniformity of the centralizing impulse that he exhibits elsewhere.

Not only does Lambarde exhibit a keen interest in the particular places of Kent, he also makes them a priority in his organizational scheme (and by extension his ordering of the land). As noted earlier, the *Perambulation* contains a deliberate division between the general 'Estate of Kent' and the much longer and more particularized perambulation that follows.[50] One reason for the relative brevity of the general shire section is that Lambarde often postpones his coverage of people and events to later entries. For example, after briefly discussing the reigns of the Kentish kings Ethelbert and Eadric in the general section, Lambarde defers other Saxon kings to subsequent entries: 'as for the rest, I passe them over to their fit titles, as things rather perteining to some peculiar places, then incident to the body of the whole shyre' (16–17). The implication is that if certain events or characteristics are not equally applicable to the entire county, then they need to be treated in relation to their own smaller spheres. But this is not the same as simply relegating less important details to the back – remember, 405 out of 535 pages of the *Perambulation* are devoted to individual place entries. Instead, these less pervasive details are still pertinent and still have their 'fit titles.' The meticulous work of antiquaries like Lambarde reveals that particularization – of noteworthy singularities as well as more mundane details – is not simply a matter of generating some sort of giant appendix for everything that cannot fit into a county stereotype. It is a conscious investment in minutiae, even if the details unearthed cannot be directly linked to a more general or universal trend. Thus, one may find details on ancient kings and important battles in the pages of sixteenth- and seventeenth-century chorographies, but one is just as likely to find a transcription of a Saxon will, a description of a village's 'holy wells,' or a list of local proverbs.[51] The particular is valued and even treasured by these writers.[52] It is also the means to an alternative order that lies at the heart of many of these chorographies. For particularization, despite its lack of uniformity and potential for fragmentation, can be a way of creating order.

We see this construction of knowledge most directly in the Renaissance writers of 'anatomies.' Their assumption is that an encyclopedic cataloging of everything relevant to a given subject (no matter how particular) will yield insight. But there is no attempt in the *Anatomy of Melancholy*, for instance, to fuse its voluminous findings into a unified statement. Somehow, accounting for all of the different causes of melancholy has brought a level of awareness that will be of service to the reader. We can also see the particularizing impulse at work in Bacon's inductive method, where an intimate knowledge of the particular is seen as the key to greater knowledge. Of course, this epistemological investment in the particular was current long before Burton, Bacon, and even Lambarde. Jonathan Sawday finds its roots in the 'scientific revolution' of the continental Renaissance that 'encouraged the seemingly endless partitioning of the world and all that it contained.'[53] In *Chorographia: or a Survey of Newcastle Upon Tine* (1649), William Gray undertakes a description of this city precisely because England's previous national and county chorographies have failed to 'attain unto the perfect knowledge of all passages, in all places.'[54] Gray's assumption, like that of other chorographers, is that a more exhaustive focus on the particular will yield a more 'perfect knowledge' of English places.[55] In this way, the genre emerges as part of the 'culture of dissection' spawned by Renaissance science in which the county, city, or hundred – like the body – 'has to be opened out, displayed, so that its interior dimensions are truly known and experienced.'[56] Thus, Lambarde trades the clear lines and neat categories of generalization for the overlapping variety of particularization. In doing so, he gains a different type of certainty: one that is more specific and in some ways more accurate. He also arrives at a different vision of order. Though Lambarde elsewhere imposes order on the landscape by projecting uniformity onto its surface, here order emerges as an aggregate, in which constituent parts of the landscape give shape to the whole. As we shall see, such an approach has much more in common with an older, more feudal form of English order in which the land is a patchwork of distinct entities.

For one thing, the author's structural and topical emphasis on specific places has a fragmenting effect. The implication is that Kent is not so much a county unit as collection of its diverse topographical and human features. There is a certain gazetteer-like quality to the *Perambulation*'s structure; each place is a distinct entry, disconnected from the larger geographical fabric of which it is a part. Such a structure, combined with Lambarde's use of place as a determining factor for content – 'I deeme it impertinent to my purpose, to speake further of any thing, than the very place in hand shall iustlie give me occasion' (87) – effectively partitions Kent into discrete geographical units.

Lambarde's apportioning mentality is especially evident in his treatment of history. In terms of both subject matter and space, the Kentish past dominates the *Perambulation*. But what sort of county history emerges? Beginning with the county's first inhabitants, Lambarde does provide a general overview of Kent's history in the 'Estate of Kent' section. But this narrative breaks off at the Conquest in 1066; thus, there is no generalized county history for the most recent 500 years. The perambulation proper fleshes out some details from this period, albeit in a piecemeal manner. The entry on the Cinque Ports, for instance, lets us know that continental invasion was a major concern in this period, and that Kent was an important part of the royal defense network. By mentally collating the various entries, a reader could arrive at a pretty thorough account of Kent's history. But Lambarde makes no attempt at such a larger application. Instead, he leaves the historical detail scattered throughout his place entries. The end result is something like 84 individual historical narratives, rather than one systematic county history. Lambarde devotes 13 pages to the history of Kent as a whole, and around 400 pages to the histories of the individual places within Kent.

But Lambarde's historical narrative is even more fragmented than these numbers suggest. Only in the entries for large towns like Canterbury and Rochester does the author provide anything like a uniform chronology of local history. Usually, he simply includes whatever disparate elements he happens to have knowledge of. Thus, some place 'histories' skip hundreds of years, and others have only one noteworthy event detailed at all.[57] Such entries are much closer to antiquarian remains than what could be termed a historical narrative. Even when one historical chain of events is thoroughly described, it too can be particularized – as when a single event is spread out over multiple place entries. In the entry for Wingham, the reader hears that Archbishop Baldwin came here 'at such time, as hee had contention with his Covent of Christes Church, for making a Chappell at Hakington, as in fit place you shall finde more largely disclosed' (240). Although

Baldwin's actions are brought up in relation to Wingham, the reader must wait until the Hackington entry (44 pages later) to learn the cause. For Lambarde, the observance of 'fit place' seems more important than narrative cohesiveness.[58] The author's treatment of Thomas à Beckett is even more parceled out. Much of the archbishop's history is reserved quite naturally for the Canterbury entry, but supplementary details are also found in the entries for Hyde (162), Saltwood (164), Romney (179), Harbledown (288), Strood (356), Lessness (394), and Otford (460). As a result, Beckett's full history emerges piecemeal through the lenses of the various Kentish places that had a role in its making. It is a decentralized way of presenting history because it disperses a central historical narrative into its constituent parts. In the case of the *Perambulation*, this dispersal is dictated by place. While it is unclear why Lambarde sticks so doggedly to place, he does seem to want to tie his historical subjects to the settings in which they occurred.[59] Perhaps he is only making a claim that each place has its own historical legacy – or its own 'antiquities,' as Lambarde would have put it – that isn't simply subsumed into a larger county (or national) narrative. In any case, Lambarde's fragmented treatment of history tends to undermine the more uniform ordering that he elsewhere asserts. In terms of its political implications, such a narrative dispersion has much more in common with a distributive model of local government than a monolithic county community.[60]

Significantly, Lambarde's chorography does take a keen interest in sub-county government and administrative arrangements. The beginning of the *Perambulation* specifies that 'The whole Shyre hath long been, and is at this day, divided into five partes, commonly called Lathes . . . which also be broken into Hundrethes, and they againe parted into Townes and Borowes, most aptly for assemblie and administration of justice' (3). From the outset, then, Lambarde asserts the fundamental importance of sub-county divisions, and links them with effective administration.

In the place entries that follow, Lambarde describes these local government mechanisms and the particular offices, privileges, and customs that they codify.[61] We have already noted Kent's diverse composition of liberties, franchises, charters, manorial courts, and conventional county government, so it is not surprising that the arrangements described by Lambarde vary in age, origin, and function. Some areas of the county fall under special laws: Romney Marsh is 'governed by certaine lawes of Sewers' while the Weald falls under the 'Statute of Woods.' Particular towns are likewise noted for special privileges (Cinque Ports), exemptions (Chatham), or jurisdictional arrangements (Milton and Genlade). Sometimes, Lambarde just likes to point out some pieces of the invisible web of connections that tie local places together. In his entry for Swanscombe, for instance, he notes: 'The Manor of Swanscombe, is holden of Rochester Castle, and oweth service toward the defence of the same, being (as it were) one of the principall Captaines to whome that charge was of auncient time committed, and having subiect unto it, sundrie Knights fees, as petie Captaines (or inferiour souldiours) bound to serve under her banner there' (434). Together, these local arrangements are a fascinating mix of ancient custom and recent innovation. In many cases, the Crown had expressly set up these local arrangements and continued to maintain (or at least not disallow) these privileges.[62]

Whatever their source, such privileges and administrative arrangements serve as maintainers of local order in the *Perambulation*. On a literal level, they are the means by which particular towns, villages, and land areas are governed. And within each entry, they provide an appropriate receptacle for the narrow focus and detail of Lambarde's description. Presumably, these specialized structures are well suited to manage the particular concerns that have been generated by the place's history and current singularities. One example is the privilege of 'wreck of the sea,' which determined who was entitled to the spoils if a vessel wrecked at sea and washed up on the coast. Though the beneficiaries varied from place to place, the privilege established proper claimants in advance and – by preventing a chaotic free-for-all – helped bring order out of potential disorder. Nor were such local guidelines easily discounted, even by the royal prerogative. When William the Conqueror founded Battle Abbey in Sussex, he granted the monks 'wreck of the sea' on a portion of the Kentish coast. Before long, the monks' privilege was put to the test – and validated – in the reign of William's son, Henry I:

> [A] ship laden with the Kings owne goodes was wrecked within the precinct of this libertie, which his Officers would have seised and saved to his use: but Geffray (then Abbat of Battell) withstoode them, and that so stoutly that the matter by complainte came to the Kings owne hearing: who (to make knowen how much he valued his fathers graunt) yeelded the matter wholy into the Abbats owne courtesie. (257–258)

By emphasizing local arrangements, Lambarde disperses the maintenance of order into Kent's constituent communities. Whereas the county unit was the primary receptacle of the centralizing order discussed earlier, here it is the smaller units of Kent's hundreds, towns, and villages that bring order from within. Each place is treated as a discrete unit that then forms part of a broader, more aggregate order. Such a vision of order appears all the more natural because these places have already been distinguished by their separate historical narratives and endearing singularities.

Even though the result is an order that is not built on sameness or uniformity, Lambarde makes it clear that fragmentation and diversity need not lead to instability. In fact, gavelkind – the Kentish inheritance practice to which Lambarde devotes a special section of the book – could be said to contribute to a sort of aggregate order. Since land is divided up amongst all children instead of being handed down via primogeniture, land holdings naturally become smaller and more fragmented. Yet for Lambarde such fragmentation actually leads to greater stability. Because of gavelkind, 'every man is a freeholder, and hath some part of his own to live upon'; as a corollary, 'no where else in all this realme, is the common people more willingly governed' (7–8). Similarly, the *Eirenarcha* affirms that diversity is no threat to order. In clarifying what is meant by 'the maintenance of the peace,' Lambarde observes: 'Justices of the Peace were not ordained (as some have thought) . . . to reduce the people to a universal unanimitie (or agreement of minds) . . . Neither is it any part of their office, to forbidde lawful suites and controversies . . . but to suppresse injurious force and violence, moved againste the person, his goods, or possessions.'[63] Here, creating order is not about reducing everything to 'universal unanimitie' or sameness. Instead, Lambarde allows for differentiation and distinctiveness (even disagreement) so long as they do not erupt into any kind of disorderly threat. Even though these passages apply specifically to the duties of a JP, they also encapsulate something of Lambarde's approach to ordering Kent in the *Perambulation*. He is not so invested in uniformity and regularity that he reduces Kent to one landscape and one common history. Rather, he allows and even treasures the particular differences that he finds.

Conclusion

In the *Perambulation*, then, can be found two very different strategies for bringing order to the places and features of Kent. We have seen Lambarde's tendency towards an imposed uniformity in the first part of this chapter. It is characterized by a carefully pursued literary method, the use of oversimplification to carve up landscape, a desire for uniformity in government and religion, and an emphasis on general characteristics common to the whole county. Here the creation of order hinges on asserting regularity and establishing the wider context of the county or nation. But we have also seen Lambarde's penchant for recording local particularities. His entries are full of singularities of place, disparate historical narratives, and specialized administrative arrangements. Here, order is aggregate and emerges from an investment in the particular.

As a narrative characteristic, this dual mindset is intriguing. But it is not simply that Lambarde cannot decide which vision of order he wants; rather, the *Perambulation* is a reflection of the historical moment in which its author was living. If chorographies suggest how people ordered the world around them, and especially how they thought about local places in relation to the nation-building that was occurring at the time, then the *Perambulation* is a striking historical/political document. It reflects the tension between an ancient organic order that was being slowly replaced by a more centralized national government. The Crown was the impetus behind this new county government, and before long William Lambarde (who became a JP in 1579) would lend his cooperation. Lambarde, of course, was a loyal servant of the Crown throughout his life, but something – perhaps his practical experience as a local official or his antiquarian nostalgia – made him cling to some features of the old order as well. Or perhaps Lambarde's duality is best seen as compounding the advantages offered by each model of government. In the *Perambulation*, centralization offers stability, political and religious uniformity, and the best protection against the specter of rebellion. Traditional local government, on the other hand, offers a more exact form of administration. Not only are its specialized structures well suited to address local concerns, they also contribute to the 'noteworthy distinctiveness' that defines and distinguishes the local in the first place. Together, the central and the local offer disparate but equally valuable enticements.

Ultimately, Lambarde turns to the gentry to mediate between the competing claims of a centralized and a dispersed order. The Kentish gentry are ideal governors for Lambarde because they are able to bridge two worlds. As appointees of the Crown charged with executing legal, fiscal, and administrative tasks, they have one foot solidly in Westminster. But as native gentlemen born and bred in the areas they serve and sensitive to local needs and peculiarities, they have another foot solidly in the local community. Peter Clark articulates their position more broadly: 'the gentleman's primary function in county society was as an intermediary between different concepts of the community – the local gentleman mediating between village and hundred, the more important landowner mediating between hundred and county, and the county grandee mediating between shire and kingdom.'[64] Because of his position as intermediary, one could argue that the gentleman is able to maximize the strengths of each model of order. He is an instrument for imposing uniformity from the top down, but he is also sensitive to local differences and able to convey local concerns. Lambarde seems aware of this middle ground in an important passage of the *Eirenarcha* that discusses the discretion that is reserved for justices of the peace. After making it clear that JPs are bound to the law and do not have a lot of room to maneuver, he then concedes that 'the Justice of the Peace may exercise sometimes Legis actionem, and sometimes Judicis officium, or (which is all one) Judicium and Discretum, as the case shall offer, and the law will suffer him.'[65] Thus, as the gentleman JP enforces abstract laws, he may also need to consider the particular circumstances of the case. In other words, Lambarde allows for discretion to operate within a larger legal framework. While we should not exaggerate such discretionary freedom in the formal duties of an Elizabethan JP, it is certain that it was an important part of his unofficial duties. Justices of the peace were often called upon to settle disputes and offer informal arbitration at the local level. Lambarde himself says that a gentleman should be as much 'a compounder as a commissioner' of the peace.[66] One look at the *Ephemeris* – Lambarde's personal journal of his JP activities – reveals unofficial arbitration and mediation to be an important part of his daily office.[67] In this sense, the gentry are ideal orderers because they are already mediating the competing claims of uniform adherence and local application.

A key passage in the *Perambulation* exemplifies Lambarde's blending of these two models of order. In the entry for Rochester, the author includes a long section on the maintenance of the bridge spanning the Medway River. The original bridge was composed of nine arches and numerous planks, '[t]oward the reparation and maintenance whereof, divers persons, parcels of lands, and townships . . . were of dutie bound to bring stuffe, and to bestowe both cost and labour in laying it' (352–353). In other words, the bridge was parceled out 'by tenure, or custome, or both' (353) and various localities were assigned to the maintenance of a specific section. It is a striking image of diverse communities combining to form something cohesive. Around the year 1300, this wooden structure was 'borne away with the Ise [ice]' (344), and a new stone bridge was built by Sir Robert Knolles. This bridge's upkeep depended on a similar division of labor, which continued to function effectively.

Some local men even contributed to the beautification of the bridge independently: Sir John Cobham erected a chapel at one end, and Archbishop Warham adorned some of the masonry with iron bars. But at some point, the bridge's maintenance was neglected, and the structure began to fall into disrepair: 'For, besides that the landes contributarie to the repaire thereof were not called to the charge, even those landes proper were so concealed, that verie fewe did know that there were any such to support it: the revenewe being so converted to private uses, that the countrie was charged both with Tolle and Fifteene, to supplie the publique want, and yet the woorke declined daily to more and more decaie' (355). For whatever reason, there simply was not enough initiative and/or authority present to continue what had heretofore been an effective arrangement. According to Lambarde, Queen Elizabeth learned of the bridge's poor condition while on progress in Kent 'in the fifteenth yeere of her Raigne' and began a process that led to the bridge's rejuvenation. She set up a commission composed of William Cecil, 'certaine Lords,' and 'divers knights and Gentlemen' of the county to look into and try to improve the bridge's maintenance. The result was a new statute and a reformed arrangement, though one still founded on the shared upkeep of many of the same nearby people and communities. The bridge, Lambarde happily reports, is now doing better than ever.

Overall, the basic method of bridge upkeep is still very much in line with a decentralized and aggregate vision of order. The integrity of the local unit is preserved, so much so that a group of people visiting from Gillingham (for instance) could look at the structure's second pier and declare, 'that's *our* section.' Out of these separate contributions, a cohesive and useful structure is able to emerge. But Lambarde's emphasis on the Crown's recent role is also significant. Without Elizabeth's concern and call for action, 'it was to be iustly feared,' says Lambarde, 'that in short time there would have beene no Bridge at all' (354–355). Thus, the Crown's authority and resources were key elements in restoring what was almost lost. Yet it is also worth noting that Elizabeth did not take over the maintenance of the bridge; rather, she provided the impetus and structure for change (through the commission and the resulting statute), but then left it once again in the hands of the local community. The bridge's current healthy condition then is a result of both traditional local arrangements and central royal authority. Not surprisingly, the native gentry have played a key role in this fusion. The bridge was built by Sir Robert Knolles, beautified by Sir John Cobham, and reformed (via the commission) with the help of local knights and gentlemen. Afterwards, the gentry continued to be involved in the collection of money and upkeep. In fact, William Lambarde himself would go on to serve faithfully on the Rochester Bridge Corporation from 1585 to 1601.[68] Overall, the bridge's maintenance is a fit emblem for William Lambarde's multifaceted approach to order in the *Perambulation of Kent*. He clearly values the local and its particulars, but he also sets this sort of decentralized approach to order within a larger context of the more centralized and uniform state that was emerging in England.

3
Michael Drayton and Jacobean Court Culture

The *Perambulation of Kent* and the chorographic genre that it helped establish came to exercise a significant influence on the poetry of Michael Drayton. Born in 1563, Drayton was a contemporary of Camden and Lambarde and was directly affiliated with the antiquarian movement.[1] In other words, he was well aware of the ways in which local places were coming to be valued and described in the second half of the sixteenth century. But as a writer, Drayton was probably influenced more directly by Edmund Spenser's poetic engagement with chorography, which Bart Van Es describes as 'a mode that surfaces recurrently in Spenser's prose and poetry.'[2] Spenser seems especially drawn to chorography's use of the contemporary landscape as 'a springboard to the past.'[3] In works like *The Ruines of Time* (1591), *Colin Clouts Come Home Againe* (1595), and the *Faerie Queene* (1590, 1596), he appropriates this basic feature of chorographic narration to create his own mythical histories of England, Ireland, and Wales. As a young poet, Drayton seems to have been particularly inspired by the marriage of the Thames and Medway episode in Book IV of the *Faerie Queene*.[4] But what is an occasional feature of Spenser's verse becomes a central concern in the works of Michael Drayton. In the analysis that follows, I will explore Drayton's engagement with the fertile link between land and history that chorography helped bring to the forefront of the English imagination.

This chapter will focus on the early works of Michael Drayton from the 1590s to the publication of the first half of *Poly-Olbion* in 1612. In particular, I want to explore the author's conception of heroic literature. The first half of the chapter will investigate Drayton's heroic and note the persistent bond between the history that he depicts and the place or location in which it occurs. Drayton invests in the local landscape, I will argue, to help access, create, and sustain the heroic virtue that his poems seek to inculcate. The final two sections will show how the Jacobean Court threatened Drayton's heroic, and spurred him to develop further the local landscape of England and Wales – in *Poly-Olbion* – as a heroic alternative to the unheroic Court.

Heroic history

Although Drayton is well known for his varied poetic output, English history is his most pervasive subject. Early in his career he published four legends (*Peirs Gaveston*; *Matilda*; *Robert, Duke of Normandy*; *Legend of the Great Cromwell*), a set of historical letters (*Englands Heroicall Epistles*), and a long historical poem (*Mortimeriados*) that was soon expanded into a historical epic (*The Barons Warres*). Towards the end of his life, Drayton produced the *Battaile of Agincourt* and the *Miseries of Queene Margarite*. And, of course, the middle part of the poet's career was dominated by Drayton's imaginative shaping of English history into *Poly-Olbion*. It is little wonder that one critic has called Drayton 'the historical poet of the English Renaissance.'[5] But why was Drayton drawn to English history? And what uses did he make of it?

Like most early modern historical poets, Drayton is prone to embellish and transform his raw source materials to suit his larger poetic purposes. But these larger purposes are not primarily didactic. In the *Barons Warres* (1603), for instance, Drayton provides nominal warnings of the dangers and consequences of factionalism and rebellion, but there is very little assigning of blame. In fact, the poem provides a sympathetic treatment of the various faction leaders – the Mortimers, Edward II, and Queen Isabella – on both sides.[6] And although he writes 'legends' in the *Mirror for Magistrates* tradition, he is not primarily interested in depicting the whirling wheel of Fortune.[7] Nor does Drayton's treatment of history seem motivated by the sort of cause/effect analysis that was coming to characterize the new political histories.[8] Drayton may draw from the many traditions of history writing that were current in his historical moment, but he is ultimately after a different sort of effect.

Richard Hardin has argued convincingly for a different approach to understanding the historical poetry of Drayton: '[I]t may best be described as monumental history, the effort to derive a pattern of greatness from contemplation of the past. More important than its admonitory purpose . . . was its epideictic function. The monumental historian, through the vision of the past, reminds his audience that greatness, having been possible once, may be so again.'[9] The primary function of Drayton's histories is the depiction of greatness. Throughout Drayton's works, the basic building block of this monumental vision of history is the heroic: the charismatic personalities and captivating actions of the past. 'Like Pindar, and Homer before him,' notes Joan Grundy, 'Drayton worships *arete*, heroic excellence, the great spirit manifesting itself in great deeds.'[10] In fact, Drayton is one of the earliest English poets to register the influence of Pindar; the twelve odes that he published in 1606 are generally credited with introducing the classical ode into English poetry.[11] Not surprisingly, part of what attracts Drayton to the ode is Pindar's 'transcendently loftie' use of the form to '[consecrate] to the glorie and renowne of such as returned in triumph from Olympus, Elis, Isthmus, or the like' (II:345).

This fascination with the heroic permeates many of Drayton's early works. Drayton introduces his Legends as 'being a Species of an Epick or Heroick Poeme, [that] eminently describeth the act or acts of some one or other eminent Person' (II:382). By 'Epick or Heroicke Poeme,' we are not to expect a rigid genre with formalized conventions, for that notion of the 'epic' had not yet developed in England.[12] What defines the category is not conventions and structure so much as its lofty spirit. It is this spirit that pervades *Englands Heroicall Epistles* (1597) and allows these fictitious love letters to earn the tag of heroical poetry. As Drayton explains in the preface to this work:

> though (Heroicall) be properly understood of Demi-gods, as of Hercules and Aeneas, whose Parents were said to be, the one, Caelestiall, the other, Mortall; yet is it also transferred to them, who for the greatnesse of Mind come neere to Gods. For to be borne of a caelestiall Incubus, is nothing else, but to have a great and mightie Spirit, farre above the Earthly weakenesse of Men. (II:130)

For Drayton, there is something almost divine about 'a great and mightie spirit,' and it is this that he hopes to raise from the past and hold before his readers. 'The concentration upon the acts of "some one eminent Person" . . . is something Drayton sought instinctively,' observes Joan Grundy. 'And beyond the act, he sought the spirit of the act. Because this is so, Drayton's historical poems are in a sense interesting more for their reach than for their grasp. They are charged with a love of the heroic, and a desire to isolate it, to capture its pure essence.'[13]

But in practice, Drayton's heroic turns out to be quite flexible. Predictably, he uses this conception of the heroic to depict pious Crusaders like Robert Duke of Normandy and glorious English battles like Agincourt. But it is also elastic enough to accommodate the heightened passions of noble lovers in *Englands Heroicall Epistles*, a heroically chaste woman in the *Legend of Matilda* (1594), and a long-suffering if manipulative queen in the *Miseries of Queene Margarite* (1627). In other words, Drayton's heroic is far from monolithic. It can center on romantic love, religious piety, military valor, chastity, and even such morally ambiguous qualities as cunning and pride. The heroic, Drayton shows us, can even characterize deeply flawed characters like Mortimer, Peirs Gaveston, and Thomas Cromwell. In the depiction of Mortimer, for instance, 'the stress . . . is . . . much more on greatness than goodness.'[14] Such historical characters may be forces of disorder and emblems of pride in Drayton's works, but they are still acting on a grand stage, and like Marlowe's overreachers, there is something intoxicating about their audacity.[15] The Earl of Essex, himself an overreacher, articulates the appeal of such heroic spirits to Drayton and his contemporaries. After defending his participation in 'forraine imploimens and actions of the warre' in his *Apologie* (1600), Essex feels compelled to justify (more generally) his 'friendshippe to the chiefe men of action and favour . . . to the men of warre.'[16] He associates with such men because he 'love[s] them for their vertues sake, for their greatnesse of mind: For little mindes though never so full of vertue, can be but a little vertuous.'[17] Such an assessment seems to capture something of Drayton's approach to his English heroes: even with their flaws, their much larger capacity for greatness can still be exploited.

Drayton depicts past heroes not only for their own sakes, but also to inspire great deeds in the present. In 'To George Sandys,' he says that 'brave numbers' are 'able to awake . . . men at armes' and ''Gainst pikes and muskets were most powerfull charmes' (III:208). Similarly, the ode 'To the Virginian Voyage' (1606) promises that the reading of heroic deeds 'shall inflame / Men to seeke Fame' (II:364). Ben Jonson's prefatory poem to 'The Battaile of Agincourt' (1627) anatomizes the effect that Drayton is after. First, he praises Drayton's lengthy catalog of transport ships and 'list of aydes, and force' for their exhaustive sense of detail. 'And when he ships them where to use their Armes,' Jonson continues, 'How do his trumpets breath! What loud alarmes!' Here, Jonson exalts in the vividness and energy of Drayton's depiction of history. But perhaps most importantly, the moment of Agincourt is brought forward into the present so that it can inspire anew: 'This booke! it is a Catechisme to fight, / And will be bought of euery Lord, and Knight, / That can but reade; who cannot, may in prose / Get broken peeces, and fight well by those.'[18]

But the sort of reaction that Jonson predicts cannot be evoked simply by chronicling the past. Rather, history must be treated poetically before it can become heroic. In *Matilda*, poetry is celebrated for its ability to record great acts and engrave them in the memory through stately rhyme (I:243). In the legend *Robert Duke of Normandy* (1596), Drayton says that the poet works by 'casting life in a more purer mold' and that the heroic is 'Truth in Arts roabs, adorn'd by Poesie' (I:285). The poet, then, not only embellishes truth with his art, but works to isolate and intensify that heroic quality that is worth preserving in the first place. In Drayton's poetry, this process relies on, among other things, dramatic characterization, epic similes, orations, apostrophes, extravagant scene painting, and the compression and amplification of the historical record.

The local landscape

And yet there is another factor at work in this dynamic that bears attention; the heroic is often closely associated with the specific geography of its occurrence. Drayton's argument for the fourth canto of the *Barons Warres* exemplifies the prevalence of place names to be found in his historical poetry:

> The Queene in Henault mightie Friends doth win,
> In Harwitch Haven safely is arriv'd,
> Garboyles in England more and more begin,
> King Edward of his Safetie is depriv'd,
> Flyeth to Wales, at Neath received in,
> Whilst many Plots against him are contriv'd;
> Lastly betray'd, the Spensers and his friends
> Are put to Death: with which, this Canto ends. (II:68)

Here, Drayton is not just concerned with recording that Queen Isabella and Mortimer invaded England from France and that King Edward fled to Wales; he goes out of his way (in the Argument, no less) to specify that the Queen found favor in *Henault* and landed on the Essex coast at *Harwich*, and that Edward II fled specifically to *Neath Castle* in Wales. The poet is even more obviously devoted to place when he enters into extended chorographical descriptions in the midst of the action. Thus, a twenty-line account of the Trent River region precedes the Battle of Burton Bridge in canto II. And later, when the Queen and Mortimer have their court in Nottingham, Drayton offers a forty-line description of the city, the castle, the vales and meadows, and the forest of the region (II:107–108). Even in *Englands Heroicall Epistles* a sense of where the letters are written (and received) is quite pervasive – place details are even supplemented by annotations at the end of each letter.[19] In other words, a sense of place permeates Drayton's historical poetry and seems to play a key role in creating and sustaining the heroic. But why should this be so?

Despite the vibrancy and ennobling power of heroic action, it is an unstable and vulnerable quality. In several passages, the poet complains about the oblivion with which time afflicts great men and women. Drayton laments that Peirs Gaveston's 'name hath been obscured so many yeeres' (I:158) and has Matilda plead: '. . . I crave my life may be reveald, / Which blacke oblivion hath too long conceald' (I:214). Human action – even heroic action – is transient and fleeting. Even when it is occurring contemporaneously or is immortalized in verse, the heroic (like Iago's 'honor') is 'an Essence that's not seene.' Or, as Falstaff appraises it, a mere word that may amount to no more than the 'ayre' that is used to utter it. Drayton, of course, has no such misgivings about the *existence* of honor, but he is acutely aware of the problems that its immaterial nature can generate. *The Legend of Robert Duke of Normandy* voices this anxiety in Fortune's taunt about the transitory nature of Fame:

> Thou art an Eccho, a by-word, a wind,
> Thine ayrie bodie is composd of breath,
> A wandring blast, within no place confin'd,
> Which oft of nothing, silly somthing saith,
> Yet never canst speake well till after death;
> And from imagination hast thy birth,
> Unknowne in heaven, & unperceiv'd on earth (I:258)

The charge of Fortune – and fear of Drayton – is that fame (and the heroic which accompanies it) will either be 'unperceiv'd' or ephemeral. Poetry, Fame later responds, can provide a written monument to halt some of these attenuations. But heroic verse is still, one might argue, 'composd of breath' and (even for Drayton) perhaps a bit too reliant on imagination. Drayton therefore addresses the need for the heroic to be in some 'place confin'd' by turning to the land itself. It is a tangible, specific, and relatively unchanging surface on which to graft the heroic. Beginning in the 1590s, therefore, Drayton uses England's geography to help re-infuse tangible, stable meaning and value back into the moral abstractions associated with heroic virtue.

When Drayton's poetic career began in 1591, his antiquarian contemporaries were already enlisting the land's help in recovering the past. The land holds tangible traces of the past like ruined walls, old coins, fields where armies once clashed, and redolent place names. In other words, the land – because it possesses remnants of what went before – is a reservoir of history. Such a realization was at the heart of the sixteenth-century antiquarian movement that sought to take stock of and describe the 'antiquities' that were still physically present throughout England. As we have seen, these antiquarians used the historical remnants that they found to construct new histories of their cities, counties, and nation.

Drayton may be working from this same antiquarian impulse, but his literary productions take it a step further by bringing the poetic imagination to bear on English places. In the *Barons Warres*, the barons' defeat at Borough Bridge results in a permanent alteration of the landscape so that grass no longer grows around the bridge. To this day, Drayton tells his readers, the bare ground serves as a 'marke of their Mischance' (II:40) and bears witness to this bloody episode in English history. In the *Legend of Peirs Gaveston*, the Forest of Arden provides similar access to the distant past. When Peirs is executed at nearby Blacklow,

> Oke-shadowed *Arden*, fild with bellowing cries
> Resounding through her holts and hollow grounds,
> To which the Eccho ever-more replies,
> And to the fields sends forth her hideous sounds,
> And in her Silvan rude untuned songs,
> Makes byrds, and beasts, for to express my wrongs. (I:204)

In Drayton's estimation, the mysterious sounds of the contemporary forest are actually doleful cries associated with Gaveston's death. Clearly, Drayton's topography provides access to past events in a much more imaginative way than it does for the prose chorographer.

Indeed, at times, Drayton personifies the land and makes it an actual participant in historical events. To the historical fact that the King and his barons were camped on opposite sides of the Trent before the pivotal Battle of Burton Bridge, Drayton adds: '. . . the Trent was risen so betwixt, / That for a while prolong'd th' unnaturall fight, / With many Waters that it selfe had mixt, / To stay their Furie, doing all it might' (*Barons Warres*, II:30). Much later, in the *Miseries of Queene Margarite*, Towton Field is affected by but also contributes to the carnage of the Wars of the Roses: '[the field] With the hot gore of her owne Natives wet, / Sends up a smoke, which makes them all so mad, / Of neither part that mercy could be had' (III:106). The creative license that Drayton takes in making the River Trent and Towton Field 'characters' in his historical drama could be dismissed as mere poetic fancy. But such personifications also emphasize the land's connection to the past. The human participants of these bloody battles had been dead for centuries, but Drayton's readers could still access other 'participants' by wading into the Trent or visiting Towton Field. In this way, many of Drayton's works dramatize the land's potential to put us in more direct contact with the heroic.

Seen holistically, the land serves as a mediator between history and the poetry that heroicizes it. On the one hand, the land preserves history and provides a tangible link to events and actors that might otherwise be remote and obscure. Because of this, the land gives the poet concrete material on which to work, and can even serve as a catalyst for the poetic imagination. Ultimately, the land not only helps connect history and poetry; it comes to function as a receptacle of the heroic. Monumental history, once it is created by the poet, is projected back onto the land, where it becomes a constant, visual reminder of the heroic. In this sense, the land becomes for Drayton a sort of map of heroical memory. Like the Brunonian memory system that Frances Yates describes, its power is rooted in its status as a 'striking' image that is 'able to stir the memory emotionally' and even 'arouse the passions.'[20]

Drayton's treatment of Berkeley Castle in the *Barons Warres* epitomizes this complex dynamic. Edward II was cruelly murdered at Berkeley Castle in 1327, but Drayton – writing in 1603, some 276 years after the fact – insists that the occurrence is continually projected into the present:

> Let thy large Buildings still retayne his Grones,
> His sad Complaints by learning to repeat,
> And let the dull Walls, and the senselesse Stones,
> By the impression of his Torment sweat,
> And for not able to expresse his Mones,
> Therefore with Paine and Agonie repleat,
> That all may thither come, that shall be told it,
> As in a Mirror clearly to beholde it. (II:102)

On a basic level, this passage begins with the idea that the land is a historical source, that it bears the imprint of those events that have occurred upon it. In this case, a king has died here and the place will forever be associated with the infamous act. At this point, we are not very far from the way in which the antiquarians might approach the land as a histori-cal source. But unlike its role in antiquarian works, here Berkeley Castle spurs Drayton's *poetic* faculties and invites him to bring his *imagination* to bear on the scene. When he does this, the poet begins to create corre-spondences that tie physical remnants to emotional responses. Thus, the walls sweat in 'impression of his Torment' and the buildings echo with Edward's moans. While such associations may not be strictly true, they transform Berkeley Castle into a more evocative historical source and an enduring, visual reminder. For Drayton, to walk through Berkeley Castle is to be instantly and powerfully reminded of the mighty (and in this case, tragical) deeds of Edward II's reign. The castle has been transformed from historical site to highly charged heroic scene.

But Berkeley Castle and other historical sites are meant to take on new meaning not only for the poet, but for 'all [that] may hither come, that shall be told it.' The visitor to Berkeley Castle will now have a heightened sense of Edward's spirit and the suffering to which it was subjected. Though this awareness was forged in the pages of the *Barons Warres*, the castle has become its physical locus. Drayton's monumental history has now become a permanent part of the English landscape. A similar transferral takes place near the end of *The Legend of Matilda*. In this work, Drayton locates Matilda's virtue and John's tyranny not just in his heroic poem, but in the village of Dunmow in Essex. This village is where Matilda was poisoned and where John performed his penance, and so, Drayton imagines, where 'all the world' will remember 'And quote the place, (thus ever) passing by, / Note heere King Johns vile damned tyranny' (I:244). Dunmow has become a 'living' associa-tion of the history that occurred here and the dramatic shades in which Drayton has depicted it.

Drayton's use of place to locate and stabilize heroic virtue would get its fullest expression with the publication of *Poly-Olbion* in 1612. In this voluminous poem, Drayton aligns hundreds of English places with their historical events (and corresponding heroic values). But even in the first two decades of his poetic career, Drayton's treatment of land already has a localizing tendency. We have already noted Drayton's habit of linking his historical subjects with particular places. Typically, this occurs in dramatic fashion near the end of the poem. The implication is that although 'great deeds' may have a universal application, they are best accessed 'locally' through particular places – Matilda in Dunmow, Edward II at Berkeley Castle, Gaveston in the Forest of Arden, and so on. Drayton, it seems, is willing to shrink the scope of heroic access in order to increase its intensity. As a result, certain English places come to embody certain aspects of heroic virtue. For Drayton, this is not only a function of specific historical events (e.g. Dunmow's claim to Matilda's exemplary chastity); particular heroic virtues may also cohere from more traditional associations. In the beginning of the *Barons Warres*, Drayton carefully describes the taking up of arms all across England. But rather than specify who fought on which side, Drayton catalogs the military skills in which different regions of England specialize:

> From *Norfolke*, and the Countries of the East,
> That with the Pike most skilfully could fight;
> Then those of *Kent*, unconquer'd of the rest,
> That to this day maintaine their ancient Right;
> For courage no whit second to the best,
> The *Cornish* men most active, bold, and light;
> Those neere the *Plaine*, the Pole-axe best that wield,[21]
> And clayme for theirs the Vaward of the Field. (II:19)

In a subsequent stanza, Drayton goes on to detail the martial proclivities of soldiers from Wales, Lancashire, Cheshire, and the North.[22] Each county/region of England is thereby associated with a particular heroic tendency.

Indeed, part of what makes English geography such a fitting receptacle of Drayton's heroic virtue is that both contain an infinite variety. We have seen that Drayton's conception of heroic virtue is not monolithic; it can take the form of love, piety, military valor, chastity, political action, or almost any other human virtue elevated to a grand stage or realm of action. We have also seen that such virtues are frequently commingled with (and even heightened by) suffering, tragedy, and character flaws. Though in Drayton's mind these various threads might be unified under the name of 'heroic,' the category's heterogeneity runs the risk of making the heroic an admired but ambiguous quality. But the land mirrors and is able to accommodate the variety that is found in the heroic. Its churches provide links to the religious past, its villages endure as hallowed birthplaces, its castles bear the marks of great sieges, and its arbors still echo with the vows of noble lovers. The individual components of the land provide a natural means of itemizing and parceling out the different aspects of heroic virtue – as Drayton overtly performs in the county catalog of the *Barons Warres* – and of making them more accessible to the reader. Such a project would be fully realized in *Poly-Olbion*, but it is significant that Drayton's early works already explore and assert a connection between the local landscape and heroic virtue.

The Jacobean Court

In the same year that the *Barons Warres* was published, James ascended the English throne. Despite his initial attempts to secure the patronage of the new king, Drayton had an estranged and sometimes hostile relationship with the Jacobean Court.[23] In various works, he satirizes the Court in general and James in particular, and in an elegy to William Browne he characterizes the entire reign as 'the evil time.'[24] While many have noted Drayton's disenchantment with the Court of James, few have recognized its *heroic* origins. For a number of reasons, the reign of James proved antithetical to the type of heroic poetry that Drayton espoused. It is this 'crisis of the heroic' – more so than any issue of patronage or personality – that accounts for Drayton's frustration with the Court and his eventual development of the local landscape into a full-fledged heroic alternative to the unheroic Court.

First of all, James's foreign policy was harmful to Drayton's conception of heroic action. The King began his reign by making peace with Spain. After two decades of intermittent war that had drained the treasury, peace was probably inevitable and might even have been brokered by Elizabeth if she had lived long enough. But the immediacy with which James made peace and the resilience he displayed in maintaining it throughout most of his reign was a dramatic (and sometimes unpopular) departure from the previous monarch. Under Elizabeth's leadership, England emerged as the chief defender of the Protestant faith, and the Queen came to be celebrated as the embodiment of England's religious values, maritime power, and dynastic ambitions. But James's pacific ideals required significant adjustment to this paradigm. From his London entry in 1603 to the masques of the 1620s, the King was associated with British unity, internal prosperity, and law-giving.[25] But the King's foreign policy was not to everyone's liking. And Drayton seems disappointed that, among other things, James was failing to assert England's might abroad. Not only did the King fall short of the standards set by previous English rulers (many of whom Drayton had written about), his pacifism had also made contemporary heroic action difficult by removing one of its main theaters: war. In the closing lines of the *Ballad of Agincourt* (1606), Drayton yearns for a return to the days of Henry V: 'O, when shall English Men / With such Acts fill a Pen, / Or England breed againe, / Such a King Harry?' (II:378). As the last word suggests, Drayton's hopes were in the more militaristic and anti-Spanish son of James: Prince Henry. It is Henry to whom Drayton dedicated *Poly-Olbion* in 1612, including an engraving of the prince in full armor.

Another potential theater for heroic action in Drayton's works is the realm of overseas exploration and colonization. In his ode 'To the Virginian Voyage,' the poet exclaims: 'You brave Heroique Minds, / Worthy your Countries Name, / That Honour still pursue, / Goe, and subdue, / Whilst loyt'ring Hinds / Lurke here at home, with shame' (II:363). Drayton pointedly contrasts the heroism of these trans-atlantic adventurers with the shame of those who remain at home in England. Later, in Song XIX of *Poly-Olbion*, Drayton catalogs, describes, and celebrates English voyages and daring feats at sea – borrowing both Hakluyt's stories as well as his grandiose tone. The problem, for Drayton, is that the new monarch by and large 'took measures to dis-courage such adventures.'[26] He halted English piracy and never really supported English overseas expeditions.[27] In other words, he refused to sanction what was, for Drayton, another avenue for the contemporary pursuit of heroic action. With the twin theaters of war and empire shut down, the heroic action (to which much of Drayton's poetry hoped to inspire its readers) was severely limited. '[I]n this latter Time, it hath beene said, / The tongue doth all . . .' complains Drayton in *The Owle* (1604), 'Vertue, whose chiefe prayse in the Act doth stand, / Could wish the Tongue still coupled with the Hand' (II:513).

For Drayton, the King's inaction in these areas was made worse by his action in other areas. In his first few years in office, James's selling of titles increased the size of the peerage, and – in Drayton's eyes – decreased its worth.[28] It enabled the rise of a man who 'Never durst looke upon his countreys foe, / Nor durst attempt that action which might get Him fame with men,' complains Drayton in the elegy 'To William Browne' (III:210). 'This Drone yet never brave attempt that dar'd, / Yet dares be knighted, and from thence dares grow / To any title Empire can bestow' (III:210). James's sale of titles, combined with his pusillanimous foreign policy, had created a state in which people become knights without ever proving their mettle. To make matters worse, the system also caused worthy men to be overlooked: 'The vertuous man depressed like a stone / For that dull Sot to raise himselfe upon' (III:210).

Despite Drayton's bitter attacks on the Jacobean Court, he is not criti-cal of all courts. In a long passage at the beginning of the *Legend of Peirs Gaveston*, Drayton paints an idealized picture of Edward II's Court. At least initially, it is an ideal combination of learning, military arts, and public service, from which machiavels, atheists, and pettifoggers are banished. It rewards virtue, merit, and honor with both the trappings and titles of nobility; it is a place where 'good men as rare pearles were richly prized.' In contrast to more recent courts, no doubt: 'Pride was not then, which all things overwhelms: / Promotion was not purchased with gold, / Men hew'd their honor out of steeled helms: / In those dayes fame with bloud was bought and sold' (I:161). All in all, Edward II's Court was an environment where heroic action was both fostered and rewarded. Throughout Drayton's works, the heroism of past times is celebrated and held up to inspire his contemporaries. But as first James's and then Charles's reigns unfold, there is an increasing resignation that this sort of heroic action is no longer possible. Drayton's 1629 commendatory poem for Sir John Beaumont's *Bosworth-field* is characteristic: 'But that brave world is past, and we are light, / After those glorious dayes, into the night / Of these base times, which not one Heroe have, / Onely an empty Title, which the grave / Shall soone devoure; whence it no more shall sound, / Which never got up higher then the ground' (I:505).

According to Drayton, not only did Jacobean court culture discourage heroic action, it also rejected the literary means by which men might be reawakened to great deeds. Jean Brink has observed that '[Drayton's] conception of the poet as a guardian of heroic values and a spokesman for virtue, unmistakably diverged from those of Jacobean patrons who expected poets to compose witty compliments and clever entertainments for court ceremonies.'[29] While this assessment oversimplifies the richness and complexity of the literature of James's reign, it does capture something of what Drayton himself expressed in his preface to the first part of *Poly-Olbion*:

> In publishing this Essay of my Poeme, there is this great disadvantage against me; that it commeth out at this time, when Verses are wholly deduc't to Chambers, and nothing esteem'd in this lunatique Age, but what is kept in Cabinets, and must only pass by Transcription. In such a season, when the Idle Humerous world must heare of nothing, that either savors of Antiquity, or may awake it to seeke after more. (IV:v)

For Drayton, both the shrinkage in scope and subject matter of Jacobean poetry represented an abdication of the poet's public duty. This trend has been caused by but also reflects a current literary state in which 'These [courtiers] boldly censure, and dare set at nought / The noblest wit, the most Heroike thought (*The Owle* II.497). The dearth of heroic action and the decline of heroic poetry have become inextricably linked.

Drayton's brand of historical poetry was also being undercut by new developments in historiography. Starting in the sixteenth century, historians began to approach their sources more critically and write histories that prioritized truth and accuracy over more traditional moral and aesthetic ends.[30] Of course, as Drayton's own works show, history and fiction were not completely separated by the early seventeenth century. Even so, the collaboration of the historian Selden and the poet Drayton in the first part of *Poly-Olbion* reveals the gap that was opening up between the two pursuits. Much of Selden's commentary serves as a corrective to Drayton's rather loose treatment of English history and myth – though Selden's tone is good-natured rather than overly stringent.[31] Selden's prose commentaries also underscore the extent to which poetry and history were beginning to part company. Carew is indicative of this trend in his 'Answer of an Elegiacal Letter . . . from Aurelian Townsend' when he politely defers the celebration of the military deeds of the King of Sweden to chroniclers and prose writers. Although some poets did continue to take up historical subjects, by the 1630s, 'strict respect for fact had become established as a standard of historical poetry.'[32] Obviously, neither the avoidance nor the unimaginative treatment of history was desirable for a poet of Drayton's mold. And though James and his Court could hardly be blamed for such a general development, it no doubt contributed to Drayton's sense of frustration.

Whether or not his charges are justified, Drayton *does* repeatedly blame the Jacobean Court's policies, values, corruption, and literary tastes for creating this 'evil time.' Yet possibly the most alarming feature of the Court to Drayton was the fact that this same malevolent influence was actually increasing in size and importance. James's Court was physically larger and spent more money than previous English courts. It also controlled patronage much more directly than had Elizabeth's studied, decentralized approach, as Smuts has shown.[33] Now, in order to exercise the sort of public, poetic vocation that Drayton desired, one had to be associated with the Court much more directly than had Drayton's idols Sidney and Spenser only a generation before. In many ways, the Court was becoming more of a national institution. And yet, paradoxically, the Jacobean Court was in other ways becoming more isolated from the rest of the country. Smuts has shown that during the early Stuart era, the Court became 'more firmly anchored in London, more distinct from provincial landed society in its outlook, and more sympathetic to the Baroque cultures of Europe.'[34] This assessment fits nicely with Drayton's tendency to paint the vices of the city and the Court with the same brush, and to charge them both with threatening to contaminate the rest of England.[35] In James's reign, the Court was coming to emblematize

England more and more, yet it was also (in Drayton's mind) increasingly disconnected from the heroic values that had shaped it in the past and should continue to guide it in the future.[36]

Poly-Olbion

In the ninth year of James's reign, Drayton published *Poly-Olbion*, a poem in which the author's dual interest in heroic virtue and English geography takes center stage. In some ways, the work is merely a natural outgrowth of the connection between history and land that Drayton had already explored in his earlier works. But in other ways, it seems particularly calculated to respond to the 'crisis of the heroic' that the Jacobean Court had precipitated. Drayton's disenchantment, I would argue, explains his voluminous effort to invest in the local landscape as a heroic alternative.

In doing so, *Poly-Olbion* develops and expands the localizing tendency that characterizes Drayton's earlier depiction of the land. The standard critical assessment of this ambitious work is that it is a nationalistic, patriotic poem that celebrates the landscape of England. Even though critics dispute the type of nationhood to which *Poly-Olbion* gives rise, they still tend to approach Drayton's masterpiece as a nationalistic work.[37] Here, I will argue that *Poly-Olbion* is at its heart a local poem. Although Drayton does give a tour of all of England and Wales, it is a tour that is organized by local geography, rooted in local distinctions, and delivered by local spokespersons. As he catalogs and celebrates the heterogeneity of the landscape, Drayton does not present the reader with a unified vision or a single cohesive meaning. In fact, the poem's most celebrated feature – its minute topographical and historical detail – has also been its downfall in the eyes of some readers; they are simply overwhelmed by the length and lack of focus of its 15,000 lines.

Poly-Olbion is a strange poem by almost any standard. It is topographical in nature, but it also contains a significant amount of English history. And these historical events are blended with everything, from Ovidian mythology to lists of agricultural products. The thirty songs that compose the poem are sung by a bewildering variety of personified rivers, hills, forests, marshes, and other landscape features. Finally, each poetic song is accompanied by a fantastical map and antiquarian commentary.[38] As the structure of this chapter has attempted to emphasize, the key to understanding Drayton's choices in *Poly-Olbion* is to allow Drayton's other works – and the historical context in which it was composed – to illuminate the many features of this poem that might otherwise appear as peculiarities. Viewing *Poly-Olbion*'s treatment of land, history, and poetry in the context of Drayton's earlier odes, epistles, legends, and other historical works will tell us how and why Drayton embraces the local landscape.

Like Drayton's *Legends*, *Heroicall Epistles*, and *Barons Warres*, this work takes heroic history as one of its primary subjects. Angus Vine has written of the poem's extended 'literary engagement with antiquarian scholarship' and Homer Nearing has observed that despite *Poly-Olbion*'s other features, 'it is the poetic energy of these historical passages that gives life to the massive poem.'[39] As with his earlier works, Drayton is interested in transmuting that history into heroic poetry. Drayton himself refers to *Poly-Olbion* as a 'Herculean labour' in the preface and goes on to invoke the British bards because of their heroic associations:

> O memorable Bards, of unmixt blood, which still
> Posteritie shall praise for your so wondrous skill,
> That in your noble Songs, the long Descents have kept
> Of your great Heroes, else in Lethe that had slept . . . (IV:118)

Drayton may well think of himself as a modern-day bard, because he too will recount, catalog, and dramatize the heroic personalities and events of Britain's past.[40]

The result is a grand pageant that combines the various types of heroism seen in Drayton's individual works. Soldiers, saints, kings, conquerors, magicians, lovers, explorers, and even mythical giants all mingle together in *Poly-Olbion*'s verses. Such variety confirms the earlier suggestion that Drayton's heroic is multifaceted and non-monolithic. And yet the occurrence of these heroes together (sometimes in the same historical narration) shows that the various aspects of the heroic need not be mutually exclusive. In Song XXII, for instance, Drayton transforms the scourge of civil war into something sublime and magnificent, so that all of its historical participants – even Richard III and the Irish – are praised for their boldness and valor.

One way that *Poly-Olbion* is able to contain so much heroic diversity is by associating different heroic virtues with different places. As in his earlier works, Drayton looks to the land as a reservoir for history, tradition, and myth. It is the land that contains visible traces and distant echoes of what has come before, and it is this connection to history that Drayton is so eager to explore in each area that the poem traverses. In each of the thirty songs, Drayton focuses on a one- to three-county area. As the Muse progresses through each region, she takes a particular interest in the natural landscape (rivers, mountains, forests, caves, marshes, plains, valleys, lakes, springs, vales, stones, heaths, plants, and animals) and man-made features (ruins, cities, mines, agriculture, livestock, dykes, gardens, hunting, and customs) that characterize each region. In almost every song, the land is then associated with the particular historical events that it has 'witnessed.' The River Dart tells of Brutus and his founding of Britain, Wrekin Hill sings of Saxon military might, and the topographical features of the northern border tell of England's centuries-old clashes with the Scots.

As these examples suggest, *Poly-Olbion* is able to dramatically fix these associations because the land itself is the primary mouthpiece of historical narration. Drayton turns the rivers, hills, forests, marshes, and other landscape features into personified spokespersons that sing of the history that they have 'witnessed.' In fact, hardly any of the many speakers that Drayton employs to deliver his topographical descriptions and historical accounts are human or even man-made.[41] Instead, voice is given to the land itself. The setting of Song XVII is London, yet it is the River Thames, not the city of London, that records the exploits of England's monarchs since the Norman invasion. Similarly, Sherwood Forest is entrusted with the tale of Robin Hood, and the River Avon sings of Guy of Warwick's deeds. In making the land itself the primary narrator, Drayton dramatizes and develops the 'voice' that he only occasionally attributed to the land in his 1590s works.

This effect is strengthened by Drayton's treatment of places as fully developed 'characters' in their own right. His spokespersons aren't just generic voices; they are embodiments of the places they represent. One of the most memorable characters in *Poly-Olbion* is Song XXVI's old lady of the Peak district:

> A withered Beldam long, with bleared watrish eyes,
> With many a bleake storme dim'd, which often to the Skies
> Shee cast, and oft to th' earth bow'd downe her aged head,
> Her meager wrinkled face, being sullied still with lead,
> Which shee out of the Oare continually refines (IV:530–531)

Like the Peak district, this 'withered Beldam' is ancient, beaten down by storms, and adept at mining. Appropriately, her physical characteristics actually reflect the features of the land that she embodies. Throughout *Poly-Olbion*, Drayton refers to his embodiments of place as nymphs. The concept, of course, stretches back to classical mythology, where nymphs are minor deities who inhabit and sometimes personify the characteristics of the trees, streams, and mountains in which they dwell. In his poem, Drayton seems to emphasize the nymphs' taking on of the characteristics of the places they represent. He also provides a visual representation of this relationship. Thus, the 'withered Beldam' of the Peak is actually depicted on an accompanying map. She is a stooped-over old lady in matronly garb who is wielding a walking stick. This drawing corresponds to the text and provides a visual identity for this memorable character.

Indeed, almost every landscape feature mentioned in the poem (and certainly all the ones that speak) are represented as quasi-mythical figures who are sitting, standing, and frolicking across the maps that precede each of the thirty songs.[42] The maps were intended, Drayton tells us in the preface, 'for the further understanding of my Poeme.' Specifically, they are for 'delineating to thee, every Mountaine, Forrest, River, and Valley; expressing in their sundry postures; their loves, delights, and naturall situations' (IV:vi). As the latter part of this passage suggests, the figures on the maps embody the same distinctive characteristics of place that have been highlighted in the text. All of the personifications occupy poses that are appropriate for their sphere: river nymphs pour water or emerge from rivers, forest nymphs hunt, dykes recline horizontally, and moors sit down flat on the map. Despite some of these languid poses, the maps seem alive with activity and vitality. There is much gesturing, pointing, and posing; it is as if Drayton wants to dramatize their roles in verbalizing the landscape. And although some regularity is maintained in the presentation of similar personifications – for example, all of the city-figures are standing and their heads are crowned with buildings, and all of the hills are topped by male walkers with staffs – no two representations are exactly alike. Each one has a slightly different pose or accoutrement. Even the river nymphs – the most frequent depiction on almost every map – are individualized. Most are engaged in similar activities and don't have any clothes, but their arms are all placed in slightly different positions. Considering the quantity of rivers included in the poem, it is clear that Drayton has gone out of his way to maintain individual distinctions in the maps. Together, the maps serve as visual embodiments of the local associations that Drayton is affirming in the text. They also help develop the idea that each place has its own local heroic spirit that can function as an alternative to the Court.

We know that these local claims are important to Drayton – and not merely convenient – for we find him going out of his way to establish the particular qualifications for many of his speakers. Thus, the general praise of English virtues (in answer to the preceding panegyrics on the ancient Britons, Songs IV–X) is handled in Song XI, but only after Cheshire itself has been shown to be the embodiment of self-sufficient, yeoman sturdiness and brave military service. Such a careful justification not only reveals Drayton's commitment to tie even the most generalized history to a particular place, it also implies that each geographical area of England has a rightful 'claim' to some sort of heroic history. In Song XVIII, Drayton puts the history of English warfare in France into the mouth of the Medway, reasoning that this river has the greatest claim to speak on their behalf:

> This Medway still had nurst those navies in her Road,
> Our Armies that had oft to conquest borne abroad;
> And not a man of ours, for Armes hath famous been,
> Whom she not going out, or coming in hath seen:
> Or by some passing Ship, hath newes to her been brought,
> What brave exploits they did; as where, and how, they fought.
> (IV:366)

Even more tenuous is the Great Ouse's chronicling of all the civil war battles fought in England in the past 500 years (Song XXII). This claim stems not from having witnessed them all (no single landscape feature could boast that), but because, according to tradition, the irregularity of its tides once prophesied the Wars of the Roses. Here, a peculiar feature of the Ouse has been combined with larger events to give this river special importance – and a special identity – in English history.

Although the heroic deeds recounted in the various songs of *Poly-Olbion* would seem to be applicable to all English readers, Drayton insists on a local point of access. His local alignments may therefore suggest that they possess a special relevance for the people of that area. The mythical figures of Brutus and Arthur, for instance, have long been associated with the West Country. Indeed, their legacy has undoubtedly contributed to that region's traditional fashioning of itself as a remote and fiercely independent area. When Drayton broaches the contemporary skepticism about the authenticity of Arthur and Brutus, it is significant therefore that the erosion of heroic values has a local manifestation. For it is the River Dart and the Camel River that first align themselves with these mythical figures and then complain that they 'the envious world doth slander for a dreame' (IV:9).[43] Arthur and Brutus have a particular potency as heroic vehicles for the West Country; it is therefore the West Country that suffers when such values are undermined.

The notion of local places as separate – and even exclusive – entities is underscored by the competition in which various landscape features engage. In Drayton's chorographic sources, such rivalries take the form of single authors making assertions about the pre-eminence of their subject locale. In *Poly-Olbion*, they are conducted via impassioned debates between the actual competitors. Mountains proclaim their supremacy over valleys, forests vie with downland, and plains strive against marshes. There are also disputes among characters that belong to the same landscape category. For instance, Redhorse Vale, the Vale of Ringdale, and the Vale of Bever all give lengthy explanations to support their claims as England's most beautiful valley. Other competitions are interspersed in the text, ranging from the specific – two areas of Lincolnshire jealously compare their local bird populations – to the sustained rivalry between the Celts and the Saxons that plays out over several songs. Such verbal banter can be read as a manifestation of the local pride that accompanied the emergence of local consciousness. When Hampstead and Highgate compete for 'noblest hill' in Middlesex in Song XVI, one can't help but wonder if it reflected an actual rivalry between neighboring human populations. Regardless, the rivalries also serve another, and in some ways more important, end for Drayton: the creation of a heroic dynamism. A passage in *Robert Duke of Normandy* implies that fame arises from peril, and a similar assumption governs the competition and rivalry here. Striving is a key ingredient for Drayton's heroic, and that is exactly what we find the land (in personified form) engaging in. It is the same method that Spenser uses to transform abstract morals into heroic virtues: by plugging them into a context of struggle and striving. But for Drayton (unlike Spenser), it doesn't matter who wins these contests – and that is why he never declares winners.[44] What matters to Drayton is the creation of an England where the very land exudes a heroic spirit – both in its own 'actions' and in the ancient history of which it sings.

Another byproduct of dramatizing rivalries without declaring winners is that Drayton leaves the reader with a keen sense of the differences among the various counties and regions of England. *Poly-Olbion* is meant to be a celebration of England and Wales, but the focus is not on homogeneity. Rather, Drayton revels in the diversity found in the topography, history, and culture of various parts of the island. The full title of the work indicates this intended heterogeneity: *Poly-Olbion. or A Chorographical Description of Tracts, Rivers, Mountaines, Forests, and other Parts of this renowned Isle of Great Britaine, With intermixture of the most Remarquable Stories, Antiquities, Wonders, Rarityes, Pleasures, and Commodities of the same: Digested in a Poem.* Drayton's great theme throughout the poem is variety and differentiation, and he constantly puts before the reader the 'wonders, rarities, [and] pleasures' that inhabit the different parts of the island. Nor is he only concerned with cataloging well-known features and popular stereotypes. In an illuminating passage in Song XXIX, Pictswall (Hadrian's Wall) grumbles that the Muse has lingered on 'every petty Brooke' and almost forgotten himself, one of England's 'longst-liv'd monument[s.]' But that is exactly the point. Drayton has been endeavoring all along to capture and present the hundreds of smaller, less conspicuous features that make England so diverse. He wants us to look closely and celebrate the particular. Drayton describes the distinctive products and industries of areas like the Cotswolds (sheep), Yarmouth (fishing), Lemster (wool), Chatmosse (turf bricks), Rutlandshire (cattle), and Peryvale (wheat). He lingers on the natural beauties that are specific to each region: the seven natural wonders of the Peak, the flowers of the Golden Vale, and the views from Mt. Skiddow. The poet also describes the various animals that make different areas distinct: West Country hounds, Severn valley horses, Lincolnshire birds, and Isle of Lundy coneys. Even man-made features of the landscape – like the Cambridgeshire dykes and the Roman ruins of Essex – are important components in Drayton's pageant of variety.

What, then, is the broader vision that Drayton offers of England and English heroism? *Poly-Olbion* has been traditionally read as a nationalistic and patriotic poem. While there are features of *Poly-Olbion* that support such a reading – especially the frequently discussed frontispiece – a nationalistic reading does not always accord with the multifaceted and heterogeneous land that Drayton offers us. Andrew Hadfield has usefully argued against the unity that others have seen in the poem, though he reads the diversity of *Poly-Olbion*'s voices as a source of anxiety, skepticism, and even chaos.[45] But I would argue that Drayton *revels* in the diverse topography, history, and culture that he finds in various parts of the island. The very title of this poem – 'Poly-Olbion' – is indicative of such a focus, with 'poly' signifying 'more than one, or many' and 'Olbion' or 'Albion' the ancient name of England. Thus, 'many Englands' or 'England's variety.' Either way, the emphasis is on embracing the *variety* that the island holds. Although diversity need not preclude national vision, Drayton does go to a lot of trouble to emphasize what makes each part of England distinct from all others – the skills of Cornish wrestlers, the wonders of the Peak, the wisdom of Oxonians, and Northamptonshire's specialized hunting methods. And by embodying these distinctions in personified characters (that also appear visually on *Poly-Olbion*'s maps), Drayton solidifies the perception that these places have their own discrete identities. Finally, the competition and rivalry into which the poet places the land generates a heroic dynamism and adds a sense of exclusivity and local pride to these distinctions. All in all, the poet's use of distinctions, personifications, and rivalry imparts a localizing tendency to the depiction of the land.

If *Poly-Olbion* is a nationalistic text, it is surely one that draws strength from diversity and arrives at the celebration of the general (England) by proceeding through the particular (the local). Drayton has expanded his earlier association of land and the heroic so that *each* part of England now has its own heroic history and its own contemporary embodiment of heroic spirit. No longer must the path to the heroic deeds of the past and the inspiration for the present run through James's Court. But the result is not so much an alternative to a corrupt court as a corrective to it. Since most courtiers had country estates to which they returned for large portions of the year, perhaps Drayton is simply trying to awaken them to the heroic greatness in their own 'backyards.'[46] In firmly locating the heroic in the rural landscape, Drayton also seems to counteract the stereotypes of the idle country gentleman and the country as a place of passive retirement. *Poly-Olbion* finds valor, passion, and nobility in every forest, stream, and vale. Through this heroic and localized landscape, the poem would inspire contemporary native inhabitants to emulate the great actions of their predecessors.

The resulting forms of heroism are united in one literary work, but this need not mean that they are subsumed into a single heroic vision. The personified landscape features are not presented as minor, submissive spokespersons who are trotted out to do the Muse's bidding as it flies over all of England. Instead, they retain their own personalities and concerns. In Song II, the River Itchen's praise of Bevis of Southampton develops into a rather long digression. The river's tributaries, sensing the impropriety (and the Muse's desire to move forward), plead with the Itchen to desist. But the Itchen goes on to give 120 more lines of Bevis's history before she is finally interrupted by the New Forest. The Muse's larger agenda notwithstanding, this obscure river will have its say. There are plenty of other proud, assertive, and querulous voices in *Poly-Olbion* that are never quite reined in. But as the narrative is passed around to (and sometimes seized from) various spokespersons, the effect is one of ebullience rather than frustration. The land itself becomes a channel of the greatness of spirit and heroic striving that Drayton has been unable to find in a monolithic court or in any other single vision of England.

4
George Herbert and Caroline Religious Uniformity

The concept of nationhood became even more contested in the two decades following the 1612 publication of *Poly-Olbion*. The commencement of Charles I's Personal Rule in 1629 did little to assuage the fears of a monolithic nationhood and, indeed, seemed to confirm Michael Drayton's particular complaint about the disproportionate influence of the royal Court. As we shall see, there were initiatives afoot to reduce the national religious landscape to a greater uniformity as well. Such political and religious issues came to dominate public discourse, and it is easy to look back at the 1620s and 1630s as a time of national polarization. But against this highly charged backdrop, contemporaries continued to turn to the local to mediate ideological conflicts. The same heterogeneity that Lambarde and Drayton endorsed in their works was also found serviceable to a new generation of writers. In this chapter we will consider George Herbert's investment in the local parish as a strategy for negotiating national religious controversies about appropriate forms of worship. As with the previous two chapters, the author's deployment of the local is intimately tied to his historical moment – in this case, the rise of Laudianism.

The rise of Laudianism continues to absorb historians of the Stuart Church. Despite disagreement over the movement's origin, nature, and primary architect, most historians agree that its *effect* was to polarize rival factions in the Caroline Church and erect ideological battle lines that hastened the descent into Civil War. Kevin Sharpe, however, has posited a non-ideological factor that helped determine contemporary reactions to Laudianism: 'When attitudes and reactions to ceremonies were strong they may well have been more affected by changes in circumstance and local custom than by any concerted position or opposition among the parishioners. Because episcopal practice had

long varied, local reactions were quite different.'[1] By Sharpe's estimation, the inertia of parish tradition – rather than complex theological
or liturgical positions – played a significant role in determining local
perceptions of and reactions to Laudianism. In addition, the reminder
that 'episcopal practice had long varied' suggests that a certain degree
of local variation may even be viewed as a feature of the *via media* that
had defined the Church for decades. If the Jacobean Church can be seen
as an accommodating consensus that allowed for some degree of local
variety, by the 1630s an emerging Laudianism (intent on conformity
and uniformity) was creating a more prescriptive version of Church doctrine, liturgy, and worship – with less local variety. As Sharpe's assertion
implies, it may well have been Laudianism's encroachment on local
'prerogative' rather than 'the beauty of holiness' that most antagonized
its opponents.

   This chapter will argue that George Herbert's major prose work,
The Country Parson (c. 1632), registers contemporary anxieties about
Laudianism's impact on parish religion. Herbert's vision of the ideal
parson has been variously treated by critics as character sketch, conduct
book, and autobiography. In most of these treatments, *The Country
Parson* (like Herbert's poetry) is used to sound the author's theological views, establish his liturgical preferences, and claim him for a faction of the English Church.[2] Some, like Achsah Guibbory, have more
usefully focused on Herbert's 'equivocal' attitude towards ceremonial
conflicts.[3] But I will argue that Herbert's vision of parish religion is not
so much concerned with revealing his personal religious tastes as it is
with endorsing a concept of local variety that had been a feature of the
Jacobean Church. Given the climate of the 1630s, Herbert cannot be
too overt about this endorsement – and he certainly does not have his
parson ignore canons or confute bishops. Instead, he uses what Annabel
Patterson has called 'disguised discourse' and 'oblique communication' to present a tacit challenge to the Laudian remaking of the local.[4]
Again and again, *The Country Parson* dwells on distinctions among
parishes and emphasizes the parson's need to consider these differences
in ordering the religious life of the parish. Moreover, the ideal parson
repeatedly consults particular circumstances and individual experience
(rather than broad rules) for epistemology, moral judgments, and even
Church ritual. In my reading, it is not really that Herbert objects to the
'beauty of holiness' or other elements of the Laudian program. It is that
these changes are being insisted upon across the board for all parishes.
In this sense, *The Country Parson* constitutes a plea for traditional local
'autonomy' in the face of an increasingly rigid Laudianism.

This chapter will begin by historicizing the local variety contained within the Jacobean Church. It will then chart the impact, beginning in the late 1620s, of the Laudian program on parish religion. I will then offer an extended reading of *The Country Parson* as a response to these changes. Finally, I will assess the nature of Herbert's localism in terms of his larger vision of the English Church. My objective throughout is to bring the wealth of recent scholarship on Stuart Church history to bear on *The Country Parson* and to show how this text both reflects and addresses an overlooked aspect of its cultural moment.

The Jacobean Church

James inherited a church characterized by a wide spectrum of belief. Despite his considerable interest and skill in theology, the King had no intention of constructing rigid definitions of orthodoxy. His main objective was to secure the supremacy of the Crown in church affairs and root out political subversion. Because of this, he was much more concerned with 'extracting proof of loyalty and obedience than in the small print of regular conformity.'[5] Thus, James required the clergy to subscribe to the legality of the Prayer Book and the bishops. In doing so, he effectively drove a wedge between moderate Puritans (who were willing to subscribe) and those who were of a more radical bent. But beyond this litmus test, James cared little for defining religious orthodoxy. Even though 141 canons (most of which were holdovers from Elizabeth's reign) were ratified anew in 1604, the King did not focus his attention on stringently enforcing them.[6] After an initial drive in the first few years of his reign, James did not enforce full conformity in the localities.[7] Instead, his approach could be characterized as a reciprocal arrangement that James struck with moderate Puritans. He was willing to trade a certain amount of flexibility and variety at the local level in exchange for overall loyalty. In this way, the Jacobean Church sought to accommodate as many as possible and avoid conflict.

Nor was James the only architect of this arrangement. As Peter Lake has pointed out, the toleration of occasional conformity also depended on a 'sympathetic hearing' from 'powerful men in Church, State and university' who could mediate or soften official policies with 'tact and discretion.'[8] This included local godly gentry who supported lecturers and had a say in Church livings. But it also extended to the bishops themselves. Collinson has written of the 'Grindalian episcopacy' of the early English Church, which Fincham describes as 'a style of government practised by Calvinist bishops which overlooked divisive issues of nonconformity in favour of the common endeavour of bishop and puritan to spread the gospel and resist Roman Catholicism.'[9] Such an arrangement was rooted in shared Calvinist doctrine and maintained for the sake of Protestant unity and the larger evangelical goals of the Church.[10] This ideological unity, it was judged, was not worth jeopardizing by an over-insistence on minute conformity and the subsequent alienation of tender Puritan consciences. Lake has written this arrangement as a *de facto* 'series of nudges and winks' between ecclesiastical authorities and local clergy that benefited both sides.[11] A certain amount of local autonomy in the exact observance of Church ritual and liturgy was tolerated in exchange for the larger unity of the Church.

Even if Lake's claims of such a tacit agreement are overstated, authorities would have found it very difficult to monitor the localities and enforce conformity. The royal supremacy notwithstanding, 'ecclesiastical government . . . was fundamentally devolved and decentralised' and periodic visitations could only go so far in effecting change.[12] It was much easier – and more productive in the eyes of many Jacobean officials – to draw the line at occasional conformity.[13]

The result was a system of Church government that some have praised for its inclusiveness, but others have decried for its introduction of a subversive 'fifth column' within the Church that was one of the major causes of the Civil War. But whatever its ramifications down the road, it was an arrangement that made a distinct mark on the Jacobean Church: 'The strength of [the Jacobean] Church lay in the incorporation of diverse and competitive threads in English protestantism, and its acceptance of the ambiguities of official formularies which could produce rival readings of the English reformed tradition.'[14] While such rival readings were generally contained under the umbrella of a Calvinist consensus, they did lead to some distinct variations in local practice. The Church's 'toleration of a certain variety of liturgical practice'[15] meant that some clergymen directed worship exclusively from the Prayer Book and minutely observed canon prescriptions – like kneeling at communion, making the sign of the cross at baptism, and wearing the surplice[16] – while others, like John Rogers (a godly minister in Essex) 'refused the surplice and used the ceremonies minimally, perhaps meeting the canonical requirement of reading the divine service and administering the sacraments twice a year using the Prayer Book ceremonies.'[17] Moreover, such disparities could even be found in the same diocese, where parishes in which 'the Canons of 1604 had made very little impression' jostled up against 'islands of canonical conformity.'[18] Local standards of conformity were subject to a host of factors, including 'religious topography,' the temperament of bishops, and even 'pressures from influential patrons.'[19]

Some of this latitude arose from ambiguity in Jacobean canons and other official formulations. For instance, the canon dealing with the placement of the communion table presumably allowed parish churches to decide where it sat when not in sacramental use. Some parishes moved it around while others (even before Laud) set it permanently at the east end. When the Laudians attempted to prescribe this and other practices in the 1630s, their directives often flew in the face of earlier variations.

Minimal enforcement also ensured a diverse religious landscape. Moderate Puritans, so long as they subscribed to the legality of the Prayer Book and the bishops, flourished during James's reign. They also increasingly pursued voluntary religious activities – like fasting, household meetings, and lectures – that provided an alternative religious focus away from the ceremonialism of the official Church.[20] Yet this arrangement was flexible enough to hold. Patrick Collinson has remarked: 'the Jacobean Church had the capacity to contain within its loose and sometimes anomalous structures vigorous forms of voluntary religious expression.'[21]

Local congregations not only benefited from these developments, but they also became important sites of negotiation. Early modern conformity, Michael Questier and Peter Lake remind us, should be thought of 'not so much as a static grid of rules and regulations,' but 'as the end product of the process whereby those rules and regulations were enforced.'[22] In the flexible approach of the Jacobean Church, local communities were free to approach conformity as a 'series of negotiations mediated through a variety of political, ideological, institutional, even geographical and personal structures or sets of circumstances.'[23] In other words, standards of parish conformity could be and were actively shaped on the local level. Such a process produced some parishes that were very much in line with 1604 Canons, but it could also function as an important and depressurized outlet for those individuals and communities who found themselves in less than total agreement with national orthodoxies. As Judith Maltby, John Fielding, and others have shown, these local negotiations were not without ideological conflicts.[24] But this does not mean that factions of Puritans and Anglicans or Calvinists and Arminians were battling each other for supremacy on the local level. The Jacobean Church, Peter White reminds us, was more of a broad spectrum of belief than a pair of polarized camps.[25] And although the higher ecclesiastical authorities were sometimes necessary to broker peace, most local communities reached consensual accommodations that reflected the shaping hands of local clergymen and congregations.[26] In short, local flexibility was a big reason why the Jacobean Church was 'a fairly comprehensive one, in which different viewpoints and different groups had worked out mutual accommodations.'[27] In effect, parishes had a certain latitude to fashion their own version of Anglicanism.

Part of the Anglican tradition bequeathed to George Herbert, then, was a level of pastoral 'autonomy' in determining the forms of worship of the parish. Despite indications that James began to tighten conformity after 1622, this is by and large the Church in which George Herbert grew up and first considered taking orders.[28] Occasional conformity and local variety may have originated out of concerns for tender Puritan consciences, but that did not mean that one had to be a Puritan to appreciate this arrangement. By the end of James's reign, it had become a defining feature of the English Church, and something that everyone (including non-Puritans) had come to expect.

The rise of Laudianism

Much changed in the English Church after the accession of Charles in 1625. Recent scholars have taken great pains to identify the primary architect of Caroline Church policy (Charles, Laud) and determining the most appropriate label for it (Carolinism, Arminianism, Laudianism). While I am not primarily interested in these distinctions, I will follow Peter Lake in calling this movement 'Laudianism' and treating it as 'a coherent, distinctive and polemically aggressive vision of the Church, the divine presence in the world and the appropriate ritual response to that presence.'[29] However, my main concern is to sketch how the Laudian program affected the local variety that we have noted in the Jacobean Church. Here, there is less disagreement, since even critics of the 'rise of Arminianism' theory (like Kevin Sharpe and Peter White) grant that the 1630s saw a heightened emphasis on conformity. Whether or not critics see the program of 'Thorough' as innovative or merely enforcing traditional canons, most agree that it represented 'a marked discontent and indeed discontinuity with the immediate past' of Jacobean accommodation.[30]

Why were churchmen like William Laud, Richard Neile, William Peirs, and Matthew Wren so intent on creating greater uniformity across the parishes of England? First and foremost, they – as well as King Charles I – tended to view Jacobean 'unity' as illusory. For them, flexibility and accommodation really only masked disorder and division; this they sought to rectify with a program of order, obedience, and uniformity.[31] Charles was not without political motives in this shift. Clashes with the Puritan House of Commons in the 1620s did little to assuage the King's fears of Puritan subversion, a danger from which the 'Arminians' promised to rescue him. But uniformity was also central to a larger ecclesiastical vision. Laudians sought a more inclusive national church in which all – not just the predestined or Elect – could theoretically be saved. Because of this, the sacraments took on added significance as a means to salvation and a focus of corporate worship. The end result was a new insistence on the uniformity of worship. For Laud, 'The unity of the visible church required one set form of worship. In the departure from the canons and the diversity of local practice tolerated by some of his predecessors and especially by Abbot, Laud believed the decline of piety had its roots.'[32] There was much at stake, then, at the local level, and it is little wonder that it became the focus of Laudian efforts.

The implementation of Thorough on the local level was enabled by such measures as the expansion of episcopal powers, more stringent visitations, and the suppression of non-beneficed lecturers.[33] The overriding aim was a more exact enforcement of church canons, including church fabric, ceremonies, and liturgy. 'No longer were the authorities satisfied with the Jacobean requirement of formal obedience,' says Fincham, 'whereas once a puritan divine such as Richard Bernard had enjoyed some indulgence in view of his preaching and pastoral gifts, now, as Dee of Peterborough observed, "no man's learning and piety shall excuse . . . his unconformity."'[34] As bishop of London, Laud developed a system of local informants to ferret out nonconforming ministers and 'he followed up his information with a greater energy and diligence than his predecessors had displayed.'[35] As archbishop, Laud demanded full reports from each bishop on the progress of 'reforms' in their diocese.[36]

Margaret Stieb's study of the diocese of Bath and Wells has shed much light on the Laudian approach to the local. In this 'laboratory' of Laudian practice, she observes a 'new atmosphere' that was characterized as 'a general tightening up of activities.'[37] These included the extirpation of unauthorized theology, tidying and streamlining church courts, and harsher punishments for violations.[38] At least in this diocese, there is little doubt that Laudian churchmen both demanded and attempted to enforce a more minute uniformity. Significantly, the impulse for change came from above, as Stieb found 'the involvement of higher officials in events normally dealt with on a parochial or diocesan level.'[39] The marked increase in presentments of local church-wardens who themselves failed to present shows the extent to which ecclesiastical authorities were willing to bypass the traditional manner in which nonconformists were detected and reported.[40]

Under such scrutiny, occasional conformity became increasingly untenable. But it is not simply that the Laudians were better able to expose the skillful evasions of nonconformists. Webster and Lake suggest that the Laudians actually forged a new, more rigorous definition of conformity. The dilemma of some who ran afoul of the Caroline Church was really 'an incomprehension of Laudian policy; while the ministers were striving to present themselves as "conformable", committed Laudians were looking for conformity without exception: it was no longer sufficient to show willing by using sections of the liturgy, or wearing the surplice occasionally.'[41] As Tyacke puts it, the concept of ecclesiastical conformity was undergoing a shift from 'sometimes' to 'always.'[42]

Although the timing and intensity varied, it became clear that the Laudians meant to apply these standards to local congregations throughout the realm. In fact, measures were even taken to extend heightened conformity to English merchant and military communities abroad.[43] Whether at home or abroad, the Laudians sought to fundamentally reshape the local. This goal can be seen at the administrative level, where Laud unsuccessfully petitioned to break up some of the larger dioceses into smaller units in order to enable greater episcopal control.[44] It can also be seen in the Laudian notion that parish churches should model themselves after the cathedral in their diocese. This 'idea of the cathedral as exemplar' was especially evident in the Laudian campaign to fix the position of the altar at the east end of the church.[45] But the underlying assumption, that the parish church should surrender its peculiarities and become a copy of a single model, represents quite a departure from the Jacobean legacy of parish tradition and adaptation.

Perhaps more alarming to contemporaries was the related notion that the Chapel Royal should be a 'prototype' for the parish church.[46] As Peter Heylyn, chaplain in ordinary to the King, put it: 'The king's chapel . . . or the king's practice in his chapel . . . is the best interpreter [of the] rubrics, laws and canons of the Church.'[47] This assertion implies not only that the Chapel Royal should function as a model, but that it should also serve as the source for determining conformity standards. Using this rationale, Charles hoped to enlist 'the parish church as the main vehicle for the propagation of his sacramental kingship.'[48] Here there seems to be much more at stake in the Laudian attentions to the local than just heightened scrutiny or the 'donnish hectoring of Laud.'[49] Part of the Laudian program seems to have been to transform the local unit by way of erasing its distinctions and integrating it into a more centralized and uniform whole.

The crucial years of this shift coincide with George Herbert's writing of *The Country Parson* (c. 1630–1632), just prior to his death in 1633.[50] Any interpretive approach to *The Country Parson* should therefore begin with a careful consideration of Annabel Patterson's first hermeneutical principle: 'the importance of an exact chronology in determining what any given text was likely to mean to its audience.'[51] How far along was the Laudian transformation of the local in 1630? The rise of Laudianism is often associated with 1633, the year of Laud's elevation to arch-bishop.[52] But the movement was already well underway in the previous decade.[53] The House of Commons debates of the 1620s reflect the belief that 'a general Arminianization of the English Church was in process' – particularly with regard to ecclesiastical preferment and ceremonial-ism.[54] In an attempt to enforce previously dormant canons, visitation articles were also becoming more stringent in the 1620s.[55] Laud himself was promoted to the bishopric of London in 1628 and 'rapidly became the principal royal adviser on religious affairs.'[56] One of the first things he orchestrated (along with Harsnett) was the Royal Instructions of 1629. The Instructions, 'concerneing certaine orders to be observed and put in execution by the severall bishopps in his province,' were aimed at restricting lecturers, tightening ordination procedures, and increas-ing the presence of the liturgy – particularly the practice of catechiz-ing.[57] Although they were fairly specific in their intended applications, the royal orders signal a much larger shift in Caroline Church policy. 'The Instructions,' observes Davies, 'constituted a radical, if somewhat disorganized programme to subordinate the pulpit to the liturgy, and to uproot nonconformity within the Jacobean Church.'[58] Moreover, they were intended to effect change at the local level; not only do they include instructions for local regulation, but they were widely dissemi-nated to parsons and churchwardens in each parish.[59]

As a newly ordained parson just settling in at Bemerton (Wiltshire) in 1630, Herbert would have been acutely aware of the 1629 Instructions – and the larger changes that they intimated. In Herbert's neighboring diocese, more dramatic changes were already underway. In London diocese, Bishop Laud was already applying a corrective to the '*laissez-faire* attitude towards nonconformity' that had been tolerated by his pre-decessors.[60] By 1629, partial conformity in London diocese was already becoming both 'ideologically and administratively unavailable.'[61]

The prosecution of Thomas Hooker, a lecturer in Chelmsford, Essex, encapsulates these changes, and also suggests the broader perceptions that individual cases could generate.[62] Even in dioceses like Herbert's Salisbury, where Laudianism had not fully arrived, there could still exist an 'atmosphere of confrontation' and 'fears of imminent persecution.'[63] Or as Davies remarks: 'Although the king's policies did not have a uniform impact upon the country, their effects transcended ecclesiastical boundaries and created deep scruples of conscience, which led contemporaries to question the demands of authority.'[64]

Herbert may never have openly questioned the demands of authority, but he was surely aware of the impact that the Laudian program was beginning to exert on the local level, and the polarized resistance that it was engendering – even if his own Bishop of Salisbury, John Davenant, was notably moderate. And as a newly ordained parson just taking up his duties, Herbert would naturally have been concerned with defining what religion should look like on the local level. Herbert's personal situation, combined with the Caroline Church's renewed focus on parish religion, make *The Country Parson* ideally suited to speak to its historical moment.

The Country Parson

Given the highly charged moment in which it was written, the first thing that one notices about *The Country Parson* is what type of manual it is not. 'In the atmosphere of the early 1630s,' observes Ronald Cooley, 'a book written primarily to gain ecclesiastical preferment, or even merely to avoid provoking the authorities, would have been an emphatically Arminian book: one that emphasized the sacramental and ceremonial aspects of worship and de-emphasized the public godliness that had become associated with Puritanism. But this is not at all the sort of book Herbert wrote.'[65] In Cooley's estimation, what *The Country Parson* does *not* do is itself suggestive. But if it is not 'an emphatically Arminian book', what is it and how does it fit into the religious controversies of the 1630s?

Herbert's succinct 'Author to the Reader' provides some answers. Annabel Patterson has demonstrated that early modern prefatory material often functions as a 'kind of signal' that addresses itself to 'reader expectations' and even 'alert[s] the reader to his special responsibilities.'[66] In the first two sentences, Herbert seems to acknowledge the danger of his project by his attempt to qualify its intention: 'I have resolved to set down the form and character of a true pastor, that I may have a mark to aim at . . . Not that I think, if a man do not all which is here expressed, he presently sins and displeases God.'[67] Herbert's initial claim is that he is offering a private and 'indifferent' model; that is, *The Country Parson* should not be viewed as a rigid or contentious statement. And yet, Herbert's very disavowal also signals a potential application. The possibility (and perhaps intention) of a broader application is made more explicit in the third and final sentence: 'The Lord prosper the intention to myself and others, who may not despise my poor labours, but add to those points which I have observed, until the book grow to a complete pastoral' (190). The language is still humble and non-contentious, but the focus is no longer on 'the true pastor' as a private model. Herbert is now envisioning a readership of 'others' whom he imagines will emulate and 'add to those points' in some sort of collective enterprise. The goal of this enterprise – the creation of 'a complete pastoral', or 'treatise dealing with the duties of a pastor'[68] – seems rather benign. But such a project, as a 1630s readership would no doubt have recognized, was bound to comment on some of the fundamental assumptions of the Laudian program.[69] Herbert wants his readers to think about *The Country Parson* as part of a larger vision that needs to be added to and perfected – not only within the pages of his book, but also perhaps within the English Church.

It is significant that Herbert's treatise begins by subtly undercutting the ecclesiastical hierarchy on which so much of Laudian uniformity depended. The first line of the first chapter asserts that 'A pastor is the deputy of Christ for the reducing of man to the obedience of God' (191). This is a seemingly innocuous formulation, but one that – especially given the choice of the word 'deputy' – noticeably bypasses archdeacons, bishops, other ecclesiastical officials, and the Crown itself in order to derive the pastor's authority directly from God. As if to emphasize this point, Herbert affirms that 'this is the complete definition of a minister' and that the link between Christ and pastor 'contains the direct steps of pastoral duty and authority' (191). All pastors, presumably extending to the most humble parson, derive their authority directly from God. The author then clarifies the particular pastoral scope of his manual: 'Of pastors (intending mine own nation only, and also therein setting aside the reverend prelates of the Church, to whom this discourse ariseth not) some live in the universities, some in noble houses, some in parishes residing on their cures' (191). This is one of the few passages in *The Country Parson* where Herbert actually mentions the higher ecclesiastical authorities by name. They are respectfully acknowledged – 'the reverend prelates of the Church' – but then jettisoned as irrelevant to the 'discourse' that will follow. Herbert will limit his scope to the local level; a space, he implies, within which these prelates are of little concern.

Such an opening dovetails neatly with Herbert's later depiction of the ideal parson as largely self-sufficient. Herbert's prototype is well-rounded, 'full of all knowledge' (193), and capable of almost anything. He 'desires to be all to his parish, and not only a pastor', but also a lawyer, physician, and judge (219). The parson's wide-ranging capabilities are not only convenient, they are what justify his 'deputization' and assist him in guiding the flock entrusted to him. He is still, of course, subject to the higher ecclesiastical authorities; however, there is a sense that, ideally, he should not need to rely on them. One could even argue that the parson's knowledge and skills qualify him to actively shape the religious experience of his parish rather than simply enact whatever directives are passed down from above.

From the beginning, then, Herbert sets up a self-reliant parson who is well-qualified for a certain degree of independent action. But what are Herbert's motives for doing so? Does it signify a deep-seated antipathy for bishops and church hierarchy on the part of the author? Is it proof that Herbert opposes the theological and liturgical underpinnings of the Laudian program and wants to empower parsons (like himself) to resist or soften its directives? A close examination of *The Country Parson* reveals something less dramatic but more fundamental: Herbert's implicit valuation of the local sphere. The parson is to be 'father to his flock' and is to care for the same 'as if he had begot his whole parish' (211). Such a formulation moves beyond the realm of official responsibility and takes on an air of paternalistic concern. Indeed, Herbert actually recommends that the parson, 'his parish being all his joy and thought', hardly ever leave the geographical confines of his parish (212).

Nor is the local sphere a fitting receptacle only of the parson's devotion; the men and women in his charge also benefit from and are fulfilled by the local church. The parish, as Herbert describes it, becomes the concrete realm in which practical Christianity comes to life. It is there that the biblical command to 'love thy neighbor' takes on a literal significance.[70] For Herbert, as we can see from his instructions guiding charity (207, 214), Christian love and community begin at home, literally with one's neighbors: 'Neighbourhood being ever reputed, even among the heathen, as an obligation to do good, rather than to those that are further, where things are otherwise equal' (214). With the help of the parson, almost every aspect of parish life – worship, labor, social gatherings, charity – can increase the bonds of love among parishioners

and engender a true sense of Christian community. Herbert is so committed to this vision of parish community that '[t]he parson's punishing of sin and vice is rather by withdrawing his bounty and courtesy
from the parties offending, or by private or public reproof . . . than by
causing them to be presented, or otherwise complained of' (215). The
preference for handling sin and vice within the parish (rather than
presenting the offender to the higher authorities) bespeaks the closed
nature of this community. But the assumption that such a practice rests
on – that there exists some sort of parish bond or fellowship that would
be painful on the part of the sinner to lose – is even more telling. The
local church, Herbert seems to be asserting, is the primary Christian
community for most people, and it should be valued accordingly.

As we have seen, the Laudians place a similar emphasis on the parish
as a key site of Christian community. But there are significant differences in how the parish bonds of Laud and Herbert are constructed. For
Laud, the rituals of the Church – corporate worship, public prayer, and
the dispensation of the sacraments – are the vital elements in inculcat-
ing virtue and forging community. In this vision, the 'physical acts of
reverence and piety, choreographed by the liturgy and performed at the
promptings of the priest' united the congregation in worship and even
'made it possible for the Laudians to equate an active lay piety with
mere assiduous attendance at and participation in the services of the
established Church.'[71] Although Herbert certainly values corporate worship, the parish bonds that he depicts are much more informal and personal. They derive from social intercourse (200), charitable action (207,
214), and daily conversation as much as formal worship. For instance,
the parson 'likes well that his parish at good times invite one another to
their houses, and he urgeth them to it: and sometimes, where he knows
there hath been or is a little difference, he takes one of the parties, and
goes with him to the other, and all dine or sup together. There is much
preaching in this friendliness' (238–239). The final sentence highlights
the effectiveness (and holiness) of informal modes of interaction. Parish
unity might even arise from old customs like perambulation of the parish bounds, which Herbert partially characterizes as a form of charity in
'walking and neighbourly accompanying one another' (238).

Both Laud and Herbert, then, are heavily invested in the cultivation
of parish communities. But their divergent methods also carry different
implications for their visions of the national Church. For Laud, parish
unity arises from following rituals and ceremonies that (given their role
in grace and salvation) were not surprisingly becoming more carefully
delineated and insisted upon to ensure decent order. In fact, it had

even resulted in what Lake has called 'the Laudian obsession with the forms of public piety in the parish church' and the 'absolute necessity of ceremonial conformity.'[72] The Laudian goal was not to be oppressive; it was just that parish ritual was increasingly tied to national canons and injunctions that spelled out decent order. The parish was a vital realm for the Laudians, but it was to be a local enactment of the same dynamic to be found in other parishes. Such uniformity, the Laudians felt, strengthened the whole, but it also ensured that local religious experiences were practically interchangeable.

Herbert's communal bonds, on the other hand, derive more from human interactions, and often take place outside of church. They may revolve around universals like love, forgiveness, and charity, but they are not experienced through subscription to national formulations. Moreover, these bonds do not conform to exact patterns, and each parish may exhibit different dynamics. The parson is to ensure that beggars do not go hungry in his parish, but there are many paths of charity from which to choose: 'This [charity] he effects either by bounty, or persuasion, or by authority, making use of that excellent statute, which binds all parishes to maintain their own. If his parish be rich, he exacts this of them; if poor, and he able, he easeth them therein' (207). In other words, the relative affluence of the parish determines the proper show of love. Herbert's local is less yoked to external forms, and more decentralized in the formation and execution of communal bonds. It is important here to acknowledge that while the specifics of Herbert's approach are not incompatible with Laudianism (i.e. Laud would not fault the parson for showing charity in this manner), Herbert's privileging of communal bonds at the very moment when the Laudians were elevating the more formal bonds of public worship is highly suggestive.[73]

Given his investment in communal bonds, it is understandable that Herbert's parson takes a more active role in shaping parish religion. But surprisingly, the parson often proceeds by *adapting* to what is already there. Herbert is constantly aware of the parson's rural audience, so he emphasizes strategies of appealing and relating to them. Such adaptation is most clearly seen in his preaching and teaching, where he often relies on 'stories and sayings' (197) to connect with his parishioners. To further appeal to his audience, the parson 'condescends even to the knowledge of tillage and pastorage, and makes great use of them in teaching' (193). The parson also adapts church ordinances to his rural flock, including 'a slighter form of catechizing, fitter for country people' (195). Again and again, Herbert posits a link between the parson's local knowledge and his successful execution of his pastoral duties. If he is to successfully handle tricky cases of conscience, he must start by study-ing 'the particulars of human actions . . . which he observeth are most incident to his parish' (195). Nor is it merely a matter of preparing for a generic rural audience, but – as *'his* parish' implies – the parson has to carefully consider the distinct features of his particular flock. This includes an awareness of the different types of audiences that may share the same parish. Thus, 'The Parson in Circuit' shows the parson adapt-ing his discourse to various audiences *within* the parish that he meets along the way.

Not only does he appeal and relate to his country audience, but at times the parson must actually *conform* to local standards and expecta-tions. In his own life, the parson must be most careful about 'those things which are most apt to scandalize his parish' (193). Some, like drinking alcohol, might be frowned upon in a parson anywhere. But others, like dressing plainly and being strict in keeping one's word, arise from a desire to project a persona that conforms to local expecta-tions. The important point here is that the parish itself takes a role in determining the standards of propriety for the parson – they are not just fixed, universal ideals. In fact, local conditions may even dictate something as important as the parson's matrimonial state: 'The country parson, considering that virginity is a higher state than matrimony, and that the ministry requires the best and highest things, is rather unmar-ried than married. But yet as the temper of his body may be, or as the temper of his parish may be, where he may have occasion to converse with women, and that among suspicious men, and other like circum-stances considered, he is rather married than unmarried' (200). Thus, even ideals may have to be adjusted for parish realities.

All of these adjustments to accommodate the local situation may seem natural to a modern reader, but they are philosophically at odds with the Laudian program that was gaining momentum in 1630. Whereas Laud compels the parish to conform to national standards, Herbert has his parson adapt to his parish. In fact, Herbert begins with local differences, and constructs the parson's preaching, conversation, and behavior accordingly. The result is a 'custom fit' that allows for the local to flourish.[74]

But Herbert's strategy of adaptation is not one of merely personal convenience or practicality; rather, it is a part of a deeper epistemo-logical and philosophical position. For Herbert, the sort of contingent approach taken by the parson is superior to the systematic rules and prescriptions that characterize Laudian initiatives. Cases of conscience are a frequent concern throughout *The Country Parson* and emerge as one of most important duties of a local clergyman.[75] Like Donne, Herbert is sensitive to cases and situations where normal standards cannot be evenly applied.[76] Even seemingly clear-cut concepts like sin and holiness can be cloudy. For instance, that which constitutes the sin of gluttony may vary from person to person, depending on such factors as 'knowledge of their own body, and what it can well digest' and 'the feeling of themselves in time of eating' (225). The guidelines for religious fasting are similarly contingent. The parson generally endorses the tradition of 'eating no flesh,' but also qualifies it – 'since fasting in Scripture language is an afflicting of our souls, if a piece of dry flesh at my table be more unpleasant to me, than some fish there, certainly to eat the flesh, and not the fish, is to keep the fasting day naturally' (205). The parson also excuses the weak and sickly from the potentially harmful practice of forgoing meat.

The point is not to undermine religious imperatives or to reduce them to relativity. Rather, Herbert wants his parson to be sensitive to the *intent* of rules and the *context* within which they are being applied. This is why casuistry is characterized as a positive good rather than a source of vexation: 'He greatly esteems . . . cases of conscience, wherein he is much versed. And indeed, herein is the greatest ability of a parson to lead his people exactly in the ways of Truth' (195). Far from undermining religious imperatives, these special cases provide the opportunity for a more 'exact' Truth.[77] And it is the parson, armed with a broad knowledge of virtue and vice but also a familiarity with his individual parishioners, who is best equipped to give the right spiritual judgments on issues like gluttony and fasting. He is not content with formulating and enforcing general directives, but is willing to descend to the particulars of each case. Elsewhere, Herbert notes that 'exactness lies in particulars' (231). And indeed, the particular becomes a sort of Baconian epistemological foundation for the parson's work in the parish. Like other 'local' texts we have examined, *The Country Parson* exhibits a marked distrust of overarching systems and monolithic approaches. A careful consideration of particular circumstances and conditions guides not only cases of conscience, but the parson's interaction with his parishioners and, ultimately, the execution of his duties.

The parson's emphasis on contextualization can even be seen in something as fundamental as his approach to Scripture. It is not enough just to read something in the Bible and act on it as truth. Instead, the parson must carefully consider its context. To avoid error, Herbert recommends a 'diligent collation of Scripture with Scripture,' noting that 'an industrious and judicious comparing of place with place must be a singular help for the right understanding of the Scriptures' (194). The benefit of seeing a passage in the context of other passages (rather than adopting it blindly) is 'right understanding,' which sounds a lot like the 'more exact Truth' furnished by the parson's casuistry. This approach to Scripture also shows that the parson's focus on the particular need not be an isolating exercise that operates at the expense of universals. As we see here, the 'judicious comparing of place with place' is what actually illuminates the true *spirit* of Scripture. Similarly, the parson's casuistry may undercut the letter of the traditional definition of gluttony, but it allows its true spirit to emerge in a more exact way for each person.

Like the discernment with which William Lambarde equips his jus-tices of the peace, Herbert is eager to give the parson a certain amount of 'dexterity' in executing his pastoral duties (235). He never directly challenges the ordinances of the Church, but he does volunteer that 'in any country-duty, [the parson] considers what is the end of any com-mand, and then he suits things faithfully according to that end' (213).[78] At first glance such a formulation seems quite complaisant: the parson should faithfully execute the Church's commands. But a closer exami-nation of Herbert's method – 'he suits things faithfully according to that end' – reveals Herbert's apparent preference for the spirit rather than the actual letter of these commands. As Ramie Targoff has observed, '[H]owever important . . . external proscriptions may have been for maintaining order in the church, they ultimately reveal Herbert's more pressing concerns about the worshipper's internal condition.'[79] There are also times, Herbert seems to imply, where the strict execution of a canon might trample on tender consciences or create controversy that might destroy the original goal of a canon.

The taking of Communion is a case in point. The Laudian insistence that parishioners kneel when taking Communion was opposed by those who felt that this smacked too much of popery. Herbert's position is one of studied ambiguity: 'The feast indeed requires sitting, because it is a feast; but man's unpreparedness asks kneeling. He that comes to the Sacrament hath the confidence of a guest, and he that kneels confes-seth himself an unworthy one, and therefore differs from other feasters; but he that sits or lies, puts up to an Apostle: contentiousness in a feast of charity is more scandal than any posture' (218–219). The passage displays a sensitivity to tender Puritan consciences, even as it seems to endorse the official line of kneeling.[80] Yet the last line condemns the contentiousness surrounding this issue for a familiar Herbertian reason: the spirit of the feast should not be sacrificed by wrangling over the letter of the law. In this way, Herbert downplays the ideological importance of the issue (and the parson's necessity of adopting a clear position) and instead asserts the spirit of Communion as the key concern. While Herbert does not exactly say that each parson should do what he finds meet, he does suggest that the parson may need to put up with some nonconformity.

If Herbert's Communion practices are done to mediate contentiousness, his adjustments to the catechism are done to render it more meaningful and effective: 'When once all have learned the words of the catechism, he thinks it the most useful way that a pastor can take, to go over the same, but in other words' (216). Herbert gives detailed examples of potential alternate questions that a parson might ask. Perhaps he knows that he is treading on shaky ground, because he is very careful to qualify his adjustments with 'when once all have learned' and ensure that 'the order of the catechism would be kept, but the rest varied' (216). Herbert's motive for these changes is a familiar one: upholding the intent of the catechism, and not just the catechism itself. '[F]or many say the catechism by rote, as parrots, without ever piercing into the sense of it,' Herbert observes (216). The parson's alterations are meant not to defy authority, but to help that authority accomplish its goals. Nevertheless, the parson's adjustments do represent an investment in a certain level of local adaptation.[81]

In fact, Herbert goes so far as to critique those churchmen who formulate directives without taking the local into account: 'And scholars ought to be diligent in the observation of these, and driving of their general school rules ever to the smallest actions of life; which while they dwell in their books, they will never find; but being seated in the country, and doing their duty faithfully, they will soon discover: especially if they carry their eyes ever open, and fix them on their charge, and not on their preferment' (224). Parish particulars, or as Herbert calls them, the 'smallest actions of life,' should inform any attempt at 'general school rules.' But as this passage asserts, these particulars are only really accessible to parsons who are 'seated in the country, and doing their duty faithfully.' Those engaging in religious rule-making beyond the parish have an incomplete and inexact perspective that doesn't descend to practical realities and circumstances.

In place of 'general school rules,' Herbert seems to gravitate towards the proverb or aphorism: a pithy saying drawn from observation and experience. As Brian Vickers has shown, the aphorism was an important Renaissance form that was often associated with the keeping of commonplace books.[82] And indeed, Herbert both collected and wrote proverbs from an early age. After his death, over 1,000 of them were published as *Outlandish Proverbs* (1640). Some are pretty conventional, as in 'Empty vessels sound most' and 'One stroke fells not an oke.' Others are more truly 'outlandish,' as in: 'Ever since we weare cloathes, we know not one another.'[83] Pithy formulations like these pepper Herbert's poetry and prose as well. They are the dominant mode of the 'Church Porch' section of *The Temple*, for instance, and a poem like 'Charms and Knots' takes pleasure in encasing the aphorism's natural pithiness in rhyming couplets. While Herbert's reliance on proverbs can seem glib or even quaint, he employs it for serious purposes. The proverb avoids the generalized abstraction of school rules because it is drawn from personal observation, yet it is also an active and adaptable form. 'The value of a proverb,' says Diana Benet, 'resides in its . . . indeterminacy of meaning' and 'its openness to different interpretations . . . A saying might encapsulate Herbert's own instruction to his audience in memorable form, but it also had the capacity to lead his auditor to self-instruction, to become a rule or guideline uniquely tailored to his own various circumstances.'[84]

The aphorism holds a similar value for Francis Bacon, who chooses it as the building block of the new science. Its discrete units free it from the danger of an overarching system, and (as for Herbert) invite further inquiry and application. 'Aphorisms, representing a knowledge broken, do invite men to enquire farther,' affirms Bacon, 'whereas Methods, carrying the shew of a total, do secure men, as if they were at furthest.'[85] But if Bacon's eventual goal is to erect a system of knowledge (or at least some sturdy maxims), Herbert's proverbs are meant to assist the reader in fashioning his own meaningful faith. They provide the 'truth' of experience without dictating the terms of application.

In *The Country Parson*, the proverb is emblematic of the parson's sensitivity to and cultivation of parish religion. It is gleaned from close observation and experience, and conveyed in open-ended manner that avoids a one-size-fits-all mentality and invites personal application. Such an approach also shares much with Herbert's devotional poetry and helps account for its widespread popularity amongst Laudians, Puritans, and Catholics alike. The poems are born of Herbert's intensely personal experiences, but the subjects are generalized enough to invite export and application into the reader's own life. This is one of the reasons why, as Targoff has shown, there are so many correspondences between *The Temple* and the Book of Common Prayer.[86]

Herbert's poems also betray an anxiety about modes that are overly formulaic. 'Jordan I' is generally noted for its renunciation of secular poetry in favor of a more simplified, religious poetic:

Who says that fictions only and false hair
Become a verse? Is there in truth no beauty?
Is all good structure in a winding stair?
May no lines pass, except they do their duty
   Not to a true, but painted chair?

Is it no verse, except enchanted groves
And sudden arbours shadow coarse-spun lines?
Must purling streams refresh a lover's loves? (lines 1–8)

Embedded in this complaint against secular poetry is also a critique of the formulaic. It is not just that 'enchanted groves,' 'sudden arbours,' and 'purling streams' imply secular and even sensory pleasure, it is that these hackneyed phrases have hardened into conventions that are no longer able to convey authentic sentiments. Part of the poet's frustration, then, is with forms that have been passed down and stripped of their meaning. Herbert's alternative – 'My God, My King' – is one that asserts not only a religious muse, but also a plainer form that is more comfortable and genuine for the speaker. As we have seen, the same tendency to discard formulaic conventions in favor of developing a more tailored approach to worship also informs *The Country Parson*.

Conclusion

The Country Parson, while not an overt refutation of Laudian practice, does present an alternative vision of parish religion. Like Laud, Herbert places enormous importance on the parish unit as the key site of communal bonding and religious experience. For Laud, this community is forged by a corporate ritual whose uniformity both validates it and connects it to the larger national Church. Herbert's communal experience, as we have seen, is more relational and informal. Because of this, the parson must carefully consider parish particulars in order to forge an effective religious experience. While not necessarily incompatible with or hostile to a national church, this vision (in contrast to Laud) is predicated on the parson adapting his own behavior and duties to local conditions. Nor is such adaptation merely a case of convenience or practicality; rather, there are epistemological and philosophical reasons for endorsing such an approach. The parson prefers contingency because an attention to local contexts and circumstances leads to a more exact truth and better preserves the spirit of the law. For Herbert, this is superior to a prescriptive approach in a whole range of religious areas, including epistemology, propriety, judgment, doctrine, and methodology. Such philosophical underpinnings share much with Herbert's devotional poetry, where individual experience is the primary subject, and over and over again we see that knowledge, insight, and salvation arise from individual wrestling.

Significantly, Herbert makes the *parish* the exemplar of this approach in *The Country Parson*. Smaller than Lambarde's county and more clearly delineated than Drayton's topographical units, Herbert's parish is an ideal sphere that allows religious complexities to be crystallized and acted on with greater certainty. There, religious experience can best be calibrated to the particular needs and circumstances of parishioners, and the intention (if not the letter) of Church directives can be more fully achieved. Such a model puts a great deal of faith in the parson's sensitivity to parish conditions and discernment in making edifying choices. As such, the parish emerges as the site where the bifurcated selves of *The Temple* (as described by Debora Shuger[87]) can be integrated; the artful, performative, public persona of the 'The Church Porch' is taken on by the parson in order to cultivate the private 'pneumatic' selves of his parishioners.

However, it is also clear that Herbert is not explicitly (or even implicitly) recommending that parsons resist conformity and operate subversively. Indeed, Herbert says very little to dispute contemporary Church injunctions, even if some of his endorsements are rather lukewarm.[88] Yet against these moments of formal acceptance (or perhaps resignation) can be set the almost constant emphasis on the importance of meeting local congregations on their own ground. If not a radical argument against the new uniformity, *The Country Parson* at least seems to question the basis on which it is demanded and the wisdom for doing so. In this last moment before Laudian strictures make open discourse impossible, Herbert is perhaps trying to bring the fragile Jacobean synthesis and accommodation into Charles's reign.

Such a goal is registered in 'The British Church,' one of the few poems in which Herbert speaks expansively of the national Church.[89] Here is a clear endorsement of the Church of England and a celebration of its basic characteristics.[90] Herbert even ends the poem with a clear acknowledgment of its exclusivity: 'Blessed be God, whose love it was / To double-moat thee with his grace, / And none but thee' (28–30). But on what grounds does the British Church earn such high praise? According to the poem, it is the Church's moderate status as a middle way between the extremes of Geneva and Rome. Yet the defining features of the British Church are never really articulated, other than to say that its aspect is 'Neither too mean nor yet too gay,' its looks split the difference between 'painted' and 'undressed,' and its elevation is somewhere between the extremes of 'hill' and 'valley.' Rather imprecise praise, since the poet proceeds by defining the Church by what it is not, rather than tying it to particular ceremonies or rituals. As a result, a pretty wide swath of middle ground is left for the British Church to occupy. Indeed, Herbert's use of the word 'British' implies just that, since it seems to incorporate the relatively different religious experiences of England, Wales, and possibly even Scotland.[91] In other words, Herbert's middle ground seems to be anything but a narrow strip of inflexible real estate. It is as if he wants the Church 'moated' to guard against these extremes, but seems otherwise satisfied with (and perhaps even invites) a certain nebulousness within these parameters. '. . . [W]hat those miss, / The mean, thy praise and glory is, / And long may be,' is about as specific as Herbert gets in this poem. But here 'the mean' is not an exact average in the mathematical sense. Rather, since it is what *both* Catholicism and Calvinism 'miss,' it is more akin to moderation – which also implies that (by definition) this middle ground is not something that is rigid or fixed.

All of this seems consistent with the ecclesiastical vision that is hinted at in *The Country Parson*. The Church of England provides the foundation, authority, and essentials needed to secure the middle ground. But beyond that, the particulars are best left to the parishes. It is the parson responding to local conditions and needs who cultivates the middle ground and makes it habitable for his flock. 'The British Church' also seems to register some of *The Country Parson*'s awareness that this delicate balance is under fire. The phrase 'The mean, thy praise and glory is, / And long may be' seems to betray an anxiety (or warning) that this moderation is even now beginning to slip away.

Such a reading of 'The British Church' need not reduce it to a reactionary poem that seeks merely to maintain or return to the Jacobean *via media*. Indeed, Herbert's vision of parish religion – as set out in *The Country Parson* – seems not so much a transplanted version of Jacobean accommodation as an amalgam of approaches. If he endorses the local adaptation and variety that was possible in James's reign, he is also attracted to the Laudian elevation of the priesthood. Whether or not he is presented as a sacerdotal figure, Herbert's ideal parson is at least well educated, respected, and at the center of his local social, moral, and intellectual community. More importantly, Herbert assumes that the parson has real authority over his parishioners and that he is the primary shaper of local religious experience. Ironically, such an 'ideal' situation was only becoming possible on the heels of Laudian efforts to suppress non-beneficed lecturers and other local clergymen who were only marginally affiliated with the Church of England. Herbert's vision would have been difficult to realize in the Jacobean Church because such figures would have kept the parson from wielding full influence in the parish. Thus, Herbert seems to embrace (or at least rely on) the elevation and exclusivity with which the Laudians were investing the parson's office, for it is these qualities that allow the parson to have the sort of shaping power that Herbert envisions.

Of course, Herbert differs from the Laudians in making the *parson* the primary beneficiary of these levelings. The Laudians cleared local impediments to ensure greater ease in carrying out Church of England directives and reforms (as we have seen, this was one of the primary purposes of the 1629 Instructions) and heighten uniformity. It also gave increased shaping power to the bishop or royal chaplain. Herbert, however, would entrust this shaping power to the parson because of his intimate knowledge and local involvement.

Yet the authority with which Herbert invests his parson ultimately ends up serving another key Laudian goal: the mitigation of subversion within the English Church. For if Herbert is willing to allow for some variation *between* parishes, he seems less open to variations *within* the parish. His parson may be sensitive to the perspectives (and tender con- sciences) of his parishioners, but it is the parson who ultimately formu- lates and establishes religious experience on the local level. Dissenting individuals and local factions are not simply left alone to their own devices. Thus, 'The Parson Arguing' details the parson's diligence in approaching 'any of his parish that hold strange doctrines,' and 'The Parson Punishing' describes the appropriate response when these inter- ventions fail. However decentralized parish religion may appear in *The Country Parson*, it is the parson's authority – along with his loyalty to the English Church in larger matters – that keeps Herbert's vision from becoming too radical. In fact, the parish itself still attains a high degree of uniformity; it is only that this uniformity is not minutely insisted upon across the other parishes of the realm.

Assessing Herbert's vision of parish religion is not, then, simply a matter of returning to the Jacobean *via media*. Herbert shares with the Laudians a belief in the dignity of the clerical office, a wariness of sub- versive elements within the Church, and an interest in homogeneity within the parish. But unlike the Laudians (and more like his pre- decessors), Herbert stresses the adaptive role of the parson and makes him – not the bishop or royal chaplain – the most effective arbiter of religious experience. He is, Herbert suggests, best suited to gauge the parish temper and circumstances and to order worship accordingly. And indeed, the parson may even choose to put up with some nonconformity (for instance, with regard to kneeling) in order to better execute the spirit of the canon and avoid alienating elements of his flock.

Positioned between Jacobean accommodation and a more rigorous Caroline uniformity, Herbert does seem to belong to the *via media* for which he has often been claimed. But in my reading of *The Country Parson*, it is a middle ground based not so much on theology or liturgical taste but on Herbert's approach to the local parish (and its parson) as a mediator and adapter of religious experience. It is this traditional element of the English Church that Herbert draws from and attempts to fashion anew in order to meet the challenges of his historical moment.

5
Izaak Walton, Lucy Hutchinson, and the Experience of Civil War

George Herbert's death in 1633 prevented him from seeing the further erosion of middle ground – not only in the Church, but in other aspects of political, religious, and social life. Within a decade, England was plunged into civil war. The English Civil War was fundamentally a national event. Unlike, say, the Wars of the Roses, it was waged in every county and involved people from all levels of society. Moreover, it was fought primarily in order to arbitrate national issues like the proper relationship between King and Parliament and the ideal form that the state Church should take. Although there were many answers to these questions, only one vision could prevail at any given time – which is precisely why the stakes were so high. The Civil War also forced people in the provinces to think nationally. In many cases, they had to pick a side or at least play a role in events that they didn't necessarily seek out.

But the Civil War also helped to foreground the local. As the country fragmented into pockets of Royalists and Parliamentarians, particular places came to be associated with each party. Oxford hosted the royal Court, the Severn valley staunchly supported the Crown, and northern cities like York and Newark maintained important Royalist garrisons. In London and the southeast, Parliament held sway. Cities further afield like Hull, Nottingham, and Exeter also became notable Parliamentary holdouts. Military combat made other, previously obscure, places like Naseby, Marston Moor, Edgehill, Newbury, and Rowton Heath into household names. The crucible of Civil War thus helped to impress new associations and distinctions on local places. This was true even on an individual level. Contemporary associations of Oliver Cromwell with his 'reserved and austere' East Anglian roots were both a way of describing the Protector and projecting his personal characteristics back onto the region that produced him.[1]

Away from the theater of action, the local sphere was embraced by individuals from both major parties. Royalist communities are probably most commonly associated with rural retirement in the 1640s and 1650s, but they were joined by a number of prominent Parliamentarians, particularly after the rise of the New Model Army and accession of Oliver Cromwell.[2] The experience of both groups is supported by literary output that explores the possibilities of the local sphere, ranging from Herrick's 'To the King, Upon His Coming with His Army into the West' to Marvell's reflections on the retirement of Parliamentary general Lord Fairfax in 'Upon Appleton House.' This chapter will examine two particular writers from opposite ends of the ideological spectrum: the Royalist Izaak Walton and the radical Puritan Lucy Hutchinson. Both witnessed the Civil War firsthand and both were involved in national events, yet both ultimately attempt to mediate this experience by appealing to and investing in the local. While some people were engaged in these years with 'writing the English republic,' other English men and women turned to the local to help negotiate the experience of Civil War.

Izaak Walton

Izaak Walton's *The Compleat Angler* (1653) would seem to fit naturally into the aforementioned category of Royalist retreat literature. After all, it is written by a Royalist, set in the country, and concerned with the leisurely pastime of fishing. But a close examination of the text reveals a more complex notion of retreat than simply removing oneself to the country. As I will demonstrate, *The Compleat Angler* localizes retreat in a particular setting that is crucial in both articulating a set of values and rendering them attainable for a specific Royalist audience. Even the practical fishing instruction could be said to endorse a 'localized' mindset that eschews larger claims of authority and epistemology and instead finds meaning, comfort, and recourse in the finite.

At first glance, *The Compleat Angler* seems to be a pretty straightforward work. It is, first and foremost, a fishing manual. Walton devotes page after page to the practical concerns of catching fish: where to find them, when to fish for them, what bait and tackle to use, how to catch them, and even how to cook them. As these recommendations vary depending on the species of fish, Walton devotes separate chapters to the salmon, chub, trout, grayling, pike, carp, bream, tench, perch, eel, barbel, gudgeon, and roach. But *The Compleat Angler* is also much more than a fishing manual; otherwise, it would not have gone on to become one of the most frequently reprinted books in the English language.

Chief among its literary attractions is the dialogue frame that Walton creates for the dispersal of all of this fishing knowledge. The dialogue begins when Piscator (an angler) falls in with Venator (a hunter) and Auceps (a falconer) as they walk along a river, and each of the three agrees to give a 'commendation of that Recreation which you love and practice.'[3] Piscator's exalted defense of the art of angling has such an impact on Venator that he declares his 'ambitio[n] to be your Scholar' (83) and learn about all of the finer points of angling that Piscator can teach him. For the next four days (and the duration of Walton's book) Piscator imparts his considerable knowledge as the two men walk, talk, and wet their hooks. In addition, both the angling and angling instruction is 'in several places mixt . . . [with] innocent, harmless mirth' (19–20). The fishing instruction is interrupted with rain storms, singing milkmaids, and character sketches of exemplary English anglers. At night, Piscator and Venator gather with other anglers in a tavern where they drink and sing songs. Here and elsewhere, Walton breaks up the text by interspersing ballads and poems by recent authors – including Drayton and Herbert. Finally, Walton has Piscator tell amusing stories, engage in frequent digressions, and even share scientific musings and experiments. Clearly, there is much more to *The Compleat Angler* than the simple transfer of fishing knowledge from master to scholar.

Although the work's generic variety has invited a number of different critical approaches, I am most interested in exploring what *The Compleat Angler* (and its invocation of the local) meant in the highly charged historical moment in which it first appeared.[4] Jonquil Bevan characterizes Walton's work as 'a book of consolation addressed to deprived and forfeited Anglicans and Royalists.'[5] And, indeed, some of Walton's intended audience appears directly in the text as the subjects of anecdotes and authors of poems – including many Anglican clergymen who were living in forced retirement.[6] Thus, Piscator's invocation of the 'brotherhood of the angle' is (as Greenslade has shown) not only a reference to an angling audience, but an Anglican audience.[7] The topicality of *The Compleat Angler* goes beyond this subtle pun, of course, and more recent critics have been keen to show how Walton's work speaks to a common set of values espoused by sequestered Royalists in the 1650s. Earl Miner notes that the work exemplifies cavalier notions of friendship and the good life.[8] Steven Zwicker has written in more detail on the social vision of *The Compleat Angler*, showing how its claims about social harmony and coherence, mirth and conviviality, innocence and simplicity, tradition and authority fit the dominant Royalist ideology of the commonwealth.[9] Such a vision includes an implied and sometimes overt critique of the values of those currently in power. Cooper has shown how the book 'hid[es] under its general air of innocence and simple piety a sharp criticism of the Puritan and Parliamentary ethos.'[10] Thus, when Piscator dismisses the 'grave serious . . . money-getting-men' (36) who disapprove of anglers, Cooper connects them to 'the Puritan merchants and tradesmen that [Walton] had known in London.'[11]

Clearly, a lot of useful critical attention has been paid to the *type* of Royalist community that *The Compleat Angler* imagines. But what about the *place* in which Walton anchors this community? In the very first sentence of the dialogue, Piscator creates the setting: 'You are well overtaken, Gentlemen, a good morning to you both; I have stretched my legs up Tottenham-hill to overtake you, hoping your business may occasion you towards Ware this fine fresh May morning.' Venator and

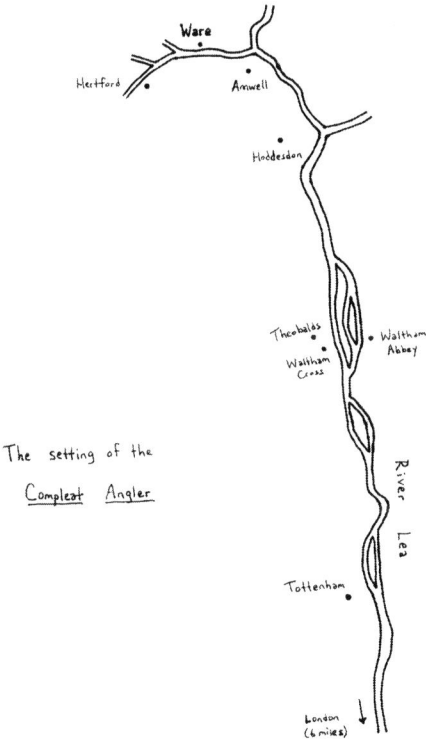

Figure 4 Map of the River Lea between Tottenham High Cross and Ware

Auceps each respond to Piscator's opening query by stating exactly where they are heading. Venator plans to 'drink my morning draught at the Thatcht House in Hodsden' and ultimately to hunt otter on Amwell Hill. Auceps, on the other hand, is only traveling 'as far as Theobalds,' at which point he will 'turn up to a friends house who mews a Hawk for me.' Topographically speaking, these are pretty exact cues. Piscator's opening statement puts the travelers near the Middlesex village of Tottenham High Cross, about 6 miles north of central London. Piscator declares his intention to walk to the town of Ware, which is about 14 miles further along the River Lea. Venator plans to take refreshment at the Thatcht House, an inn on the High Street in Hoddesdon, before continuing on to Amwell Hill, a Hertfordshire village about one and a half miles southeast of Ware. Auceps is only going as far as the royal palace at Theobalds, so he will turn off even before the others arrive at Hoddesdon for their 'morning draught.'[12] Rather than placing his characters in a generic and boundless countryside, Walton has gone to great pains to establish an authentic and limited setting. All of the places mentioned by these three characters actually exist – even the inn at Hoddesdon – and their spatial relationships are so accurate that they 'may be charted on a map.'[13] Although the action is spread over several locations, all of them can be found on a 14-mile stretch of the River Lea between Tottenham and Ware (Fig. 4).

The specificity of place names and geographical accuracy continues as the narrative unfolds over a five-day period. On the morning of the first day, Auceps does indeed take his leave when he comes in sight of the 'Park-wall' of Theobalds house (52). Venator observes that 'we have yet five miles to the Thatcht-House' (53) and invites Piscator to continue his description of angling as they walk along. After refreshing themselves at the aforementioned inn, the two agree to meet at Amwell Hill the next morning and spend the day hunting otter. On the third day, they 'do nothing but angle, and talk of fish and fishing' (73), and then lodge at Bleak Hall, 'a rural inn on the banks of the river Lea, about a mile from Edmonton.'[14] At this inn they are joined by Piscator's brother Peter and his friend Coridon for an evening of drinking, singing, and other merriment. On the fourth day, the two pairs go opposite directions on the River Lea – Peter and Coridon 'go up the water towards Ware' while Piscator and Venator 'go down towards Waltham' (113) – and then meet back at Bleak Hall for lodging and further revelry. On the fifth and final day, Piscator and Venator walk back towards London and part at Tottenham High Cross, though not without agreeing to meet back in one week in the same spot for another fishing expedition. Thus, the characters' movements are carefully plotted out and noted at various points throughout the text. If Piscator and Venator do '[wander] through the countryside, singing songs and increasing their blood-alcohol levels,' Walton is careful to record exactly where they go.[15] Nor are the local references only limited to character movement. Walton adds further local color via the stories and digressions of the dialogue. Thus, when Piscator is talking about a band of beggars he encountered on an earlier fishing trip, he reports that one of them 'was that night to lodge at an Ale-house (called Catch-her-by-the-way,) not far from Waltham-Crosse, and in the high-rode towards London' (141). A couple of pages later, Piscator refers to a legendary trout 'near an ell long, which was of such a length and depth, that he had his picture drawn, and now to be seen at mine Hoste Rickabies at the George in Ware' (143). Such stories and local lore help to further delineate the surrounding neighborhood and create a sense of place.

But why does Walton tie his dialogue so carefully and thoroughly to this particular 14-mile stretch of the River Lea when 'the countryside' might just as easily suit his purposes? Verisimilitude is no doubt one factor. If *The Compleat Angler* is supposed to present a plausible dialogue about the practicalities of fishing, a concrete setting makes the characters and their activities all the more lifelike and natural. The River Lea is also a natural choice for Walton, given that he did spend much of his life in London and was known to fish this river.[16] If *The Compleat Angler* is supposed to distill Walton's angling experiences and capture his enthusiasm for this recreation, the choice of a river that Walton knew and loved is only natural.

But I would argue that the choice of the Lea goes beyond mere realism and personal roots. Walton's decision to locate his picture of contented retirement in an actual place keeps it from coming off as purely escapist. Setting his dialogue along the Lea implies that Walton's quietest ideal is attainable; it doesn't only exist in theory or as a part of some pastoral mirage, but it can be accessed by actual people.[17] The choice of the River Lea is crucial here, I believe. Walton could just as easily have chosen a river in his native Staffordshire, which would have had the added benefit of a location far from the political and religious centers from which Walton and his circle were so 'gladly' sequestered.[18] But for Walton, the Lea is appealing precisely *because* of its proximity to London. By setting *The Compleat Angler* here, the author assures us that the quietest values that it enshrines can be found just outside – and indeed within walking distance from – the teeming heart of London and its 'money-getting-men.' One doesn't have to retire to some obscure corner of the realm to access the contentment, peace, and social harmony proffered by the text. As a result of its setting, the book renders these values stronger, more resilient, and more attainable than they otherwise would be.

Yet critics have tended to discount the specificity of *The Compleat Angler*'s setting. According to P. G. Stanwood, the work's 'rustic world is decidedly conventionalized' and 'no more particularly descriptive . . . of England, than are other conventionally depicted literary paradises.'[19] Cooper asserts that Walton's natural landscape is shaped more by pastoral convention than direct observation and that it tends to feature 'stylized rather than naturalistic descriptions.'[20] While it may be true that some of Walton's rural details – 'adjoining Grove[s],' 'silver-streams,' and 'harmless Lambs' (98) – are derived from pastoral conventions, it is a little unfair to criticize Walton for not giving us the particular flora and fauna of rural Middlesex and Hertfordshire. After all, he is no chorographer. As we have seen, Walton does give us plenty of other authentic local characteristics in his invoking of place names and attention to spatial relations. Why then is Walton drawn to some types of local detail and not others?

For insight, we will look briefly at the biographies of Anglican clergymen that Walton composed over a forty-year period.[21] Allan Pritchard has shown that the *Lives* of Wotton, Herbert, Sanderson, and Hooker all go out of their way to link each of their subjects to a particular and highly circumscribed locale.[22] For Wotton, the emphasis is on his final years of retirement at Eton College; for Herbert it is the three years he spent at Bemerton; for Hooker, the 'obscure and peaceable life of a country clergyman at Boscombe [Wiltshire] and Bishopsbourne [Kent]'; for Sanderson, his early life as a country parson in Boothby Pagnell (Lincolnshire).[23] Moreover, Walton's biographies give these places disproportionate representation and often downplay the more populous places in which these men resided.[24] For example, Walton's claim that Hooker wrote *The Laws of Ecclesiastical Polity* in Boscombe rather than London 'runs counter to the evidence.'[25] One reason that he does this is that he is keen to emphasize the particular mindset that such quiet, peaceful places nurture. Walton's biographical subjects are all presented as 'the man of peace and the practical Christian rather than the holy warrior or the fierce controversialist . . . His ideal Anglican as represented in Wotton, Herbert, Hooker, and Sanderson is a figure of charity, peaceableness, and moderation . . . seeking conciliation and harmony, avoiding disputes and divisions in favour of practical Christianity.'[26] Significantly, it is each man's local scope that is credited with stimulating and maintaining such a mindset. For instance, the *Life of Wotton* characterizes Eton as a 'Rock . . . where [Wotton] might sit in a Calm, and looking down, behold the busie multitude turmoyl'd and tossed on the tempestuous Sea of trouble and dangers.'[27]

Although Walton clearly values such places, he offers neither a distinct portrait of them nor meaningfully differentiates them. In fact, 'it is difficult in his biographies to distinguish clearly or sharply between Hooker at Bishopsbourne, Herbert at Bemerton, Sanderson at Boothby, or even Wotton at Eton.'[28] In other words, any one of these places can be conducive to the irenic mindset that Walton is after. But this does not necessarily render all such quiet retreats interchangeable. Near the end of the *Life of Wotton*, we are told that Wotton, now living at Eton, 'went usually once a year, if not oftner, to the beloved Bocton-hall, where he would say, he found a cure for all cares, by the chearful company, which he called the living furniture of that place: and a restoration of his strength, by the Connaturalness of that, which he called his genial air' (118). That Wotton is otherwise comfortably installed in blissful retirement at Eton – yet still needs the 'restoration' of his ancestral home – is an indication that each individual's 'quiet place' is particularly his own.

For Izaak Walton himself, one of these places is the River Lea valley north of London. While he may not emphasize its unique and distinguishing features, Walton does provide specific place names and a carefully delineated scope so that he can create an authentic environment that is serviceable to the quietest mindset that he most desires. But as Walton's biographies suggest, other places throughout England are also conducive to such values, and these places might do for others what the Lea has done for him. As a result, though the *Angler*'s characters and actions are firmly entrenched between Tottenham and Ware, the dialogue ranges freely throughout the realm. Piscator doesn't just talk about fishing on the River Lea; he also refers to major English rivers like the Avon, Trent, Severn, and Thames. Even relatively minor rivers – like the Ottersey in Cornwall and the Tivy in Pembrokeshire – garner attention. In one chapter, Walton illustrates the 'bold, greedy devouring disposition' of the pike by telling the story of a woman who was attacked in Kenilworth Pond near Coventry (162). As he discusses the different types of fish and different methods for catching them, Piscator fetches stories, illustrations, and experiences from a variety of places. Some twenty-one English counties are mentioned by name, including Leicestershire, Hampshire, Lincolnshire, Staffordshire, Lancashire, Derbyshire, Norfolk, and Northumberland. He also remarks on the concentrations of fish near particular cities – for example, the 'waters [teem] with young eels near Canterbury' (203) – and bridges – 'Henly-Bridg' is good for roach-fishing.[29] Not only do such wide-ranging references broaden the scope of Walton's angling analysis, they also suggest that other pastoral sites throughout England might offer the same serenity and contentment that Walton is elsewhere ascribing to the River Lea (though perhaps not at Kenilworth Pond!).

But again, it is worth noting that Walton doesn't treat all of these places the same. In fact, he goes to great lengths to record the local variation that he finds in angling sites throughout the realm. For instance, both the size and concentration of trout differ throughout the realm, and there are certain breeds that can only be found in particular places, like the rare and mysterious Fordidge Trout (named after the town in Kent where it occurs) and the Bull-trout of Northumberland. Here, Walton's treatment of place seems more heterogeneous than in the biographies, and he even ascribes to chorographical notions of place distinction. He notes, for instance, that Sussex has four types of fish that aren't found in any other county (174), that there are an unusual number of otters in Cornwall (75), and that the Char fish is found only in a particular mere in Lancashire (209). In other parts of the text, Walton turns such distinctions into full-blown local claims of pre-eminence: Lincolnshire boasts the biggest pikes (174), the Thames 'affords the largest and fattest' roaches (230), Derbyshire has the best trout anglers (230), but Hampshire 'exceeds all England for swift, shallow, clear, pleasant Brooks, and store of Trouts' (146). Walton even takes time to record the sorts of strange and unusual 'wonders' that are so prevalent in the chorographic genre. He entertains the reader with the tale of a Leicestershire gentleman who tamed an otter (77), a description of the prodigious leaping abilities of salmon in the River Tivy in Pembrokeshire (155), and the curious prospect of fish that are 'dig'd out of the earth with Spades' in Lancashire (205). Although Walton's focus is on angling lore rather than place *per se*, these formulations do reveal how traditional chorographical categories continued to impact how people defined and thought about local places.[30] In fact, Walton draws directly from Camden in some of his accounts and even inserts some verses from Drayton that play up the worth and distinctiveness of particular English rivers.[31]

But Walton has his own reasons for asserting the uniqueness of local places. As we shall see, his insistence on the variety and heterogeneity of local places is directly related to *The Compleat Angler*'s larger methodological concerns with contingency. In order to catch fish, one must take a number of shifting variables into account. In *The Compleat Angler*, you don't just drop your line in the water and begin angling. You must first decide what kind of fish you want to catch, and then consider a myriad of factors ranging from the time of day to the temperature to the depth of the water. To some extent, these sorts of considerations are typical of all fishing manuals. But Walton's emphasis on such variables is exceptional. Gudgeon can be found in river shallows in the summer months, but they move to the deeper parts of the river in autumn (216). Fishing for trout at night is an entirely different endeavor than fishing for them in the daytime (145). Roach fish can be caught with paste in the winter, worms in April, and 'in the very hot moneths with little white snails' (230). Sometimes these complex variables operate unpredictably even within the same species. Salmon, Walton remarks, are typically active in the summer months, but in the River Wie (in Monmouthshire) are in season from September to April (22). Similarly, 'Carps . . . breed in some ponds, and not in others of the same nature' (177) – though no one really knows why.

Because of such unpredictability, Walton is hesitant to synthesize his observations into broad rules that the angler can follow. '[T]here is no general rule without an exception,' warns Piscator (157). In the brief prefatory letters (to John Offley and the Reader), Walton thrice acknowledges that 'this Discourse may be lyable to some exceptions.' That is, there will be plenty of individual cases that do not conform to the general angling rules that he is promulgating. Even traditional adages, he tells the reader, are not without exception:

> whereas it is said by many, that in flye-fishing for a Trout, the Angler must observe his twelve several flies for the twelve moneths of the year; I say he that follows that rule, shall be as sure to catch fish, and be as wise as he that makes Hay by the fair days in an Almanack, and no surer; for those very flyes that use to appear about and on the water in one moneth of the year, may the following year come almost a moneth sooner or later, as the same year proves colder or hotter.

In other words, Walton can only be so systematic without running into inaccuracies; even the most basic rule is liable to exceptions.

Not surprisingly, local places play a big role in Walton's concern with contingency. On the one hand, these places can create the diversity and unpredictability that make it so hard to formulate broad rules. '[S]ome rivers . . . breed larger trouts,' Walton explains, 'by reason of the ground over which they run' (94). Although Walton doesn't fully explain this assertion, he seems to imply a mysterious connection between local topography (or soil) and the size of fish. Elsewhere, he says that just as the quality of sheep's wool can vary significantly based on which particular pasture the sheep grazed in, so too 'if I catch a Trout in one [water] Meadow, he shall be white and faint, and very like to be low-sie; and as certainly, if I catch a Trout in the next Meadow, he shall be strong, and red, and lusty, and much better meat' (148–149). Here local variety is not only formative, but seemingly arbitrary. But if local conditions sometimes create uncertainty, a knowledge of them can also help the angler negotiate contingency. '[W]hen you fish for a Trout with a Worm,' Walton recommends, 'let your line have so much, and not more Lead than will fit the stream' (125). Here the consideration of the particular stream allows the angler the best chance at success. Similarly, Walton's discussion of bait for catching roach acknowledges that though there be many types of caseworms – 'several Counties have several kinds' – it is best to use a natively occurring specimen: '[case-worms] be usually bred in the very little rills or ditches that run into bigger Rivers, and I think a more proper bait for those very Rivers, than any others' (238–239). Again, a consideration of local circumstances proves advantageous to the angler and allows him to more effectively negotiate the complexities of landing a fish.

In *The Compleat Angler* contingency is ultimately not a malevolent influence, but part of what makes angling an enjoyable pastime. Walton's ideal angler is artful and adaptable rather than someone who can simply master a body of fishing knowledge (local or otherwise). He should have 'an inquiring, searching, observing wit' (53) so that he can be constantly attuned to – and capable of negotiating – complex and shifting variables. Piscator also encourages Venator to rely on his own creativity and resourcefulness, as when he recommends that his pupil 'vary and make [artificial flies] lighter or sadder according to your fancy' (133). Finally, practical experience must round out the angler's education – for example, 'time, and a little experience will teach you better than I can by words' (168).[32] Like other artists, anglers have to develop their own unique styles. This point is driven home on the fourth morning of the dialogue, when Venator (having caught fewer fish than Piscator) asserts that his master has 'a better Rod, and better tackling' and asks to switch equipment. Piscator's continued success proves that people – not rods – catch fish. The lesson is extended via Piscator's 'short Tale' of a preacher-in-training who borrows a successful sermon from another preacher – only to have it fall flat when he delivers it. '[T]he sermon-borrower complained . . . to the lender of it, and was thus answered; I lent you indeed my Fiddle, but not my fiddlestick; for you are to know, that every one cannot make musick with my words, which are fitted for my own mouth' (125). Such an analogy suggests the limitations of the angling instructions to be found within *The Compleat Angler*. A wholesale application may not be 'fitted' to the particular skills and local conditions of every angler-in-training. It is therefore to be adapted rather than slavishly copied. Indeed, the dominant effect of the dialogue is the elevation of a particular type of mentality rather than the mastery of a body of knowledge or set of guidelines. Perhaps more than anything else, the successful angler is marked by an ability to consider shifting variables and to adapt to them on the fly.

Such attentiveness to contingency is not only beneficial to anglers, but also to the sequestered Royalists who formed the core of Walton's original audience. Critics who read *The Compleat Angler* as a reflection of Royalist thought in the 1650s tend to invoke features like pastoral escapism and scenes of social harmony – in other words, the non-piscatory parts of the text. But Walton's angling methodology can also be seen as an element of Royalist thought.[33] The emphasis on contingency that permeates Walton's treatment of catching fish would have had particular relevance when it appeared in 1653. After eleven years of internecine conflict – including the naming of Cromwell as Lord Protector just one month earlier – *The Compleat Angler* 'appeared at a time when the limits of discourse must have been painfully obvious to anyone engaged in political life: clear and distinct arguments were met with opposing arguments equally clear and distinct.'[34] Walton's emphasis on contingency thus epitomizes the 1650s reluctance to embrace overarching maxims that are at worst flawed and at best ineffective. It also helps to provide an epistemological backing for the rest of the work. Zwicker has noted a 'patchwork' quality about the generic heterogeneity of *The Compleat Angler*, observing that it 'suggests a world that has not accounted for loose ends; there is nothing here monolithic, no general field theory of politics or society. Unlike the prophetic imagination that would organize all experience and all detail into coherent, redemptive meaning, *The Compleat Angler* allowed revision, expansion, and collaboration.'[35] The 'patchwork' quality of the *Angler* has been a source of frustration for many critics as they struggle to assimilate its various parts into a coherent whole. But for David Hill Radcliffe, such heterogeneity is part of Walton's point. He sees the *Angler*'s 'hybridity' as a conscious attempt to 'represent . . . harmony through difference,' since 'Walton's generation was well aware of the ill consequences following from demands for conformity, from whichever end of the political spectrum.'[36]

Although *The Compleat Angler*'s emphasis on contingency and hybridity suggests the benefits of intellectual cautiousness, Walton does not reduce Royalist retreat to the fruitless doctrines of skepticism and relativity. Instead, he turns to the local sphere to deliver a measure of control to his beleaguered audience. In chapter after chapter, *The Compleat Angler* offers the image of a patient fisherman carefully consulting local conditions – an image that must have been appealing to a Royalist audience in enforced retirement in localities throughout the realm. In contrast to the monolithic thought patterns and endless disputes that marked the Civil War and Interregnum periods, Piscator offers a series of discrete situations that can be comprehended and acted on exactly. By narrowing his focus to a circumscribed area, the angler can clearly discern variables and plot an appropriate course. The local is thus depicted as a sphere of action and control for a group of Royalists who sorely lacked both in the 1650s. In *The Compleat Angler*, the consideration of local places is doubly appropriate. On the one hand, local differences (in rivers and topography) are frequently depicted as causing variation – and thus necessitating the contingency that the successful angler must master. But far from remaining a destabilizing force, the local sphere becomes the site where contingency can best be navigated. By limiting himself to a careful consideration of whatever local situation the angler finds himself in, he can make an informed and effective choice and exercise deliberate control over his environment.

The suggestion that Walton's angling instructions are about far more than just catching fish is writ large in the final pages of the dialogue as Venator himself becomes one of the 'brotherhood of the angle.' In declaring that he has 'turned Angler,' Venator speaks of the philosophical doctrine he has imbibed, the virtuous life he will lead, the contentment that he will enjoy, and his 'increase[d] confidence in the Power, and Wisdom, and Providence of Almighty God' (263). It is clear that angling is not just a sport, but in the pages of Walton's work, a lifestyle. To be sure this lifestyle includes the peace, fellowship, wholesome mirth, and contemplation depicted in *The Compleat Angler*, but it also involves a particular mentality that anglers cultivate. This is perhaps why Walton makes the otherwise curious claim in his prefatory letter to the reader that 'the whole Discourse is, or rather was, a picture of my own disposition' (20). The careful contingency of the patient angler is also a picture of a beleaguered community living their lives in an uncertain time.

The Compleat Angler concludes with Piscator and Venator parting and returning to London, but not, as one critic says, so that they can 'return to their former life, enlightened and refreshed, better able to assume their accustomed roles.'[37] When the two have arrived back at Tottenham High Cross, Venator laments, '[H]ere I must part with you, here in this now sad place where I was so happy as first to meet you; But I shall long for the ninth of May, for then I hope again to enjoy your beloved company, at the appointed time and place. And now I wish for some somniferous potion, that might force me to sleep away the intermitted time, which will passe away with me as tediously, as it does with men in sorrow' (262–263). London, it turns out, is not a promising venue for carrying out the lessons that Venator has gleaned from his walk along the River Lea. Only by returning to Tottenham in a week's time can the tedium and sorrow of the Interregnum metropolis be lifted. Only in the local sphere can the patient angler re-establish some measure of happiness.

Lucy Hutchinson

Lucy Hutchinson's professed reason for writing *Memoirs of the Life of Colonel Hutchinson* (1671) was simply 'to moderate my woe' (16). Her husband, John Hutchinson, had been a radical Puritan, parliamentary Governor of Nottingham in the Civil War, and one of only 39 people to sign the death warrant of Charles I. At the Restoration, he was initially pardoned, only to be arrested on a pretense of plotting in 1663. He died a prisoner of Sandown Castle, Kent the following year. But the death of Lucy Hutchinson's husband of 26 years probably also brought into sharp relief for her the loss of the Puritan cause that they had both sacrificed so much for. As N. H. Keeble observes, 'At the time of the book's composition . . . she endured more than the private anguish of her loss. She had been no less convinced than her husband of "the righteousness of the Parliament's cause" . . . and no less committed to "the most glorious cause that ever was contended for" . . . its final collapse posed for her, as for all the defeated Puritans, a daunting case of conscience.'[38] If John and Lucy Hutchinson had been doing God's work (as they were convinced), how could that work have ended in such disaster? Had God abandoned them? Had He ever really been on their side? The *Memoirs* is thus much more than a biography of a parliamentary leader; it is an attempt to address the larger questions that haunted Puritans after the Restoration.

But what makes it such an extraordinary document is the *way* in which it sets out to provide answers to these questions. Lucy Hutchinson defends her husband's role in the Civil War neither by telling a grand narrative of the whole war nor by giving an ideological defense of Puritanism. Rather, her defense is based on reporting exactly what happened in Nottingham in the 1640s and 1650s and justifying how her husband responded to those particular events. Nottingham was *his* sphere of action – and the only sphere, she implies, to which he should be held accountable. As governor of Nottingham Castle (and eventually the town itself), Colonel Hutchinson succeeded in 'preserv[ing] for the Parliamentarian cause a town of great strategic significance situated in a predominantly Royalist area.'[39] Although Lucy Hutchinson proudly notes this achievement, it is not her primary focus; after all, the Colonel's careful safeguarding of the town would eventually be undone by the Restoration. Instead, the author's micro-history serves to demonstrate the virtue displayed by her husband and confirm that Providence both blessed the Colonel and approved of his work. Although the national outcome of the Civil War ultimately went against the Puritans, the local approach of the *Memoirs* allows Lucy Hutchinson to both defend her husband and justify his actions.[40]

Not surprisingly, Hutchinson begins the *Memoirs* by establishing the importance of Nottinghamshire to the Hutchinson family. 'They have been in Nottinghamshire for generations,' she reports, where they are as 'well beloved and reputed as any of the prouder houses in the county' (31–32). It was the Colonel's father, Thomas Hutchinson, who moved the family estate to Owthorpe and 'liv[ed] constantly in the country' (33). There, he 'furnished himself with the choicest library in that part of England' and applied his skills to 'administer justice among [his neighbors] . . . with such equity and wisdom, and was such a defender of the county's interest, that, without affecting it at all, he grew the most popular and most beloved man in the county' (33). As a result, Thomas was 'sought by the whole county to be their representative' (33) and was elected to Parliament 'several times.' In the sweep of Lucy Hutchinson's narrative, Thomas functions as something of a prototype for his son, John. He not only helps establish a family tradition of commitment to the 'county's interest,' he also prefigures some of the dangers that local service can lead to. In 1627, the elder Hutchinson was arrested by Charles I and confined in Kent, 'the good father little thinking then, that in that fatal county his son should suffer an imprisonment upon the same account' (40).[41]

Lucy Hutchinson's depiction of her husband also plays up many of the same local ties. The original title of the *Memoirs* – 'The Life of John Hutchinson of Owthorpe, in the County of Nottingham, Esquire' – indicates both the family estate and native county of her husband and helps foreground the primacy of place in the narrative that will follow.[42]

Her account of John's birth and childhood is sprinkled liberally with place names. He was 'born at Nottingham' in 1615, his mother being 'forced to remove from Owthorpe to winter in the town' (34). When he was but three, young John was involved in a coach accident on the road between Owthorpe and Nottingham, after which he was taken to his uncle's house at nearby Bullwell.[43] The local sphere of John's childhood was thus contained within a diameter of about 16 miles, with Nottingham at the center.[44] In fact, John was educated at the free school in Nottingham, though his education was eventually supplemented further afield in Lincoln (32 miles away) and Cambridge (75 miles away). Lucy Hutchinson is thus careful to lay down her husband's roots in the area of his future service. But she does so not just to familiarize the reader with these places, but to suggest their formative nature and explain why Colonel Hutchinson would come to be so committed to them.

Indeed, Lucy Hutchinson's own life attests to the continuing strength of local connections in the mid-seventeenth century. In a rare moment of personal detail, she poignantly describes her own difficulties in leaving her native London as a young bride. Shortly after their marriage in 1638, her husband's 'next design was to draw her into his own county; but he would not set upon it too roughly, and therefore let her rest awhile, when he had drawn her ten miles nearer it, out of the city where she had her birth and education and where all her relations were most conversant, and which she could not suddenly resolve to quit for altogether to betake herself to the North, which was a formidable name among the London ladies' (53). Though she jokes wryly about being sentenced to 'The North' – Nottingham is only about a third of the way from London to the Scots border – this passage reveals her deep emotional tie to her own locality as well as the gradual method that was necessary to wean her away.[45] Even amongst such well-educated and widely connected gentry families as the Hutchinsons and Apsleys, local ties continued to exercise a powerful pull on men and women alike.

The primacy of early modern local identity can also be seen in responses to the onset of the Civil War in 1642. According to Lucy Hutchinson, many inhabitants of the county were eager to stay out of national affairs and avoid the conflict altogether. Indeed, one of John Hutchinson's first forays into public service was to negotiate with Royalists over the neutrality of Nottinghamshire. Peace was also a top priority for many of the 'godly people' of Nottingham, who wanted to live quietly with their families but 'found they could not do so unless the Parliament's interest were maintained' (91).[46] And even when the inhabitants of the region were inevitably drawn into the conflict, they still tended to act in terms of local interest. The county's defense of its militia powder is a case in point. Just before King Charles raised his standard at Nottingham, the sheriff of the county came to seize the town's magazine for the King's use. But 'a good company of the county' – led by John Hutchinson – prevented him, saying 'our lives, wives, children, and estates, all depend on this county's safety; and how can it be safe in these dangerous times, when so many rude armed people pass daily through it, if we be altogether disarmed?' (79). Later, when those fears had materialized into an invading Royalist army, even the town's Royalist sympathizers 'cared not much to have Cavalier soldiers quarter with them, and therfore agreed to defend themselves against any force which should come against them' (95).

But Lucy Hutchinson is far from painting a picture of local solidarity in her account of the war. The claims of geographical proximity and community were often overridden by other priorities. Ideology was one of these, as seen in Hutchinson's complaints about the town Royalists who actively worked to undo the town. Private interest was another, as seen in Hutchinson's depiction of people acting out of a desire to safeguard their families and their property. Sometimes allegiances boiled down to strict necessity; in an attack on the Royalist garrison at Shelford, Colonel Hutchinson encounters a 'foot-boy' who started out in the Parliamentary army but faithfully served both the Royalist army that captured him and the Parliamentary army that recaptured him (201). But by far the biggest challenge to local unity depicted by Hutchinson is greed and opportunism. Again and again, the covetousness, ambition, and envy of people in and around Nottingham led them to exploit the war for their own gain.[47] As their actions are often at odds with Colonel Hutchinson's defense of the county interest, he is frequently in conflict with such individuals. The resulting waste of resources and lack of unity are constant thorns in Hutchinson's side, leading his wife to make the remarkable statement that 'he encountered no less difficulties and contradictions from those of his own party . . . than from his enemies' (120). In the crucible of civil war, other loyalties and motives could be just as strong as local solidarity.

But it is also clear that Lucy Hutchinson does not approve of such fragmentation, and that she assiduously offers her husband as a corrective. Although John Hutchinson 'became . . . convinced in conscience of the righteousness of the Parliament's cause' (75), the *Memoirs* are clear that the dual interest of town and county are paramount for him. When the conflagration of war initially broke out, Hutchinson only accepted leadership responsibilities after 'many of his honest neighbours made application to him' (76) and he did so for motives of service rather than ambition. '[W]hen he undertook this engagement,' Lucy Hutchinson is at pains to point out, 'it was for the defense of his country's and God's cause, and he offered himself and all he had a willing sacrifice in the service' (119). Unlike other garrison leaders on both sides, John Hutchinson did not despoil his enemies or encroach upon the county for his own financial gain (120). In fact, he expended considerable quantities of his own money to maintain the garrison at Nottingham (119). On one occasion, John Hutchinson is offered the chance to save his estate at Owthorpe and 'have what reward he pleased' if he will abandon his post and go over to the King's side (121).[48] His refusal serves as a clear contrast to many of his neighbors whose greed and opportunism caused them to act against the interest of their locality. As the war unfolds, John Hutchinson continues to be guided by what he feels is the county's best interest. When the self-seeking Nottingham Committee tries to force him out in the autumn of 1644, the Colonel refuses to budge, lest 'the county . . . be abandoned into the hands of persons who would only make a prey of it, and not endeavour its protection, liberty, or real advantage, which had been his chief aim in all his undertakings' (175). A few months later, John Hutchinson actively opposes a Parliamentary excise tax that he fears will oppress 'the poor county' (192). In doing so, he shows his willingness to work against central government – even a Parliamentary one – in promoting the interests of Nottingham.

Although Lucy Hutchinson firmly identifies the local sphere as her husband's chief area of concern, her narrative does pause occasionally to fill the reader in on national developments.[49] For instance, she pauses to record the King's early military success in the West (104–106), the development of Parliamentary factions, the rise of the New Model Army, and the King's setbacks in the West (160–162), and the capture of the King and the emerging Parliamentary struggle between the Presbyterians and the Army (212–215). Each time that the narrative dilates in this fashion, Hutchinson makes it clear this is but a 'short digression from our particular actions' (57) and that she will only mention what is 'necessary to be remembered for the story I most particularly intend' (84). In other words, she is not implicitly interested in tying Nottingham to the larger sphere, but believes that it is 'necessary to carry on the main story for the better understanding of the motion of those lesser wheels that moved within the greater orb' (104). In the *Memoirs*, talking about national developments ultimately serves to contextualize the local: 'that we may the better judge of things at home when we know the conditions of things abroad' (160). Together, these self-conscious phrases show the extent to which Lucy Hutchinson is committed to maintaining a local view of the Civil War.[50]

Other passages in the *Memoirs* suggest that a local narrative can actually be superior to a purely national view of the Civil War. When the author is introducing the first of her digressions into 'the state of the kingdom at that time,' she warns that 'though I cannot do exactly, yet I can truly relate what I was then able to take notice of' (57). The implication is that a national narrative may be too vast and complex for one person to give an exact account of. She considers referring the reader to more exhaustive books that have already been written on the Civil War, but then asserts that many such accounts are 'fraught with abominable lies' (57). The problem with being a Puritan and writing about the Civil War in the 1660s is that the victors had already written the history books. Hutchinson's more localized account purports to be more 'exactly' written and to help set the record straight (at least in regards to what happened in Nottinghamshire).

But Hutchinson doesn't just present the local as an oppositional alternative to national history. Rather, she suggests that it can actually help shed light on the national by explaining, illustrating, and even foreshadowing larger trends. This is especially true of the factionalism that John Hutchinson continually encountered in Nottingham. Not only did the Colonel have to contend with a lack of unity amongst those he commanded, but 'almost all the Parliament garrisons were infested and disturbed with like factious little people . . . Nor was the faction only in particular garrisons, but the Parliament House itself began to fall into the two great oppositions of Presbytery and Independency' (197–198). In Hutchinson's view, the fragmentation that developed on the local level both foreshadowed and helped explain the breakdown of a national Parliamentary consensus. In other parts of the *Memoirs*, local incidents provide concrete illustrations for otherwise abstract developments. For instance, in her handling of the rapid shifts in public opinion in 1659 – the surge of Presbyterian activity, the reassertion of the Army, and the groundswell of support for restoring the monarchy – Hutchinson provides a local episode to illustrate how each trend manifested itself in Nottingham (265, 270, 275).[51]

Lucy Hutchinson has another reason for insisting that local accounts of the war are not simply absorbed into a national narrative: she needs to show that John Hutchinson was doing God's work even though the larger cause he fought for was defeated. She proceeds in this task not just by exonerating her husband and his political ideology, but by setting up less outcome-based criteria for assessing the participants of the Civil War. Instead of judging people by the side on which they fought, people in the *Memoirs* are evaluated by how they accounted themselves in their particular spheres of action. Through this lens, some Parliamentarians were dishonorable and some Royalists were praise-worthy. Sir John Gell, though he defended the nearby town of Derby against the Cavaliers, was nevertheless 'a very bad man, to sum up all in that word' (92). Several of the Parliamentarians that the Colonel worked alongside in Nottingham also attract Lucy Hutchinson's ire: Plumtre, the scoffing doctor; Chadwick the proud hypocrite; and Charles White, who had 'the most factious, ambitious, vainglorious, envious, and mali-cious nature that is imaginable' (94). Meanwhile, the local Royalists are not without their virtues. Robert Pierrepont, 1st Earl of Kingston and former MP of Nottingham, declared himself for the King, 'wherein he behaved himself honourably and died remarkably' (85). In the *Memoirs*, virtue and honor are determined by behavior rather than ideological affiliation.

Lucy Hutchinson is eager to apply these same criteria to her husband, and in doing so, she often depicts him as faction-less. 'They very little knew him that could say he was of any faction,' she remarks, 'for he had a strength of judgment able to consider things himself and pro-pound them to his conscience' (207). Lucy Hutchinson never denies that her husband was both a republican and a religious separatist (as she is herself committed to those same beliefs), but she stresses that these affiliations come from his conscience and are not simply dictated by pre-fabricated categories. As a result, sometimes John Hutchinson is not wholly in line with any stereotype. Some people identify him as an Anabaptist; others call him a Cavalier (211). Even John Hutchinson's flowing locks – he had 'a very fine thickset head of hair' (87) – give the lie to the 'roundhead' stereotype.[52] For Lucy Hutchinson, the Colonel's thoughts and actions carry more weight in defining him than do ready-made labels. Part of what she does in the *Memoirs*, then, is to recreate a local sphere where his motives and conduct can be more clearly seen and judged. Her portrayal of John Hutchinson can be conveniently divided into three discrete periods: civil war, protectorate, and restora-tion. In all three periods, his depiction is colored by the particular local sphere in which he moves.

Lucy Hutchinson devotes almost half of the *Memoirs* to the four-year period of John Hutchinson's military service (1642–1646). Even without the detailed record that his wife left behind, John Hutchinson's service in these years was unusual. In Nottingham, 'most of the gentry of the county were disaffected to the Parliament' whereas 'most of the middle sort . . . adhered to the Parliament' (76). Thus, John Hutchinson broke class ranks in supporting the godly cause. In fact, according to J. T. Cliffe, the Hutchinsons were the only major Puritan gentry family in the whole shire.[53] Not only this, but John Hutchinson was among the only one-third of major Puritan gentry nationwide who actually saw military service.[54] After playing an active but unofficial role in the first few months of the war (e.g. the defense of the town magazine), Hutchinson was appointed Governor of Nottingham Castle in June of 1643. By September, a Royalist force had attacked and occupied the town and established a fort on the Trent Bridge. By October, Hutchinson's troops (working from within the castle) were able to retake the fort and drive the Cavaliers away. Shortly thereafter, Hutchinson was elevated from lieutenant-colonel to full colonel, and his governorship was extended to include the town of Nottingham. Over the succeeding two and a half years, the town was attacked and briefly occupied twice more, but each time Hutchinson was able to lead a successful counterattack and drive away the enemy. Nottingham troops were also periodically involved (sometimes with larger Parliamentary forces) in skirmishes beyond the town. Most notably, they participated in the crucial campaign of 1645 when they took the Royalist garrison at Shelford and assisted in the siege of Newark that effectively ended the First Civil War in the region.[55]

Not only does Lucy Hutchinson carefully detail these events, she uses them to display her husband's manifold virtues. John Hutchinson emerges as a brave fighter, careful administrator, and indefatigable presence for the Parliamentary side. As a leader, he possesses a 'native majesty that struck an awe of him into the hearts of men, and a sweet greatness that commanded love' (24). His ability to blend prudence, foresight, and judgment also make him an effective tactician. In the retaking of the Trent Bridge fort, Lucy Hutchinson shows her husband's ability to pick a favorable occasion and make careful and coordinated preparations.[56] During the assault, John Hutchinson led by example and 'stayed all night in the trenches with his men' 'which much encouraged them' (132). The Colonel also displays his cleverness in making the Royalists believe that there are more Nottingham troops than there actually are and in distracting the enemy so that covert missions can be successfully carried out.[57] This local episode provides a vivid portrait of John Hutchinson much more effectually than if the author had merely cataloged his leadership abilities.[58]

During this four-year section of the narrative, Hutchinson's local sphere of conduct varies. Though it is mostly focused on (defending) the town of Nottingham, it also encompasses 'the county interest,' and at times even expands to include the neighboring counties of Derbyshire, Leicestershire, and Northamptonshire. Nevertheless, such a relatively small scope allows the narrator to emphasize the pivotal role that John Hutchinson played and to elevate the drama and heroism that occurred in this east Midlands town. In the larger scheme of the English Civil War, the retaking of the Trent Bridge fort was not that significant. Yet this event, which pitted approximately 160 Parliamentarian soldiers against 80 Royalists is given a grand, heroic treatment that fills nine pages of narrative.

But the *Memoirs* also devotes considerable space to the Parliamentary bickering and discord that characterized the First Civil War in Nottingham. This stemmed mainly from the antagonism between Hutchinson's castle garrison and the town that worsened when the Colonel's authority was extended to the town in 1644 and culminated in a power struggle between John Hutchinson and the Nottingham Committee. The causes of the strife were varied and complex – for example, the castle made the town a target, Hutchinson was an Independent whereas most of the townspeople were Presbyterians, and the town didn't think that Hutchinson could 'continue a gentleman and [remain] firm to a godly interest' (118).[59] Lucy Hutchinson's complaint is that the resulting discord damaged John Hutchinson's effectiveness and his reputation. She sets out to ameliorate these harms by describing the squabbles in detail and vindicating John Hutchinson at every turn. In general, she tends to downplay religious and class differences as factors, and instead focuses on exposing the base motives, malice, jealousy, and ambition of her husband's enemies. She also tends to focus on the effects of their refusals to follow orders and their constant attempts to undermine his authority.

At times, both John Hutchinson and the Nottingham Committee appeal to the centralized Parliamentary authorities for arbitration. Indeed, in 1644 and again in 1645, the Colonel has to leave the local theater of war and journey to London to appear before the House of Commons. Although the centralized authorities do tend to affirm John Hutchinson's authority,[60] one of the difficulties is that no one in London really knows the local situation and so must rely on the oppositional accounts of the two parties. For instance, when John Hutchinson appears before the Committee of Both Kingdoms, a certain Mr. Millington 'had written letters, and given them such false impressions of . . . him that was a stranger to them all, that they looked upon him very coldly' (182). The implication is that one must really understand the Nottingham situation and the people involved in order to get a true picture of what transpired there. This is exactly what Lucy Hutchinson tries to provide in *Memoirs of the Life of Colonel Hutchinson*. This is also why it is not enough in her narrative for the London authorities to ratify her husband's authority. At several points in the text, she describes how John Hutchinson's former enemies eventually came round to confessing their errors and asking for his forgiveness. Mr. Millington, for instance, 'applied himself to seek a reconciliation by flattering letters and professions of conviction and repentance of his unjust siding with those men' (198).[61] The *Memoirs* thus provide the local account necessary to properly judge John Hutchinson and also help enact the local vindication that is the narrative's chief aim.

After the end of the First Civil War in June of 1646, Colonel Hutchinson helped dismantle the castle fortifications and then returned to his estate at Owthorpe for a year.[62] In the autumn of 1648, the Hutchinsons moved to London so that the Colonel could 'attend his duty at the Parliament' (230). Over the next five years, he was closely involved with national events. Hutchinson was a member of the Rump Parliament that tried and executed the King in 1649 and he later served a two-year term on Oliver Cromwell's Council of State. But Hutchinson's republican sentiments could not stomach Cromwell's increasing authority, and when the latter disbanded the Rump in 1653 and declared himself Lord Protector, the Hutchinsons returned to Owthorpe for the remainder of the 1650s. It is to this second period of John Hutchinson's local involvement that we will now turn.

As early as 1649, John Hutchinson was growing weary of 'a close and chargeable attendance' (236) on Parliament and was eager to slip off to county concerns. From about 1651 he had spent frequent time 'in the country . . . when the Parliament could dispense with his absence' (254). Indeed, Hutchinson wasn't even present when Cromwell disbanded the Rump on April 20, 1653. By this time, the Colonel seemed convinced that he was better able to 'attend the public business of his county' (255) from his own estate rather than from London. From Owthorpe, Hutchinson devoted himself 'to the administration of justice in the county, and to the putting in execution of those wholesome laws and statutes of the land provided for the orderly regulation of the people. And it was wonderful how, in a short space, he reformed several abuses and customary neglects in that part of the county where he lived . . . and all the poor in every town were so maintained and provided for as they never were so liberally maintained and relieved before or since' (253). Lucy Hutchinson thus draws a marked contrast between what

John Hutchinson was able to achieve in his corner of Nottinghamshire and the machinations and injustices of 'Oliver's mutable reign' (255). It is the local – rather than the national sphere – that offers the best prospect of administering justice, executing the laws, reforming abuses, and caring for the poor. Significantly, John Hutchinson is able to effect these changes even though he doesn't hold any public office – suggesting the superfluity of formal (and even local) government structures.[63] His activities are depicted simply as the natural care for and governance of 'that part of the county where he lived.'

It is worth noting that John Hutchinson's local sphere has shrunk in this section. Although it does include an extended neighborhood and nearby towns, it is firmly centered on Owthorpe. Significantly, the Hutchinson estate is not depicted, like so many other houses in the Interregnum, as a site of private retirement and solitude. Instead, 'his house was much resorted to, and as kindly opened to those who had in public contests been his enemies as to his continued friends' (256). Once again, Lucy Hutchinson uses the local to provide a corrective to the national; in this case, Owthorpe's 'openness' contrasts with the ideological polarization and fragmentation that the author emphasizes on the national level and within the Cromwellian government. Once again, the local sphere is the place where factional assumptions can be interrogated and even invalidated. Owthorpe is 'open to all worthy persons of all parties' (265). Its scope, like the rest of the *Memoirs*, is circumscribed enough to allow for an informed judgment of 'worthy' individuals, regardless of which side they fought on in the Civil War.

But there is also a noticeably private component to Lucy Hutchinson's portrayal of Owthorpe in the 1650s. John Hutchinson relishes the chance to return to long-neglected familial and domestic pursuits, making it 'his business to attend [to] the education of his children and the government of his own house' (255). The Colonel also finds time to pursue various cultured and edifying pursuits, including building improvements, land enclosure, art collecting, hawking, and music.[64] Despite these attractions, the Owthorpe of the 1650s is mainly depicted as a home base from which John Hutchinson can continue to impact the local community around him. When Oliver Cromwell died in 1658 and his son, Richard, the new Protector, invited the Colonel to become Sheriff of Nottingham, Hutchinson acceded to this wider area of responsibility.

Before moving to the Restoration, the third and final period in which John Hutchinson is depicted, I would like to pause to discuss the role of Lucy Hutchinson's Puritanism in her depiction of the local sphere. Up until this point, her decision to justify her husband by focusing on his sphere of action rather than the larger outcome of the war would be understandable for *anyone* performing a similar task for someone who fought on the losing side of a war. But I would now like to argue that Lucy Hutchinson's religious outlook both heightens the appeal of the local and helps determine the use that she makes of it.

The local had long been a characteristic feature of English Puritanism. Although the godly were working to purify the national Church from the 1560s, the local sphere was their main area of impact prior to the Civil War. The Puritans were integral in developing a preaching ministry (including the establishment of lectureships by wealthy lay patrons) that transformed the experience of worship in many parishes.[65] The godly were also successful in establishing and enforcing more rigorous standards of individual and communal piety. Thus, even at a time when they lacked national influence, Puritans were able to impact everything from forms of worship to communal sports and pastimes on the local level. It is not surprising that some Puritans would come to espouse religious and political ideologies that privileged local autonomy. The Hutchinsons themselves were Independents, meaning that they favored 'a congregational church system granting autonomy to each particular church and allowing a degree of authority to members of congregations' – unlike the Presbyterians who favored 'a national church system with a governing hierarchy of church courts' and 'a firm notion of theological orthodoxy and intolerance of dissent.'[66] The Hutchinsons also had strong republican political leanings, as can be seen in John Hutchinson's sympathy towards the Levellers.[67] There are obvious parallels between these separatist and republican ideals and a decentralized mentality that would seem to privilege the integrity of smaller units like the local sphere. But I want to suggest some even more fundamental religious reasons for Lucy Hutchinson's investment in the local. Namely, it helps satisfy the Puritan preoccupation with discerning and responding to the will of God. In the *Memoirs*, Nottingham is an appropriate focus of the narrative because it is the place where divine providence and the Christian conscience can best act in concert.

Lucy Hutchinson is careful to demonstrate that her husband didn't just happen to pass the war in Nottingham, but that he was *called* to serve in this sphere. Before the war began, John Hutchinson's plan to purchase an office in the Star Chamber in Westminster was prevented by a 'peculiar providence.' Afterwards, the couple and their three sons left London and returned to Nottinghamshire 'to retire to that place whither God seemed to have called him by giving him so good an interest there' (57). As the nation lurched towards war, John Hutchinson was in sympathy with the Parliament, but 'thinking he had no warrantable call at that time to do anything more, contented himself to pray to God for peace' (75). Even when his fellow Puritans were joining up with the army, John Hutchinson waited to 'find a clear call from the Lord' (89). This call came in 1643, when he was given a commission to defend the town of Nottingham. Finally, 'believing that God hereby called him to the defence of his country,' the Colonel accepted his charge (110).[68] In other words, the *Memoirs* depict John Hutchinson's work in his native shire as a divine rather than an earthly appointment. He is vocationally called to the local sphere. This idea is carried throughout the narrative and is still in place even in the Restoration, when John Hutchinson's official duties have long since lapsed.[69] His friends urge him to flee abroad, but the Colonel refuses, saying that 'this was the place where God had set him' (290). John Hutchinson's local calling has significant implications for his wife's defense of him. On the one hand, he is expected to 'improve that talent' (57) that God has given him – implying a burden of responsibility. But the biblical parable that Lucy Hutchinson invests in also places limits on his accountability; it implies that he is chiefly responsible for the talent that he has been given and not those of others. In other words, since he 'made it only his business to perform what he was called to in the station God set him' (55), then that is how he must be evaluated – not by the actions of others or the overall outcome of the war. In asserting the Puritan idea that God called John Hutchinson to a special task, Lucy Hutchinson justifies the narrow scope of her narrative and its obsession with how her husband conducted himself.[70]

But rather than leave the interpretation of his conduct up to the reader, Lucy Hutchinson repeatedly demonstrates that the Colonel acted in accordance with God's will and that he was approved by God. This she does by appealing to instances of God's providence. 'Belief in the interventions of providence . . . lay at the heart of Puritan piety' because it was a sign that God was active in the lives of his people in general and that a particular individual was one of the Elect.[71] This is also why 'the godly incessantly scrutinised events for signs of divine favour and disapprobation.'[72] Providence is a primary concern for Lucy Hutchinson in her own *Autobiography*, which she characterizes as nothing more than a record of God's 'general and particular providences exercised to me, both in the entrance and progress of my life' (3).[73] The word 'providence' occurs some 27 times in the *Memoirs*. In practice, it turns out to be a rather flexible concept. Sometimes, Lucy Hutchinson sees providence in a situation, as when John Hutchinson is given a time of quiet preparation just prior to the Civil War (54). Sometimes, it takes the form of a direct action, as when 'by a providence' of a timely storm, the Nottingham troops are prevented from walking into an ambush (103). Lucy Hutchinson applies the word to the mundane (God's bringing together two people in matrimony (47)) as well as the miraculous (a cannonball that narrowly misses the Colonel (206)). Providence also functions variously in the text. Its purpose can be to carry out God's wrath against the iniquitous (125) or to teach a lesson to His followers (147). Despite these various applications, the one constant for Lucy Hutchinson is that providence is God's hand in history, shaping events to carry out His purposes and take care of those who are acting in His interests.

In the *Memoirs*, God's hand is particularly evident in protecting John Hutchinson from those Committee members and townspeople who continually plot against him. When they devise a 'wicked design which they were secretly managing to destroy' him, 'God, by a wonderful providence, brought [it] to light' (180). A later attempt is also 'brought providentially to light' (182). Again and again their subversive efforts are 'by God's providence . . . detected' (184) so that John Hutchinson is able to carry on with his duties. It also helps that the Colonel is able to deal with his enemies from a position of authority which Lucy Hutchinson also sees as divinely ordained – his enemies 'were cast under his power by God's just providence' (179).

Providence functions in a number of ways in the *Memoirs*. First, it is a way of seeing the past that enables Lucy Hutchinson to acknowledge God's care of her husband and register her gratitude. But providence is not only a retrospective virtue. It also involves being attuned to how God's plan is unfolding in the present so that one may join Him in that work. Despite Lucy Hutchinson's desire to remain in London in 1641, she interpreted the 'peculiar providence' that kept John Hutchinson from the Star Chamber as a sign that 'she ought to follow her husband where the Lord seemed to call him' (57). But the most important function of the many providences that the author records in the *Memoirs* is the overwhelming evidence that they provide that John Hutchinson is 'confirmed in the favour of God' (303).

In all of these cases, providence is particularly connected to the local sphere. God's 'various providences' extend to even the 'smallest concernments,' asserts the author in her *Autobiography* (3). In the *Memoirs*, she affirms that 'little things were links in the chain of providences which measured out [John Hutchinson's] life' (114).[74] Not only does God reveal His hand in little things, but they are also more easily seen in the local than elsewhere. That God's hand is uncommonly evident in Nottingham in the 1640s can be seen from the above examples. But this is not only because Nottingham is the prime focus of the narrative. Lucy Hutchinson does discuss the larger picture extensively – both in her narrative dilations and when she talks about John Hutchinson's role in national events – but she seldom uses the word 'providence' in these sections. In fact, only four out of 27 occurrences refer to God's intervention in national events.[75] Instead, the word 'providence' is concentrated in the First Civil War section of the narrative (17 of 27 occurences), where it is chiefly applied to John Hutchinson's activities in Nottingham.

But why should the concept of providence be more serviceable to a local narrative? One reason may be that the national sphere is simply bigger and more muddled. It is therefore much less conducive to detecting the subtle workings of God. Another problem with the national sphere – especially from a seventeenth-century Puritan perspective – is that the Royalists ultimately triumphed. As it is more difficult for Lucy Hutchinson to discern the operations of providence in this larger sphere, she asserts it less frequently. When the Colonel was in the Tower of London in 1663, one of his fellow prisoners made a 'false, flattering petition' to secure his own liberty. Lucy Hutchinson records a portion of this man's recantation – 'that since God by his miraculous providence had set his Majesty over us, he had acquiesced thankfully under it' – and then bluntly adds that 'Mr. Hutchinson would not follow his example' (311). This response suggests the difficulty of reconciling providence with the Restoration, and perhaps explains the narrative's alternate focus on instances of local providence. Whatever the reason, the effect is to establish the local as the place where one can most easily see God, sense His favor, and participate in His work.

Another religious word that occurs frequently in the *Memoirs* is 'conscience.' If the narrative depicts providence as God's hand at work in the world, conscience is what enables people to respond to God's presence and join Him in that work. A belief in the inviolability of the individual conscience was a crucial tenet of Puritanism. A natural tendency towards self-examination combined with the conviction that the Holy Spirit was at work in the individual's life meant that the godly 'champion[ed] conscience above worldly authorities.'[76] Lucy Hutchinson offers a fairly standard – if complex – depiction of the Puritan conscience. For her, the conscience revolves around one's internal sense of right and wrong, as when John Hutchinson first becomes 'convinced in conscience of the righteousness of the Parliament's cause' (75). It is also akin to one's judgment – 'he never did anything without measuring it by the rule of conscience' (22) – though not quite the same. At times, conscience seems to imply an inner prompting that can even defy rational judgment. The Colonel knew he was 'tying himself to an indefensible town . . . yet was he so well persuaded in his conscience of the cause and of God's calling him to undertake the defence of it, that he cast by all other considerations and cheerfully resigned up his life and all other particular interests to God's dispose, though in all human probability he was more likely to lose than to save them' (102). In other words, though his decision would seem to go against his better judgment, his conscience dictated that it was the right thing to do.

As with providence, conscience is depicted in the *Memoirs* as operating most clearly in the local realm. For one thing, the concept itself is highly individualized and often contrasted with broader patterns or standards of behavior. John Hutchinson, we are told, puts little stock in popular commendation or reputation, and instead looks to his own conscience for approval (28). He also feels that 'to comply with changing government or persons, without a real persuasion of conscience' is a form of religious hypocrisy (25). Nor is it simply a matter of aligning one's conscience with some transcendent, immutable standard. In the *Memoirs*, two virtuous individuals can arrive at different conclusions, but still be true to their own consciences.[77] As Governor, John Hutchinson refrains from persecuting people in matters of conscience, even though their beliefs differ from his.[78] Even a single individual's conscience may not be consistently fixed. Over the course of the *Memoirs*, John Hutchinson becomes convinced in his conscience of certain things, implying that these things weren't clear (and that he wasn't bound by them) before.[79] Thus, far from exhibiting unwavering constancy or simply reflecting an external ideal, the conscience is fluid. It is depicted by Lucy Hutchinson as a process that involves searching, probing, and listening carefully for God's inner prompting.

For all these reasons, the *Memoirs* depicts the conscience as particularly suited to the local realm. The local, like the conscience, is inherently decentralized and often distinct from larger patterns. Moreover, the conscience operates most effectively when particular circumstances can be assessed and acted on with clarity; the local's small scope and finite factors are ideal for this process. As in Walton's *Compleat Angler*, the local offers a more exact way of proceeding that is superior to general rules because it allows the individual to detect and respond to contingency.[80] The word 'conscience' occurs 46 times in Lucy Hutchinson's narrative. Its usage is spread more evenly throughout the text than 'providence' – with quite a few deployments of conscience on the national level.[81] But the majority of occurrences (28) describe John Hutchinson's conscience and/or its operation in the local realm.

Lucy Hutchinson generally inserts the word in relation to a decision that her husband made. For instance, in the First Civil War, a local minister named Mr. Palmer wanted to form and lead a troop of soldiers to assist in the defense of the county. The Hutchinsons knew him to be 'vain-glorious, contentious, covetous, and ambitious,' though Palmer acted as if 'the honest people pressed him very much to be their captain.' When he came to the Hutchinsons for advice, they tried to dissuade him from his design, saying that he had already freely accepted 'a charge of another kind' and that he might just as well accompany the soldiers as a chaplain than as a captain. Palmer went on to accept the commission anyway and later make trouble for the Colonel in recompense, but Lucy Hutchinson defends her husband's decision, saying he 'only declared his own judgment when he was asked, as a Christian ought to do according to his conscience . . . and censured him not.' Although the episode could be skewed by the Colonel's detractors to make him look jealous of a potential rival to his authority, Lucy Hutchinson presents it as a conscientious objection. John Hutchinson was able to discern the true motives animating Palmer and determine that his intended course of action was not advisable. His familiarity with and careful consideration of the particulars of the situation helped his conscience render a just decision.[82]

But Lucy Hutchinson doesn't just invoke the Colonel's conscience as a defense mechanism or explanatory tool, she also depicts the application of conscience as a noble and fulfilling practice. Words like 'satisfied,' 'enlightened,' 'confirmation,' and 'good' are all used in close proximity to 'conscience' to characterize its operational effects. Just as Walton's angler takes pleasure in making difficult choices, Hutchinson portrays the exercise of conscience as an admirable and even artistic skill.

But in the *Memoirs*, conscience – like providence – is less viable on the national level. As we have seen, the word itself is deployed less frequently in describing the larger theater of war. This may partially be an issue of clarity, as it is more difficult for the individual conscience to arrive at a thorough understanding of all the complex factors operating at this level. But as the *Memoirs* unfolds, there is also a developing disconnect between the private conscience and the national outcome of the war. Ironically, the section of the narrative where 'conscience' appears most frequently is when Lucy Hutchinson explains her husband's complicity in the execution of Charles I. As she walks the reader through his decision, the word appears seven times in a little over a page. He prayed that God would 'lead him by a right enlightened conscience; and finding no check, but a confirmation in his conscience that it was his duty to act as he did, he . . . proceeded to sign the sentence against the King' (235). When Lucy Hutchinson was writing in the 1660s, her husband's verdict was indefensible from a national perspective – the monarchy had been restored and some of the regicides had already been killed. So Lucy Hutchinson offers a justification of her husband based purely on his conscience. She does so in an attempt to contextualize and privatize his decision, implying that this is what makes it defensible. Yet this maneuver only underscores the emerging gulf between the Puritan conscience and the national outcome. John Hutchinson's conscience may have been prompting him to act as he did, but it can no longer be countenanced from a national perspective.

In the Restoration – the third and final period that Lucy Hutchinson's narrative covers – the ties between conscience and the local sphere are further cemented. Even before the Restoration, in 1659, we find John Hutchinson growing weary of national affairs. In that year, Richard Cromwell's new Parliament was dissolved by the Army, and the Rump was recalled. John Hutchinson dutifully returned to London, but he was an irregular attendee. According to his wife, he was 'much perplexed, for now he thought his conscience, life, and fortunes again engaged with men of mixed and different interests and principles' (263). After spending six years reforming and improving his corner of Nottinghamshire without compromising his principles, John Hutchinson was hesitant to return to the national sphere. A year later, he had little choice, as he was called to London at the Restoration to account for his role in the regicide. Among other things, he told his interrogators that he regretted leaving his own 'blessed quiet to embark in such a troubled sea' where he had 'made a shipwreck of all things but a good conscience' (279). This metaphor vividly asserts the dangers of national involvement and also contrasts it with a good conscience. All of these Restoration-era statements reveal John Hutchinson's growing reluctance to expose his principles and conscience to the dangers and adulteration of national affairs.

This reluctance is mirrored by the Colonel's actual, physical withdrawal into the local sphere. When John Hutchinson was pardoned by the Convention in June of 1660 and included in the Act of Oblivion two months later, he returned to Owthorpe. Unlike in 1653, when he used his estate as a home base for impacting 'that part of the county where he lived' (253), he now lived at Owthorpe with 'all imaginable retiredness' (292). During these years, Lucy Hutchinson composed a poem that captures some of the attractions of this retirement:

> This freedom in the country life is found,
> Where innocence and safe delights abound:
> Here man's a prince; his subjects ne'er repine
> When on his back their wealthy fleeces shine:
> . . . .
> What court then can such liberty afford?
> Or where is man so uncontroll'd a lord? (31–34, 61–62)[83]

The poem extols life at Owthorpe because it offers freedom and liberty without the political relationships that threaten safety and innocence. Although the poem may be making a virtue of what was more or less an enforced withdrawal from public life, the *Memoirs* suggests that John Hutchinson's fondness for Owthorpe was heartfelt. In his retirement, 'he took up his time in opening springs and planting trees and dressing his plantations' (292). During these years, he also developed a deep bond with his new daughter-in-law, chiefly because she 'loved [Owthorpe] not as his own wife did, only because she was placed in it, but with a natural affection, which encouraged him in all the pains he took to adorn it, when he had one to leave it to that would esteem it' (292). The Colonel did not stop serving his fellow man – Lucy Hutchinson notes that he provided work for poor laborers and instructed his servants and children – but his sphere was now almost completely contracted into the world of the estate.

This idyllic existence came to an abrupt end in October of 1663, when Hutchinson was arrested for his alleged involvement in the Northern Plot and imprisoned in the Tower of London. There, he was examined but never formally tried. Instead, he was moved to Sandown Castle, Kent in May of 1664 and died four months later. Some of the people he was imprisoned with wrote petitions recanting their roles in the Civil War and gained their liberty. John Hutchinson did not. In fact, he was loath to be freed by any means that would 'fetter him in obligations to such persons as every day more and more manifested themselves ene-mies to all just and godly interests' (311). Again, the Colonel exhibits an anxiety about unduly connecting himself with people of 'mixed and different interests and principles' (263). Even if he was restored to lib-erty and the Parliamentarians were once again in power, he vowed that 'he would never meddle any more either in councils or armies' (322). At most he might be persuaded to act as a justice of the peace and rid the neighborhood of drunkards. Once again, the Colonel's ideological retreat is imagined as a physical retreat to the local scope.

During his confinement in London and Kent, John Hutchinson returns frequently – if only in his thoughts – to his native locality. Not to the county or town that he served so dutifully in the 1640s nor to the extended neighborhood that he so ably administered in the 1650s, but to Owthorpe itself. He spent his final night there before being conveyed to the Tower, and '[took] leave of his poor labourers, who wept all bitterly when he paid them off' (303). Months later, when his wife visits him at Sandown Castle, the Colonel 'gave her directions in a paper for planting trees, and for many other things belonging to the house and gardens' (327). Even though he admits that he may never see the house again, the issuing of these particular instructions affords him a measure of control at a time when he has very little. It is not unlike Walton's Royalist anglers immersed in the problem of how to catch chub in a particular stream. On one occasion, he tells his visiting wife that were he at liberty, he would avoid the conversation of all Cavaliers and 'would write upon his doors, *procul hinc procul este, profani*' (322).[84] This is a far cry from the house open to people 'of all parties' (265) that we saw in the 1650s. Owthorpe is now valued for its effectiveness in shutting out harmful influences. It has become a contracted scope where the conscience can live untainted and unfettered. John Hutchinson's Christianity is not dependent on such a cloistered setting – at one point he acknowledges that 'God is the same God at Tangier as at Owthorpe' (322) – but as the *Memoirs* has shown, it is easier both to see God's hand (providence) and join Him in His work (conscience) on the local level.

This may be why John Hutchinson was so adamant about being returned to Owthorpe for burial. According to the *Memoirs*, he made this request three times just before his death. Lucy Hutchinson confesses to being a bit puzzled. Not only is the trek back to Nottinghamshire 'about eight score miles distant,' but her husband had previously said 'in all his life time before . . . that wherever he died he would there be buried' (333). Yet this change of plans does seem consistent with the central importance of Owthorpe to John Hutchinson in this final stage of his life. Lucy Hutchinson ends up ascribing his motive to wanting to avoid the 'superstitions' of the Prayer Book burial service by being interred in the church on his estate.[85] If this is true, it serves to underscore the point that Owthorpe has (now literally) become the only place left where John Hutchinson's conscience is free to act as it would. Providence seems to have assented to the Colonel's wishes, as 'the hand of God' granted peaceful passage to his body 'through the dominions of his murderers' and home to Owthorpe (334, 333). Throughout the *Memoirs*, the local has featured as the place where John Hutchinson was called to serve, the realm in which he most effectively exercised his conscience, and the sphere where he could best detect God's affirming providence. It is thus appropriate that his life story concludes with the Colonel and God teaming up to return his body to its native locale.

The Civil War experiences of Izaak Walton and John Hutchinson could scarcely be more different. When John Hutchinson was serving on the Council of State in the early 1650s, Walton was living quietly in London and perfecting his angling craft. At the Restoration, Walton was invited to live with bishops, while John Hutchinson was imprisoned. Yet for both writers, the national conflict that they participated in served mainly to confirm the sanctity of the local sphere. Whether in the heat of battle or along a quiet river, each writer imagines the local as a welcome contrast to the confusion and uncertainty of larger events. Both the Lea valley and the city of Nottingham are finite spaces that offer clearer choices and thus a theater for meaningful individual action – whether the actor is retaking a fort on the Trent, or pulling a grayling from its watery depths. Hutchinson and Walton also envision the local as a place to safeguard values that are under threat in the larger sphere. This capability doesn't simply arise from the local's tranquillity – Hutchinson's godly virtue must still be defended from plotting townspeople and whizzing cannonballs, and Walton's innocent mirth can be soiled by lascivious innkeepers – but from the greater control that the local offers in identifying, shaping, and displaying these values. In this regard, the angler's careful consideration of contingency is not materially different from the blameless exercise of John Hutchinson's conscience. Both thrive in the local sphere because it allows for an exactness that goes beyond polarizing and monolithic ideologies. The *Angler* and the *Memoirs* even agree in ultimately positing the local as a spiritual sphere. It is a place both to see God (Lucy Hutchinson's 'providence') and reflect on His blessings (the angler's contemplation of God's natural handiwork) at a time when it seems difficult to do either on the macro-level. The local thus emerges as an anchor of assurance in a troubled time.

6
The Country House Poem and the Localization of Empire

As we have seen, the *Memoirs* portrays the Hutchinson estate at Owthorpe as not just a home, but a local sphere of operation that is serviceable to many of the same goals that motivated the Colonel's earlier defense of his city and county. While in retirement at Owthorpe in the 1650s, John Hutchinson is able to execute the laws, administer justice, and maintain an 'orderly regulation of the people' in the surrounding neighborhood. This is typical of the estate's role in the early modern period, for it was not just a private dwelling, but the center of its local neighborhood. Since it was inhabited by the ruling gentry, it functioned as political seat, administrative hub, and occasionally even religious center.[1] The estate was also an important site of social relations, where hospitality was dispensed, marriage matches made, and disputes settled. Perhaps the reason that Saxton and Speed include so many minor estates on their maps is not just to assert gentry ownership of the land, but because these estates were also important landmarks that defined their areas of the county.

The notion of the estate as a local unit is supported by its portrayal in the country house poem. In 'To Penshurst' (1612), that quintessential English country house poem, the estate is imagined in terms of the same categories of local definition that chorography helped to establish. Ben Jonson asserts the estate's distinctiveness (from prodigy houses), describes its topography (mount, lower land, middle ground), recounts its historical highlights (the visit of King James), draws attention to its local dignitaries (the poet, Sir Philip Sidney), and provides a sense of the human community that inhabits it (the Sidney family as well as their tenants and servants). This final category has been much commented on by literary critics, who focus on the social function of estates and the hospitality offered by benevolent landlords.[2] Certainly, such social

154

interactions are crucial for the poets' constructions of local community. Otherwise, country house poems would not be full of communal feasts in the great hall, charity and provision to strangers, obliging laborers, country sports and diversions, and other images of social harmony.

But equally important in forging a sense of community is the care with which these poets position the estate in the context of its geographical locale. As we shall see, most early country house poems depict particularized settings, contain references to local place names and features, and value indigenous forms of nature. These characteristics ultimately validate the social harmony asserted elsewhere in the poem by forging an even closer bond between the estate and its surrounding neighborhood. But local references also help us see the estate and its neighborhood as a distinct locality and keep us from 'reading' it simply as a microcosm for a larger vision of England.[3] The first part of this chapter will draw from the poems of Geoffrey Whitney, Aemelia Lanyer, Ben Jonson, Robert Herrick, and Thomas Carew to illustrate the extent to which the early country house poem is rooted in the specific locale of its subject estate. I will then consider how the genre is transformed to negotiate the challenges of England's developing commercial and colonial empire. From the middle of the seventeenth century, the country house is increasingly imagined as an artificial space created by its owner and teeming with foreign luxury goods. Particular attention will be paid to Mildmay Fane, whose country house poems of the 1650s and 1660s both exemplify and explain the genre's changing treatment of local space.

The early country house poem

The very first English country house poem, Geoffrey Whitney's 'To Richard Cotton, Esq.' (1586), demonstrates just how important place is to this genre.[4] The poem's Latin motto reads *Patria cuique chara*; or 'Every man's native land is dear to him.'[5] Although the poem is written about Cotton's estate, the motto is autobiographical since Whitney was born a mere ten miles from Combermere Abbey and mentions his impending return to the area in the poem's final stanzas.[6] The idealization of this particular 'native land' in the Cheshire countryside is anchored in the engraved image of a beehive. It is a conventional motif of harmony and industry, but it is also well suited for its locale, since Cheshire was known for beekeeping in the sixteenth century.[7] Kathryn Hunter argues that 'the analogy of the bees' that continues throughout the poem symbolizes 'the estate's social function in the life of the community.'[8] But in this poem, the attraction to one's native land goes beyond the people that inhabit it: '[Bees] all at night unto their home repair: / And every-one, her proper hive doth know, / Although there stand a thousand on a row' (17–18). If the hives do signify social harmony, the fact that they stand 'a thousand on a row' renders them relatively interchange-able. That each bee nonetheless returns to its 'proper hive' suggests an additional attraction. The penultimate stanza offers some insight: 'So, though some men do linger long away, / Yet love they best their native country's ground. / And from the same, the more they absent be, / With more desire, they wish the same to see' (39–42). The simple and instinc-tual desire to see one's 'native ground' is what ultimately motivates the poet's return to the Cheshire countryside.

Whitney's insistence on the primacy of place would be developed by later country house poets. Unlike sixteenth-century English pastorals that tend to feature generic rural settings, the country house poem 'is firmly located in a recognizable and specific locale.'[9] This assessment characterizes most pre-Civil War country house poems, I would argue, including those by Whitney, Lanyer, Jonson, Herrick, and Carew. In 'The Description of Cooke-ham' (1609–1610), Aemelia Lanyer's delinea-tion of the estate's walks and gardens culminates in a towering oak tree and the 'goodly prospects' that it affords of some thirteen neighboring shires. Meanwhile, Jonson provides specific details of Penshurst's trees, mount, copses, and lower and middle grounds. Such details are not, however, limited to the boundaries of the park. Instead, the particu-larized topography includes or is connected to the surrounding com-munity. In 'To Penshurst' (1612), local stone, Medway fish, and early cherries place the estate firmly within a larger Kentish neighborhood.[10] Similarly, the prospect of Cookham may belong to the Russell family (and visitors like Lanyer), but the view inspires first meditation and then action – 'feed[ing] / Your pined brethren, when they stood in need' (91–92) – that affirm the social duties of ownership and extend the estate's virtue into the countryside that it overlooks. Such local references create a richer sense of the community that the estate is supposed to concenter by connecting the estate grounds with the surrounding neighborhood.

But local features also function more conceptually, and can even be 'organized to give impetus to a central theme.'[11] Carew's use of climate is revealing in this regard. 'To Saxham' (c. 1631–1632) begins by invok-ing a winter landscape of 'frost, and snow.' Such weather may be unu-sual for a country house poem, but would have hardly been atypical for a seventeenth-century winter in inland Suffolk. But Carew's nod at win-ter weather is more than an authentic decoration of the poem; rather, it is employed to develop a central poetic theme: Saxham's social importance and its benevolent role in the surrounding community. Early in the poem we learn that 'The cold and frozen air had sterved / Much poor, if not by thee preserved' (11–12). And later, the poet depicts the 'weary pilgrim' and 'stranger' gathered in out of the cold night by Saxham's 'cheerful beams.' The harsh weather, therefore, functions as a means of bringing the local community closer together and asserting its dependence on the Crofts' hospitality.[12] But none of this could be so powerfully dramatized without the seasonally accurate winter backdrop. Another early country house poem that uses local details to launch its central theme is Jonson's 'To Sir Robert Wroth' (c. 1616). In this poem, the location of the Wroth estate along the River Lea and just north of London is crucial. Its geographical positioning – 'so near the city, and the court' (3) yet outside their potentially harmful domain – feeds into the philosophical balance between retirement and participation that Jonson asserts throughout the poem.

The country house poets of the early seventeenth century also link their subject estates to their surrounding region through their depiction of nature. Carew and Herrick, for instance, insist on the natural bounty that is indigenous to the locales of their subjects. In 'To the King at His Entrance into Saxham' (c. 1620), a Carew poem in the country house mode, the poet tells James not to expect 'Such rarities that come from far.' Instead, Carew promises, 'We'll have whate'er the season yields, / Out of the neighbouring woods and fields' (29–30). Such language creates a tone of humility appropriate for hosting a monarch, but it also conveys a certain pleasure in offering the simple virtues of the 'homely cheer' that Saxham and the surrounding countryside afford. In subsequent Carew poems, the word 'native' comes to signify this local bounty. In 'To the King,' it is the 'native sweets' on which Carew enlarges. And in 'To My Friend G.N. from Wrest' (1639), the vision of indigenous nature is even more forcefully articulated:

> Her porous bosom doth rich odours sweat;
> Whose perfumes through the ambient air diffuse
> Such native aromatics, as we use
> No foreign gums, nor essence fetched from far,
> No volatile spirits, nor compounds that are
> Adulterate, but at Nature's cheap expense
> With far more genuine sweats refresh the sense. (12–18)

In this passage, the word 'native' is applied to the botanic fragrances emanating from the earth of Wrest Park. But the term has also acquired a double meaning; 'native' is employed to denote both place of origin (indigenous, not 'fetched from far') and quality ('more genuine'). Whereas the importation of rarities was outside the capacity of the humble host in 'To the King,' here ranging from Wrest's native bounty seems not only superfluous but undesirable; there is a sort of taint and spuriousness associated with the introduction of unnatural additives.

In Herrick's 'The Country Life' (c. 1625–1648) a similar attitude towards foreign incursions predominates:

> Thou never ploughst the ocean's foam
> To seek, and bring rough pepper home:
> Nor to the eastern Ind dost rove
> To bring from thence the scorched clove.
> Nor, with the loss of thy loved rest,
> Bringst home the ingot from the west. (5–10)

Herrick acknowledges the larger world of overseas trade, but finds it incompatible with the virtues of country living. Instead, he depicts the estate owner walking around his estate to oversee and validate the local agricultural activities: 'and as thy foot there treads, / Thou seest a present Godlike power / Imprinted in each herb and flower; / And smellst the breath of great-eyed kine, / Sweet as the blossoms of the vine' (30–34).

The insistence on what is natural and native reaches a higher pitch in these poems by Herrick and Carew because of the emergence of a new – and in many ways contradictory – country house aesthetic in the mid-seventeenth century.[13] But their general preference for the native is consistent with earlier poems by Whitney, Lanyer, and Jonson. Even Jonson's highly exaggerated mode of *sponte sua* (in which nature readily offers itself up as a sacrifice) is appropriately curtailed. Carps, pikes, and eels leap from the waters of Penshurst while the garden proffers cherry, plum, fig, grape, and quince. In both cases, however, the obliging homage is paid by what actually swims in the waters and grows in the gardens of Penshurst.

Clearly, localized topography, climate, and nature are prominent features of the early country house poem. Together, they anchor the genre in the reality of time and space and keep it from succumbing to pastoral escapism.[14] The poems are ideal constructions, but whatever else they may be imagined to be, Saxham, Penshurst, and Cookham are actual buildings on actual estates inhabited by actual people. Because of their localized presentations, these estates are never solely microcosms for some sort of larger national vision. Instead, they are depicted as belonging to extended neighborhoods to which they give but also receive marks of identity.

Given the careful integration of estate and locale that we have seen in these poets, it is remarkable that less than a decade after Herrick's death, the English country house tradition could produce a poem like Charles Cotton's 'Chatsworth' (c. 1678–1681). Cotton celebrates William Cavendish's newly remodeled seat as a 'glittering pile' that is:

> Environed round with nature's shames and ills –
> Black heaths, wild rocks, bleak crags, and naked hills,
> And the whole prospects so inform, and rude –
> Who is it but must presently conclude
> That this is paradise, which seated stands
> In midst of deserts and of barren sands?
> So a bright diamond would look, if set
> In a vile socket of ignoble jet, (1315–1322)

Here, the estate's relationship to its surroundings has changed dramatically. Rather than display a sense of organic connection to its native environment, the civilized elegance of Chatsworth contrasts strikingly with the 'wild,' 'bleak,' and 'barren' Derbyshire countryside. Nor is this estate at odds only with its geographical surroundings; it is also isolated from other people. The poem fails to mention hospitality or anything resembling a social community, and Cotton actually takes solace in ancient earthworks that keep 'the Peak rabble' out. Finally, Chatsworth flourishes despite – rather than because of – local weather conditions. The 'craggy brow' of a nearby mountain shields the estate and

> Secures from eastern tempests all below,
> Under whose shelter trees and flowers grow,
> With early blossom, maugre native snow,
> Which elsewhere round a tyranny maintains,
> And binds cramped nature long in crystal chains. (1256–1260)

Thus, Chatsworth emerges as a precarious exception to the repressive, oppositional forces of the weather. Throughout the poem, Chatsworth derives many of its defining features from its locale, but only because it emerges in contrast to them. Overall, Cotton depicts an estate that is not in harmony with its local surroundings – yet he does so with a sense of ebullience. For Cotton, part of what makes Chatsworth a new

'Wonder of the Peak' is that it neither partakes of its native environment nor has much to do with the other people who inhabit it.

What has happened to the depiction of the English country house in the generation that separates Carew and Herrick from Cotton? While 'Chatsworth' is perhaps extreme in the extent to which it divorces the estate from its surroundings, it is nonetheless representative of new trends within the genre. For one thing, the omission of hospitality and class harmony in 'Chatsworth' is characteristic of many later country house poems. Such an omission has been linked to a historical decline in the feudal ideal of good housekeeping. Already on its way out in the late sixteenth century, keeping an open house for all comers became less feasible and less desirable as the seventeenth century wore on, particularly with the emergence of a money economy and the need to have the 'household economy put on a business footing.'[15] Social changes like the widening gap between owner and tenant and a more pronounced sense of privacy are also offered to explain the decline of good housekeeping.[16] While there is historical evidence for all of these changes – even in the construction of new country houses, one can see a decrease in the hall's importance and an increase of private, family rooms – their impact can be overstated. '[G]enerous housekeeping, the most visible element in that "port" required of a gentleman' continued to be practiced by the ruling classes of the seventeenth century.[17] Not surprisingly, hospitality is still depicted in some later country house poems.[18]

'Chatsworth' could also be said to represent the genre's evolving tendency to display the taste of a cultured owner. Since the emerging money economy meant that anyone could buy – and no longer need inherit – an estate, taste became a way of demonstrating that one truly belonged in the elite classes.[19] The collection and display of artwork and other luxury goods thus became a marker of class identity – and a frequent subject in later country house poems.[20] As a corollary, the estate itself became more closely associated with the character of its owner.[21] Whereas 'Jonson emphasizes Penshurst's symbolic value as something more than the reflection of its present owner's identity,' 'Chatsworth' underscores the shaping hand of William Cavendish.[22] In later country house poetry, the owner more directly creates the local rather than partaking of what is there; it is his personal taste that determines the form and it is his ownership that stamps it as his.

The decline in hospitality and preoccupation with displaying taste help explain some of the changes to the country house poem. But these explanations don't account for one of the most striking developments in the genre: an influx of foreign objects. Whereas Carew gave us 'native sweets' and Herrick eschewed the spoils of global trade, later poets glory in cataloging the far-flung origins of the objects found in their subject estates. 'Amyntor's Grove' (c. 1641) brings together Arabian perfumes (21), Italian art (31), an Oriental bowl (57), and Indian tobacco (61). 'General Hasting's Bower' (c. 1642–1646) boasts wines 'Of Spanish, French, and Rhenish vein' (29). Two Restoration odes on Belvoir Castle rapturously catalog the Earl of Rutland's Persian cloth, Turkish carpets, Parian marble, Chinese vessels, and Japanese furniture. One poem even envisions these exotic objects as tribute paid to the Earl from distant parts of the globe. In 'Caelia's Country House and Closet' (1667–1668), George Mackenzie details the contents of Anna Hamilton's cabinet of curiosities, including exotic materials (amber, coral, shells) and artwork by Dutch and Italian masters. 'Caelia' even has the figure of 'A globe, in rich mosaic marble cut' on the floor of her closet – a fitting emblem of the room's diverse contents. Flecknoe's 'On Welbeck' (c. 1664–1666) extends this eclecticism to the estate's kitchen, 'Whose cellar and whose larder seems t'have been / Of every foreign land the magazine' (5–6).

Obviously, these themes carry us a long way from the self-contained estates of Jonson, Herrick, and Carew. The local space of the country house no longer takes its identity from vernacular architecture, food, building stone, scents, and resources. Instead, it is emerging as an artificial and composite creation that displays objects from other locales. While such conspicuous consumption is meant to reflect the taste of the owner, it also attests to a growing literary and cultural engagement with the world beyond England. It is this engagement, I will argue, that is at the center of country house poem's shifting depiction of local space.

Global expansion

A recent book argues that heightened interactions with the rest of the globe were just as important to the English Renaissance as the return to classical antiquity.[23] Although these cross-cultural contacts were on the rise in the sixteenth century, it was the seventeenth century that gave birth to 'a new global consciousness' in England.[24] The colonization of the New World was one important component of this developing mindset. Following sporadic attempts from the 1570s onward, the English established their first permanent colony at Jamestown in 1607. Other settlements followed rapidly at Bermuda (1612), Massachusetts (1620), Maryland (1634), and the West Indian islands of Barbados, St. Kitts,

Nevis, Antigua, and Montserrat (1620s and 1630s). While these early colonies were a far cry from the imperial Britain that would emerge in the eighteenth century, they nonetheless provided permanent bases for global expansion.[25] By 1650, colonial populations numbered 50,000 in the West Indies, 40,000 on the Chesapeake, and another 25,000 in New England.[26] Foreign travel, though a less permanent mode of contact, was also on the rise in the seventeenth century. Courtiers, merchants, soldiers, religious dissidents, political exiles, and women all traveled abroad with increasing regularity.[27] In addition, '[B]y the middle of the seventeenth century, travel had already emerged as a normal part of the education of the young gentleman' and the more formalized Grand Tour was already taking shape.[28] For its participants, 'Travel created intellectual, social, political, and economic networks' that widened their horizons even after they returned home.[29]

But it was English commerce that really fueled global awareness. Not only did English merchants engage in trade with such diverse and far-flung outposts as India, Japan, Russia, North Africa, Iceland, the Americas, and Turkey, they brought back goods from those places to be consumed in England – thus, widening the global horizons of the vast majority of English people who never left their native land. Beginning in 1604, peace with Spain 'fostered the expansion of English trade' that continued throughout the seventeenth century.[30] These decades also witnessed the development of 'emergent capitalist structures' that made commercial expansion possible, ranging from the formation of the joint-stock East India Company in 1600 to the founding of the Bank of England in 1694. The numbers are striking: 'the tonnage of London shipping trebling between 1582 and 1629 . . . customs revenues at chief English ports more than quintupling from 1614 to 1687 . . . the pound value of London imports nearly trebling between 1621 and 1700.'[31] Significantly, these increases don't just reflect increased trade, but the expansion of markets beyond Europe.[32]

Luxury consumption was an important component of the growth of commerce. Linda Levy Peck's *Consuming Splendor* (2005) examines the process by which 'the English became enamored of foreign wares' and locates this trend in a much earlier timeframe – 1600–1670 – than previous historians.[33] She notes 'an increase in the importation of luxury goods' among the elite. Foreign furnishings were already evident in the Jacobean period, and included French wall hangings, Persian carpets, and Chinese furniture.[34] The demand for foreign – and especially Italian – art expanded in the first few decades of the seventeenth century, so much so that there was already a second-hand market for

European paintings by the 1630s.[35] The increasingly popular upper-class pursuits of architecture and gardening were also impacted by global consumption.[36] New principles of building and cultivation usually derived from the continent (especially Italy, France, and Holland), but their content – as in the exotic botanical garden that brought together plants 'from the four corners of the earth'[37] – could derive from much further. Indeed, Peck identifies a specific type of luxury consumption associated with the novel and the exotic. From the 1620s and 1630s, English collectors built specialized 'curio-cabinets' to display their collections of 'pictures, prints, sculpture, tapestries, glass, scientific instruments, or rare flora and fauna' from around the world.[38] As foreign luxury goods flowed into London and created a consumer market – retail shopping was established in the West End by 1609 – they were then disseminated into the provinces.[39]

It is no surprise, then, that foreign objects find their way into the country house poems of the mid-seventeenth century. Their presence reflects not only economic realities, but cultural trends as well. Overseas commerce precipitated a spatial as well as an intellectual 'widening of the horizons' that impacted other fields of knowledge.[40] Blair Hoxby has shown how commercial notions so permeated seventeenth-century culture that they created a new discourse for talking about the crucial political and religious issues of the period 1634–1674.[41] In fact, Hoxby suggests that '[i]n an age better known for its political, religious, and scientific revolutions, it may have been the commercial revolution of the seventeenth century that had the deepest effect on English culture and the literature it produced.'[42] Subsequent literary critics have found the animating spirit of commercialism in everything from the *Faerie Queene* to Restoration tragicomedy.[43] In this sense, the country house poem is just one of many literary genres that registers the impact of English commercial expansion. But, as I will argue, it is specially equipped to negotiate some of the anxieties created by this new globalism.

Many people were enthusiastic about the nation's expanding enterprises. In *The Web of Empire*, Alison Games points to the development of a cosmopolitan mindset whereby many English men and women were open to and curious about foreign cultures.[44] This was particularly true of merchants and early colonists who needed to learn from and assimilate into the foreign cultures in which they were working and living. Such openness was also characteristic of many elites, who 'identified themselves as cosmopolitan through the appropriation of continental luxuries.'[45] The English upper classes also evinced a more general faith in the ability of commerce to promote the 'universal improvement of manners through civilized exchange between different nations.'[46] Not only was overseas trade associated with cultural borrowing, it was also seen as something that was 'vital to the stability of the English nation.'[47] Particularly after the economic depression of the 1620s, England looked to global commerce to strengthen the national economy.[48] The appearance of economic treatises like *A Discourse of Trade from England unto the West Indies* (1621), *The Treasure of Traffike, or a Discourse of Forraigne Trade* (1641), and *England's Treasure by Forraign Trade, or the Balance of our Forraign Trade is the Rule of our Treasure* (1664) both reflected and helped shape England's global economic expansion.[49]

The reason that such a development needed to be defended in such treatises is that there was also within England 'virulent opposition to the practices and consequences of global trade.'[50] Some of these objections were as old as commerce itself: contact with heathen and 'savage' nations could contaminate England, travel corrupted the individual, luxury consumption was both idolatrous and effeminizing.[51] Other anxieties stemmed specifically from contemporary concerns: the loss of bullion would impoverish the economy, trade with Catholic nations held religious dangers, the importation of cheap goods could lead to the loss of domestic jobs and even have a leveling effect on the social order.[52] Significantly, many of these commercial fears were cast in terms of nationhood. Since cosmopolitans often 'dislodged themselves from unthinking attachments to a single nation,' this would seem to threaten the very exclusivity that made nationhood possible.[53] Some contemporaries worried that dalliances in foreign trade and empire would put England in danger of the same 'overstretching' that led to the fall of the Roman Empire.[54] Others worried that the personal indulgences of travel and luxury could 'run the risk of destabilizing the religious and social fabric' of the nation.[55] Thus, even as global commerce fostered a new 'economically based conception of the nation' it also underscored the point that commerce could never be a purely economic issue.[56] England's commercial interests became 'inextricable from English prestige and power,' which meant that those interests had to be maintained and defended abroad.[57] The series of wars that the English fought against the Dutch in the 1650s and 1660s are a prime example.[58] The national implications of trade and colonization may also explain why, according to Alison Games, the English Crown became more directly involved in both ventures as the seventeenth century progressed.[59]

The commercial revolution thus contributed to but also created problems for English nationhood. By the eighteenth century it might be possible to proclaim that 'a culture of commerce became an increasingly important part of being British,' but such a consensus had not yet formed by the middle decades of the seventeenth century.[60] The value of overseas trade and its effect on the nation were still contested concepts. The country house poem, I will argue, participates in this debate. The timing and enthusiasm of the genre's 'sudden' focus on foreign objects suggests a conscious engagement with – and even celebration of – the growth of global commerce. But far from unequivocally endorsing expansion abroad, the country house poem contracts the globe into a local space. It is here, in the carefully manicured gardens and meticulously arranged parlors of actual country houses, that foreign threats can be removed and dangers tamed. In this sense, the country house poem becomes not so much a celebration of the foreign as a celebration of the estate's ability to naturalize the foreign and subject it to the control of a cultured owner.

One way that the country house poem does this is by objectifying that which is beyond English shores. The vast and potentially unstable spaces of Arabia, China, and the New World are reduced in a poem like 'Amyntor's Grove' to Arabian perfumes, an Oriental bowl, and Indian tobacco. On the one hand, such reductionism could be seen simply as a faithful reflection of the actual objects that were increasingly appearing in country houses. But the poet's abbreviated treatment of these objects – they are often referred to briefly as a part of a larger catalog – heightens the synecdoche. There is no mention of the toil, danger, or cultural contamination that might have gone into acquiring the object; there is only the object itself. It is a little bit like the sixteenth-century advice proffered by Montaigne and Ascham to read about travel rather than to actually experience it; in doing so, one reaps the fruit of travel (knowledge) without having to expose oneself to its dangers and corrupting influences.[61] Many of the anxieties that cohered around foreign commerce in the seventeenth century are similarly absent from the country house poem. It offers only the tangible fruits of commerce.

The country house poem's display of foreign objects is not only a way of removing harms, but also a way of concentrating value. Lea Knudsen Allen describes the capacity of foreign objects to signify the value, knowledge, and beauty of the places that they have originated from and passed through.[62] The country house poem's rapid pairing of object and place is a way of invoking and displaying these resonant meanings. Value is further enhanced by concentrating objects of different origins into a single space, or, as Allen characterizes it: '[the] reduction of far-flung empires into a "little room".'[63] The concentrated objects create a density of value or 'cultural capital' that attaches to the domestic sphere in which they are displayed. At the same time, the exotic objects are themselves transformed and domesticated. Like the early modern botanical garden that brought together plants from all over the world, the country house becomes a 'site for reconstructing, owning, and naturalizing the larger world within a plot of English land.'[64]

As 'reconstructing' implies, an important part of this naturalization process is the actual arrangement of foreign objects. In systematically ordering the material culture of Asia, Africa, Europe, and the Americas, the country house poem exerts control over potentially dangerous foreign bodies. This fits with Bruce McLeod's more general observation that '[o]ut of literature's geographic bent during this period a more aggressive conception of mastering space develops' that is a direct response 'to the new worlds of capitalism and colonization.'[65] But rather than overtly constructing hegemony, country house poets aestheticize the estate's mastery of the world by arranging its objects in a unified and artistically pleasing fashion. The Dutch still-life painting of the seventeenth century is a useful contemporary parallel. These paintings often combine a group of rare and precious objects into an 'elaborately wrought and highly finished' composition.[66] For Roland Barthes, the genre 'coincides precisely and causally with Europe's imperial appropriation of the raw materials and arts of the Oriental and the Atlantic worlds' and confirms Dutch imperial power over an 'empire of things.'[67] But such a conclusion is nonetheless beautifully rendered and subtly conveyed through the arrangement and symbolic value of the particular objects in the painting. The English country house poem reveals a similar attention to the meanings and associations of the foreign objects that it sought to aestheticize.

Seen this way, the country house poem's shift from social harmony and hospitality to cultured collecting is not the abandonment of local responsibility that it might seem to be at first glance. Rather, the decidedly different characteristics of later poems can be seen as an attempt to come to terms with the global expansion of the seventeenth century and the challenges that it created for nationhood. As we saw in Chapter 2, the specter of internal disorder was the chief concern of the ruling classes in Elizabethan England. It is therefore not surprising that early country house poems attempt to naturalize and idealize rural social relations. But this threat faded over the course of the seventeenth century. Famine, the catalyst of so much previous domestic unrest, was no longer a threat after 1650.[68] Even earlier, the depression of the 1620s helped convince Englishmen that global commerce was a key to the future: 'Whereas articulate opinion had once identified the commonwealth's interests with social harmony, it now identified them more closely with advances in national productivity.'[69] It is in these decades that the country house poem begins to do a different sort of cultural work. Rather than naturalize social relations, it is called upon to naturalize the dangers of English commercial and colonial expansion. The transformation of the genre is thus not so much a withdrawal from social responsibility as an engagement with the global. But what does this engagement look like in practice, and what does it mean for the depiction of local space?

Mildmay Fane and the later country house poem

For answers, we will turn to the country house poetry of Mildmay Fane, second Earl of Westmorland. Fane is particularly relevant to this literary genre because he composed 11 of the 77 (or 14 percent) of the poems included in Alastair Fowler's collection of known seventeenth-century estate poems. In addition, Fane resided in Northamptonshire, a county famous for the quantity and quality of its country houses.[70] Finally, Fane did much of his writing during the Civil War and Interregnum – the very time in which the shift from Carew to Cotton occurred.[71]

One of Fane's earliest country house poems, 'To Sir John Wentworth, upon His Curiosities and Courteous Entertainment at Summerly in Lovingland' (c. 1648), opens with a self-conscious treatment of local space:

> Pregnant she [Nature] is, yet that must not deny
> The purest gold to come from Barbary,
> Diamonds and pearl from th'Indies, to confer
> On every clime some thing peculiar
> (For so she hath): and like a sum to all
> That curious is, seems here most liberal;
> Affording, in epitome at least,
> Whate'er the world can boast of, or call best. (7–14)

Here, Fane clearly articulates a notion of composite identity that poems like 'On Welbeck,' 'Amyntor's Grove' 'General Hasting's Bower,' and 'Belvoir' only imply with their catalogs of imported objects. Wentworth's estate distills things from other locales and concentrates them in a single location that now contains 'whate'er the world can boast of.'[72] That Fane is contrasting Summerly with more conventional notions of the local can be seen in his reference to the commonplace idea that nature 'confer[s] / On every clime some thing peculiar.' Although Fane uses global illustrations of Barbary gold and Indian jewels, he is articulating the same notion that had informed 80 years of English chorography: particular localities are defined by those few native characteristics and areas of pre-eminence that differentiate them from other places. Against this traditional notion of the English local, Fane boldly sets the aggregate quality of Wentworth's estate. The result is extraordinary:

> Now, as contracted virtue doth excel
> In power and force, this seems a miracle,
> Wherein all travellers may truly say
> They never saw so much in little way:
> And thence conclude their folly that did steer
> To seek for that abroad, at home was near
> In more perfection . . . (15–21)

This passage also reveals Fane's strategies for negotiating the anxieties of an expanding globe. He compares the estate's assemblage of treasures to 'contracted virtue,' implying an almost miraculous distillation of good qualities without the bad. This reading seems confirmed by the rest of the passage, wherein Summerly renders foreign travel (with all its dangers and 'follies') superfluous. One can safely – and miraculously – experience the wonders of the globe while remaining in eastern Suffolk.

But in order to achieve the 'perfection' promised above, the poet needs to order and unify what might otherwise remain a mere jumble of objects. To do this, Fane turns to the 'formality, symmetry, [and] elegance' of French gardening principles – yet another English import of the mid-seventeenth century.[73] Informed by notions of political absolutism, this emerging style sought to dramatize man's domination over his natural environment.[74] Seventeenth-century French gardens characteristically featured raised terraces, parterres, gravel avenues and walks, boxed hedges, topiary, statuary, canals, ponds, fountains, and vistas.[75] These gardening principles would culminate at Versailles beginning in the 1660s, but they were in vogue even earlier. Fane may have even encountered such gardens directly when he traveled in France as a young man. In any event, Fane reveals a clear understanding of the uses and effects of these principles in 'To Sir John Wentworth.' As he takes the reader on a tour of Summerly's park and grounds, he notes the disciplined lines of trees (37–38), the patterned parterres (57), and the elaborate water gardens (61–68). He also observes of the 'Walks' that 'some straight, / Others like serpents are' (57–58) – the first recording of a serpentine or meandering walk recorded in English.[76] Later on, Fane marvels at a device that triggers automated music, a common feature of mannerist gardens.[77] In embracing the French principles that underlay the garden at Summerly, Fane is making a similar claim about this estate's ability to tame and naturalize the foreign objects that Wentworth has assembled here.

But Fane doesn't just draw attention to the principles themselves, he also registers their aesthetic effect. After leading us through some of the garden features mentioned above, he pauses to declare:

> Thus like a gold chain linked, or bracelet strung,
> From carcanet pleasures on pleasures hung,
> And such delightful objects did descry
> Pursuing of each other, that the eye,
> Astonished at such wonder, did crave rest (69–73)

This passage emphasizes the *pleasure* gained in walking through the garden – an effect that is reinforced by words like 'delight,' 'astonished,' and 'wonder.' The dominant metaphor of the golden chain or bracelet is particularly well chosen. Not only is it a beautiful art object, its individual links reflect the 'succession of separate pleasures and surprises' that the mannerist garden sought to create.[78] To avoid over-stimulation, Wentworth's garden seeks to alternate the intensity of its experiences and even includes 'some space / To gather strength 'twixt this and t'other place' (77–78). As a result of these strategies, Fane not only succeeds in naturalizing the estate's foreign elements, he makes them pleasurable and exciting.

A slightly later Fane poem: 'Thorp Palace: A Miracle' (c. 1656–1666), is an encomium on the newly completed house of the Parliamentary leader, Oliver St. John. As its introductory lines suggest, the poem focuses particularly on St. John's statuary collection:

> Whoso desires, that, earnestly to see
> The statued marbles of antiquity,
> And wherewith times past imped the wings of Fame
> Ambitious is, to celebrate the same
> Let him to Longthorpe go. (1–5)

In this passage, Fane envisions Thorpe Hall as a paragon of ancient Rome – not as an exemplar of the rural countryside outside Peterborough. As we have come to expect, its depiction depends on an artificial collection of objects – in this case statues – that have been acquired by a cultured owner. Here, the visitor 'may find / Subject enough to satiate his mind' (5–6). Once again, Fane intends to create an aesthetic experience of the estate that will appeal to both the intellect ('mind') and the senses ('satiating'). But whereas 'To Sir John Wentworth' invests in mannerist gardening principles, the remainder of 'Thorp Palace' turns to the principles of landscape painting to deliver its complex aesthetic response.

Landscape painting began as mere background scenery to religious paintings and portraiture, but by the seventeenth century it had developed into an independent and popular subject matter in its own right.[79] The chief artistic pleasure of the landscape lay in its ability to depict an expansive prospect and bring together a multiplicity of scenes, people, and objects into a single, unified composition. Even when based on a real view, landscape paintings are idealizations – rather than 'photographs' – that involve artistic liberty and arrangement to create desired moods or solve compositional problems. In other words, they embody the same blend of art and nature that we have already noted in 'To Sir John Wentworth.'

Landscape paintings began to appear regularly in English art collections from the second decade of the seventeenth century.[80] Soon, landscape principles were adopted into English literature as well. As the works of Denham, Milton, and Marvell show, the influence of landscape principles was particularly evident in poetry from the 1640s onward.[81] In fact, James Turner calls landscape art a 'dominant unifying influence' for the poems of the period that 'offer[s] structural principles which could convert topography into a dazzling artifact.'[82] Fane's personal connection to landscape painting is not difficult to establish. As one of the richest peers in the realm, Fane collected art and welcomed the new aesthetic. His poem 'A Peppercorn or Small Rent' (1651) includes a lengthy catalog (and artful description) of paintings that provide clear 'evidence of Fane's connoisseurship.'[83] Since poetry and art were both interests of Fane, it is not surprising that he employs landscape principles as yet another way to organize and give meaning to the local space of the estate.

Two of the principles to which Fane is particularly attracted are the twin qualities of variety and contrast. Landscape painters implicitly value these traits because they give a sense of fullness and beauty, particularly when they are synthesized into a unified composition.[84] Ogden notes that variety and contrast as ruling principles of landscape were 'taken for granted' and that 'there is hardly a painting in this genre which does not illustrate the application of one or the other of the two.'[85] When we turn to the heart of 'Thorp Palace,' we can see the key landscape principles of variety and contrast operating in the depiction of the statuary:

> Whether he observes huntsman Adonis there
> And by him Venus' myrtle growing near;
> Or else the thunder god with threat'ning hand
> Not far from whom the sturdy oak doth stand.
> Cratippus, represented here, is one
> Was Athens' glory: moveless now as stone,
> And therefore no Peripatetikon.
> There a Romish fencer whose stern looks strike fear
> Although he hath no sword to hurt with there;
> And in the midst of these so wondrous great
> And beautiful fair Livia takes her seat.
> Not wearied with walking (as we talk)
> But Labours, Hercules o'th' right hand walk
> As guardian stands (the dragon killed) o'er these,
> And solely now protects Hesperides.
> And that these earthly trophies reach the sky,
> Behold o'th'stairs's there's winged Mercury. (9–25)

Within this passage, Fane introduces – and provides a bit of descriptive detail for – Adonis, Venus, Jupiter, Cratippus, a 'Romish fencer,' Livia, Hercules, and Mercury. Not only is there a multiplicity of individuals, but each figure embodies a different realm of human experience: love, power, philosophy, combat, chastity, heroism, and travel. These diverse embodiments of Roman virtue have been densely combined in St. John's garden, and, now, in the world of the poem. They have also been arranged to evince contrast. Just as a landscape painter might pair a barren mountain with a fertile plain, Fane sets the philosopher beside the martial combatant, and juxtaposes the quiet chastity of Livia with the heroic exploits of Hercules.

It becomes even clearer that Fane is approaching Thorpe Hall as a painterly landscape when he registers the effect of this diverse statuary: 'On every side such unity befell it / That I judge there is nothing can excel it' (30–31). In other words, the goal of all this variety and contrast is finally to create a harmonious unity. 'By selecting and placing features correctly the landscape artist created order' and made 'disparate elements . . . seem intangibly bonded,' explains Turner.[86] Fane's depiction of St. John's statuary strives for the same sense of cohesiveness. The vivid personification of the statues makes them seem like characters in a common scene. Although all are depicted in postures appropriate to their individual stations – the fencer looks sternly around, while Livia sits passively – they are not isolated figures. Their interconnectedness is established by Hercules's depiction as 'guardian . . . o'er these' and Mercury's potential role as intermediary between 'these earthly trophies' and the gods in heaven. Fane's descriptive technique also defines the statues in relation to one another. Adonis is over 'there'; Cratippus is 'here'; the Romish fencer is 'there'; and 'in the midst of these' is Livia. Such directives establish a single, fixed position from which the description originates – as if the reader were experiencing the 'scene' as a landscape painting. Finally, the pairing of statues with appropriate vegetation (the myrtle and the oak in lines 10 and 12) unifies the collection with the garden in which it has been placed. The statues may comprise a landscape of variety and contrast, but they are ultimately depicted as a unified whole. Near the end of the poem, this effect is extended to the rest of the estate as well:

> And yet these [statues] all must yield, and servants be,
> Unto the Palace; uniformity
> Sitting in triumph o'er them, and the rooms
> Enriched within with such brave encomiomes (32–35)

Here, Fane makes the description of statuary emblematic of Thorpe Hall as a whole. The 'unity' of the former has been solidified into the more weighty 'uniformity' of the latter, but both have been created by the same basic principles of correspondence and interconnectedness. The 'brave encomiomes' of the rooms no doubt partake of the same pleasing variety as the statuary, but they too are ultimately subsumed into the overarching order and unity of the estate. For Fane, landscape principles provide a way to arrange a multiplicity of objects into an aesthetically pleasing composition.

Both 'To Sir John Wentworth' and 'Thorp Palace: A Miracle' are successful in using the local space of the estate to harmonize disparate elements. But one of the tradeoffs of creating such an artificial and self-contained environment is that the subject estate becomes divorced from the countryside that surrounds it. This represents yet another contrast with earlier poems that consciously position the country house within its immediate geographical locale. But the later country house poem is not without its strategies for reintegrating the estate back into the extended neighborhood that it once concentered. In the third and final Fane poem that we will examine, the poet turns once again to the principles of landscape painting to accomplish this end.

In 'Fullbeck' (c. 1659), the estate of Mildmay's brother, Sir Francis Fane, is imagined almost purely as a landscape canvas. The poet begins with a compact description of the house, gardens, orchard, and walks – once again stressing the variety and spatial relations of these assorted components. He then arrives at the extensive view which the estate affords:

> All these and more, when duly scanned, strike sail
> Unto the nobler prospect o'er the vale,
> Where so rich soil at one view may be seen,
> Gold ears enamelled with meadows green;
> And several parishes and towns amidst
> Known and distinguished by their pyramids (21–26)

Fane describes the prospect from Fullbeck as if it were a landscape painting. The poet emphasizes the variety of the scene's colors – black (soil), green, and gold – and the multiplicity of its venues – fields, parishes, and towns. Fane's use of 'amidst' creates a sense of space, and the distant church spires ('pyramids') impart perspective. Diction like 'rich,' 'gold,' and 'enamelled' also lends the depiction a stylized, artificial tone – as if the poet were describing decorative ornamentation rather than real agriculture.[87]

The praise of a house's prospect is not a Fanean innovation; we have already noted it in a poem as early as 'The Description of Cooke-ham.' But while Lanyer's view of the surrounding countryside reminds the estate owners of their social responsibilities, Fane's prospect is almost purely aesthetic. In this poem at least, there is no sense of responsibility or interaction with the world outside the estate grounds. Instead, Fane lingers on the view and develops the visual metaphor initiated by his association of steeples with 'pyramids':

> Known and distinguished by their pyramids
> That Graves here might not judge his time lost quite
> To write of these, who of Egypt's once did write.
> What Alexandria doth commit to fame,
> Grand-Cayr or Memphis, here to Nottingham,
> Newark, and Southwell now transplanted lie,
> And claim a reverent wonder from each eye;

And fertile Nile o'ercome here by assent
Confess its water's barren to our Trent. (26–34)

In this exotic comparison, Fane asserts that the view from Fullbeck resembles a foreign landscape and that elements of the surrounding countryside approximate the architecture, cities, and major river of Egypt. In fact, the prospect is so Egyptianized that the antiquary John Greaves – author of *Pyramidologia; Or a Description of the Pyramids of Egypt* (1646) – might feel right at home here.[88] As in earlier estate poems, there are a number of local references: Nottingham, Newark, Southwell, and the River Trent. But rather than establish a sense of community or interconnection with the estate, their Egyptianization makes them seem remote and picturesque. The overriding response of 'reverent wonder' increases this sense of detached admiration. The surrounding country-side – like the estate – has become an idealized, created space. Here, it is clearly the poet who 'reads' Egypt into the prospect, but the application of landscape principles results in a treatment of local space that is consistent with other country house poems of the period. The view over the vale elicits an aesthetic delight in composing various (and especially foreign) elements into a unified whole.

Landscape principles forge a new cohesiveness in 'Fullbeck' by successfully integrating the country house, garden, park, and surrounding rural landscape into a harmonious whole. Fane's strategy is indicative of larger trends in estate building – where there was a heightened 'concern for the total environment provided by mansion, park, and garden' – and in landscape painting itself (Fig. 5).[89] At the Restoration, new genres like the 'county seat' painting and bird's eye view sought to depict English houses in their native environments.[90] According to Ogden, 'Pictures of the country house in an extended prospect from a high point of view enjoyed a considerable vogue during the later decades of the century. Such pictures showed important houses and their gardens in relationship to the surrounding countryside; the house, the gardens, and the natural scenery beyond were regarded as an artistic whole.'[91] These prospect paintings would eventually culminate in Johannes Kip and Leonard Knyff's *Britannia Illustrata* (1707), which provides a visual representation of some 80 English estates.

Given these contemporary trends, it is not surprising to find land-scape principles reshaping local space in the country house poem. But writers like Fane provide more than just images of harmonious integration; they also reveal the artistic principles – spatial relations, density, surprise, variety, contrast, compositional unity – that create these effects.

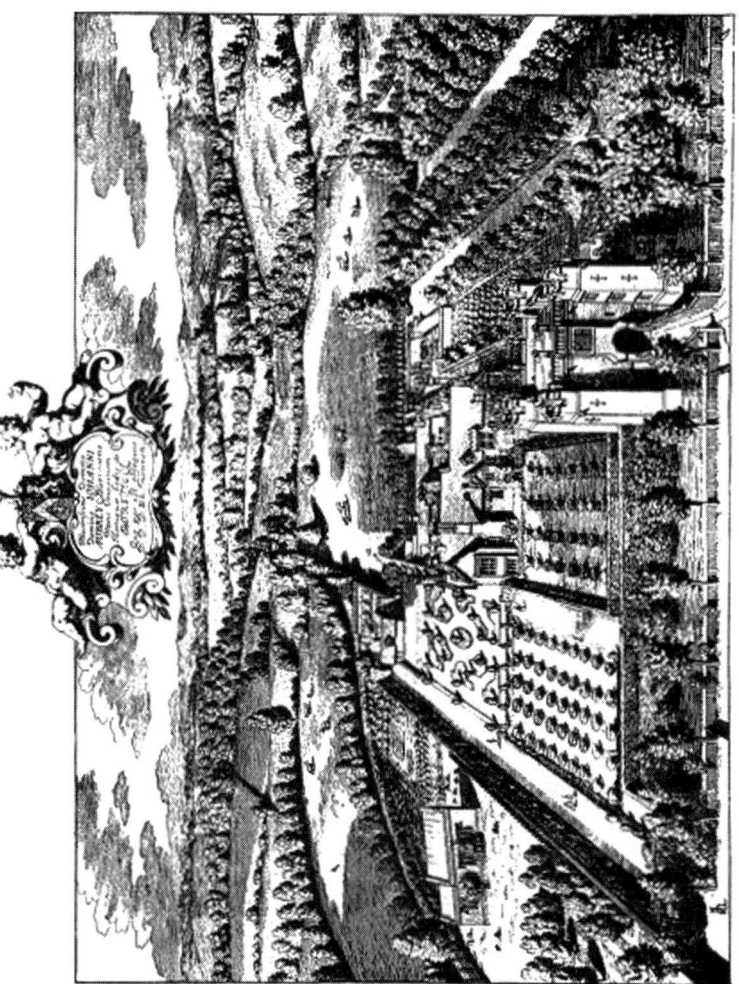

Figure 5 Boarstall, Buckinghamshire, c. 1695. M. Burghers. Published in *English houses & gardens in the 17th and 18th centuries. A series of bird's-eye views reproduced from contemporary engravings by Kip, Badeslade, Harris and others* (1908). Courtesy of Cornell University Library

Country house poets also self-consciously engage the global expansion that was both enriching the country house but also necessitating new strategies for ordering and naturalizing foreign elements. Not only do they feature a diverse assemblage of foreign objects, all three of Fane's poems are also animated by global challenges: how to embody all of Nature's bounty in one place ('To Wentworth'), how to replicate the fullness and variety of Roman civilization in contemporary England ('Thorp Palace'), and how to bring the stately splendors of Egypt to the parishes and towns of Lincolnshire ('Fullbeck'). All three poems rely on imported gardening and landscape principles to successfully negotiate these challenges. Finally, all three poems work out their solutions in the carefully controlled local space of the estate.

Although Fane brings a highly artificial approach to the depiction of local space, it is actually quite consistent with the idealizing tendency of earlier country house poets. Jonson's, Carew's, and Herrick's portrayals of hospitality and social relations – though presented as natural and organic – are no less idealized. Fane and his contemporary poets simply move in a different direction. Because of the influx of foreign luxury goods, they consciously embrace the estate as a created space rather than an organic or naturally derived one. William Cavendish – the owner of Chatsworth, Bolsover, Welbeck, and other estates featured in country house poems – published a book on horsemanship in 1657 that was liberally engraved with views of his several houses. Ogden notes that '[t]he buildings are rendered with fidelity, but the landscape around them is idealized. Hills, mountains, and even a few overhanging cliffs are introduced, so that the backgrounds sometimes resemble the imaginary scenery of Flemish landscape rather than the terrain of Derbyshire and Nottinghamshire.'[92] Such privileging of artistic license – rather than literal representation – underscores the freedom with which painters and poets were coming to approach the land. Turner, writing of the landscape aesthetic that emerged in the middle decades of the seventeenth century, reports that 'The new landscape is composite. It is not a portrait of an individual place, but an ideal construction of particular motifs.'[93]

This development risks making local spaces interchangeable. In applying the principles of gardening and painterly composition to architecture, estate grounds, and interior furnishing, owners (and poets) diminish the geographical distinctiveness that formerly defined the local. Even if these constructed spaces sometimes do provide for aesthetic unity between the estate and its surroundings (as seen above), it is a generalized union that doesn't necessarily emerge from a particular locale. Sir John Wentworth's Summerly may just as well be in the West Country as Suffolk, and Thorpe Hall's statuary could as easily be set up in Kent as Peterborough. In short, the geographical location of an estate seems less important in Restoration country house poetry.

The construction of actual country houses supports this observation. By the late seventeenth century, vernacular architecture and local stone were giving way to the more standardized principles of classicism and a greater use of imported building materials. The period also saw the rise of the professional architect who was able to apply similar designs to a multiplicity of geographical locales.[94] In fact, some architectural historians argue that the work of Hugh May and Roger Pratt constituted a 'distinctive type' of Restoration house 'that found widespread acceptance' among the gentry.[95] This is certainly not to suggest that the country house began to be mass produced in the manner of contemporary suburban houses, but these developments did tend to lessen the importance of locality as a formative influence.

And yet, despite these tendencies, writers continue to associate country houses with the counties and regions in which they are found; location does not become irrelevant. In his *History of the Worthies of England* (1662), Thomas Fuller sets out to record the notable people, commodities, manufactures, and other wonders of each county. In formulating what makes each shire distinctive, Fuller also describes 'the signal structures which each County doth afford.'[96] Thus, the section on Derbyshire mentions Chatsworth, while 'Sommerley hall' is featured in the prominent buildings of Suffolk. In the Northamptonshire section, Fuller describes Holdenby-house, Burleigh-house, Withorpe-house, and Castle Ashby, before gushing: 'Besides these, there be many others, no county in England yielding more noblemen; no noblemen in England yielding fairer habitations' (II.499). It is clear that Fuller sees country houses as distinctive structures that contribute much to the identity of the places in which they stand. They may be consciously constructed, artificial spaces, but they retain their power as identifying symbols. When Fuller mentions a 'Vineyard' near Hatfield House, he compares it to Tempe and stresses the art that has created it (two elements we have particularly noted in later country house poems). Yet, as Fuller emphasizes, it is a real place in which 'the reader must be a seer, before he can understand the perfection thereof' (II.38). This vineyard is neither natural nor organic, yet it has nonetheless come to define its corner of Hertfordshire – just as Cotton's 'Chatsworth' enshrines its estate as a new 'wonder of the Peak' region of Derbyshire. Country houses thus remain intimately associated with their native counties and regions.

The landscape aesthetic that Fane and other country house poets bring to the genre has a similar effect. It provides a way to harmonize and impart order to both the estate and the surrounding countryside in a way that is markedly different from the Jonsonian ideal. It is aesthetic rather than social, imported rather than native, composite rather than homogeneous, and constructed rather than organic. Nevertheless, the estate is still the concentering force of this local world, and it is never entirely disconnected from its geographical location. The country house poems of Fane and his contemporaries thus constitute both continuity and transformation in the depiction of the local.

Conclusion

On the title page of a first edition of *Britannia* (1586), an anonymous sixteenth-century reader has written that he cannot tell 'why [each] mans mynde in natyve soyle takes much delight' but 'that [each] mans mynde is myndfull styll of that delight: I wote that well.'[1] This observation affirms the early modern fascination with 'natyve soyle' that this book has been trying to trace – a fascination that writers like Camden both reflected and helped create. At the same time, the reader also suggests a certain inexplicability to this attraction. He doesn't know why people love their native land; he just knows that they do. This book has also attempted to shed light on that paradox, by trying to offer reasons why English writers were imaginatively drawn to the particular villages, parishes, towns, and counties that composed their larger nation.

Although England had long been characterized by topographical, geological, cultural, economic, and linguistic diversity, it wasn't until the second half of the sixteenth century that these differences began to be fully known and appreciated. Fueled by factors ranging from decreasing insularity to the proliferation of geographical works to the emergence of nationhood itself, a distinct local consciousness emerged. This phenomenon is epitomized in the chorographical genre, which not only focuses on finite geographical areas but also helps erect categories by which local places can be further known and distinguished. Local places are also invested with the imaginative potential to signify particular values. Thus, Drayton assigns different heroic values to different places, Deloney makes Newbury an exemplar of the middle-class work ethic, and Shakespeare associates Windsor with a certain type of adventurous but honest woman. As a result of such associations, it becomes even easier to value England's native diversity, because to do so is to value the different virtues that these places signify.

Faced with an emerging nationhood that was perceived to be monolithic and homogeneous, early modern writers also find local diversity serviceable to their methodological and epistemological needs. Already in 1570, we find Lambarde contrasting the uniformity of Tudor centralization with the custom fit provided by organic structures of local government. A few decades later, *Poly-Olbion* invests in 'many Englands' in order to avoid the one England of the Jacobean Court. In the 1630s, Herbert argues for religious experience that can be shaped on a parish by parish basis rather than imposed from the top down. And in the Civil War and Interregnum, both Izaak Walton and Lucy Hutchinson turn to the local to carve out alternatives to the national outcomes of war. By the time we get to Herbert and Walton, we can see that the invocation of the local is less dependent on the features of an actual place (as it was in chorography). *The Country Parson* is not a depiction of life in Bemerton, Salisbury so much as an endorsement of a *mentality* that is fostered by local places. This larger shift in the depiction of the local can be seen in the chronological structure of this book. The first three chapters are closely connected to chorographical modes of writing and they all tend to aggrandize the heterogeneity of England. The final three chapters provide a wider application for this impulse. These later writers use the local differences and lack of uniformity emphasized by chorography to establish the need for contingency in approaching the larger religious, political, and cultural changes of the seventeenth century. They imagine the local not only as a source of differentiation, but as the sphere where complexities can best be negotiated and a more exact way of proceeding can be attained. Herbert's parson, Walton's angler, and Hutchinson's Puritan conscience all invest in the finite scope and heightened clarity of the local because it provides a venue where difficult decisions can be confidently made and acted upon. That Herbert is a moderate, Walton a Royalist, and Hutchinson a Puritan illustrates the non-ideological nature of the local's appeal. But none of these writers imagines the negotiation of contingency as a burden or necessary evil. As we have seen, the parson delights in cases of conscience, the consideration of complex variables is the source of the angler's recreation, and John Hutchinson's conscience is the very thing that puts him beyond human reproach and earns Providence's approval. The fulfilling 'artfulness' of local negotiation culminates in the final chapter, where the careful arrangement of foreign objects is almost purely aestheticized.

In practice, such artistry isn't as escapist as it may sound. As we have seen, all of these writers turn to the local as a way of engaging – rather than avoiding – national developments. In fact, together, these various deployments of the local imply a particular view of the nation that was emerging in the sixteenth and seventeenth centuries – that England is and should be a heterogeneous nation. Lambarde insists on particularization, even if it creates some fragmentation. Drayton glories in the local rivalries that animate the landscape, and refuses to declare winners. Herbert endorses the usefulness of diversity in parish religious practices. Walton recommends one set of angling guidelines for the River Trent and another for the River Avon. For these writers, it is not only difficult but undesirable to reduce England to a single, monolithic meaning. Preserving local distinctions allows for more effective governance, more authentic religion, and a richer culture, but it also strengthens the nation as a whole. As we saw in the last chapter, the unity that the later country house poem exhibits is derived from the combination of diverse objects that retain their individuality and distinctiveness. In the same way, the writers profiled in these pages suggest that English nationhood is ultimately strengthened when variety and contrast are allowed to exist within its larger framework.

It is no accident that the English imagination would go on to naturalize this concept even further in the landscape garden of the eighteenth century. There, contrasting features of the land are, as Pope puts it: 'harmoniously confus'd: / Where Order in Variety we see, / And where, tho' all things differ, all agree.'[2] But if *concordia discors* generalizes and classicizes the chorographic impulse towards diversity, it remains tied to local distinctions. 'Consult the Genius of the Place in all' recommends Pope, so that local conditions continue to shape the beauty and harmony of the English landscape.[3]

One could argue that the heterogeneous vision of nationhood that emerged in the sixteenth and seventeenth centuries would later prove serviceable to British union and colonial empire in the eighteenth century. After all, both union and empire revolve around synthesizing existing differences into a harmonious composition. Helgerson has even tied chorographical diversity to parliamentary governance – 'Parliament came almost to seem a living chorography, a map made of flesh' – and asserted the role of local distinctions in the triumph of parliamentary government over royal absolutism in England.[4] But such conjectures take me beyond the scope of this book. What seems more certain is that local consciousness did emerge as a potent force in the second half of the sixteenth century. And in the decades that followed, it was invoked by a surprising number of writers working in a variety of genres to mediate the larger changes of the period.

Notes

Introduction

1. The Folger Shakespeare Library has twenty-four copies of *Britannia* that were published prior to 1611; about half of these have marginal notes.
2. Folger, STC 4503, copy 3.
3. Folger, STC 4507, copy 4.
4. Perhaps reflecting the wider readership ensured by this, the first English translation. Folger, STC 4509, copy 2.
5. Krishan Kumar, *The Making of English National Identity* (Cambridge: Cambridge University Press, 2003), 93.
6. Richard Helgerson, *Forms of Nationhood: The Elizabethan Writing of England* (Chicago: University of Chicago Press, 1992), 299.
7. See, for instance, Andrew Hadfield, *Literature, Politics and National Identity: Reformation to Renaissance* (Cambridge: Cambridge University Press, 1994); Claire McEachern, *The Poetics of English Nationhood* (Cambridge: Cambridge University Press, 1996); Gillian Brennan, *Patriotism, Power, and Print* (Cambridge: James Clarke, 2003); and Philip Schwyzer, *Literature, Nationalism, and Memory in Early Modern England and Wales* (Cambridge: Cambridge University Press, 2004).
8. These works are (in the order referred to above): Rhonda Lemke Sanford, *Maps and Memory in Early Modern England: A Sense of Place* (Basingstoke: Palgrave Macmillan, 2002); Andrew Escobedo, *Nationalism and Historical Loss in Renaissance England: Foxe, Dee, Spenser, Milton* (Ithaca: Cornell University Press, 2004); Patrick Collinson, 'Biblical Rhetoric: The English Nation and National Sentiment in the Prophetic Mode,' in *Religion and Culture in Renaissance England*, ed. Claire McEachern and Debora Shuger (Cambridge: Cambridge University Press, 1997), 15–45; Cathy Shrank, 'Rhetorical Constructions of a National Community: The Role of the King's English in Mid-Tudor Writing,' in *Communities in Early Modern England*, ed. Phil Withington and Alexandra Shepard (Manchester: Manchester University Press, 2000), 180–198; David Cressy, *Bonfires and Bells: National Memory and the Protestant Calendar in Elizabethan and Stuart England* (London: Weidenfeld & Nicolson, 1989); and Roze Hentschell, *The Culture of Cloth in Early Modern England: Textual Constructions of a National Identity* (Burlington, VT: Ashgate, 2008).
9. See, for instance, Bruce McLeod, *The Geography of Empire in English Literature, 1580–1745* (Cambridge: Cambridge University Press, 1999); Willy Maley, *Nation, State, and Empire in English Renaissance Literature* (Basingstoke: Palgrave Macmillan, 2003); Andrew Hadfield, *Shakespeare, Spenser, and the Matter of Britain* (Basingstoke: Palgrave Macmillan, 2004); Stewart Mottram, *Empire and Nation in Early English Renaissance Literature* (Rochester, NY: D. S. Brewer, 2008).
10. For an article that is representative of this tendency, see Martin Elsky, 'Microhistory and Cultural Geography: Ben Jonson's "To Sir Robert Wroth"

and the Absorption of Local Community in the Commonwealth,' *Renaissance Quarterly* 53:2 (Summer 2000): 500–528.

1   Local Consciousness in Renaissance England

1. H. P. R. Finberg, 'The Local Historian and His Theme,' in *The Changing Face of English Local History*, ed. R. C. Richardson (Burlington, VT: Ashgate, 2000), 115. Originally published as *The local historian and his theme; an introductory lecture delivered at the University College of Leicester, 6 November 1952* (University College of Leicester, 1954).
2. Eamon Duffy, *The Voices of Morebath: Reformation and Rebellion in an English Village* (New Haven: Yale University Press, 2001); David Underdown, *Fire From Heaven: Life in an English Town in the Seventeenth Century* (New Haven: Yale University Press, 1992).
3. James Horn, for instance, has written convincingly of the integrity of the hundred (an administrative unit that encompasses several parishes) in *Adapting to a New World* (Chapel Hill, NC: University of North Carolina Press, 1994), 78–84, 118–119. Many writers have asserted the existence of self-conscious gentry 'county communities' prior to and during the Civil War. See, for example, Anthony Fletcher, *A County Community in Peace and War: Sussex 1600–1660* (New York: Longman, 1975).
4. See Alan Everitt, *Landscape and Community in England* (London: Hambledon Press, 1985); and Joan Thirsk, *Agricultural Regions and Agrarian History in England, 1500–1750* (Basingstoke: Macmillan, 1987).
5. Christopher Lewis, *Particular Places: An Introduction to English Local History* (London: British Library, 1989), 35.
6. In a letter that probably accompanied Lambarde's manuscript *Description of the City of Lincoln*, Lambarde reminds Burghley that 'it pleased you (Right Honourable) this Last Terme, to demaund of me, Wheather I had written any description of Lincolne.' Lambarde says that he has 'collected some few Notes out of hystorie concerning it, which also I promised to search out, and to send you' and has also included some notes 'concernyng Stamforde your Lo. owne towne.' The letter is dated December 2, 1584. BL.Lansdowne 43, article 21.
7. Charles Phythian-Adams, *Re-thinking English Local History* (Leicester: Leicester University Press, 1987), 48.
8. Everitt, *Landscape and Community*, 1. For more on the diversity and insularity (which titles I borrow for this section heading) of early modern English communities, see Everrit's *Change in the Provinces: The Seventeenth Century* (Leicester: Leicester University Press, 1969), 6–12.
9. Barry Coward, *Social Change and Continuity: England, 1550–1750* (New York: Addison Wesley Longman, 1997), 14.
10. Ibid., 16.
11. Everitt, *Landscape and Community*, 3.
12. Coward, *Social Change and Continuity*, 15.
13. Paul Coones and John Patten, *The Penguin Guide to the Landscape of England and Wales* (New York: Penguin, 1986), 36.
14. H. C. Darby, *A New Historical Geography of England* (Cambridge: Cambridge University Press, 1973), 275–287.

15. Richard Carew, *Survey of Cornwall* (Redruth, Cornwall: Tamar, 2000), 17–18.
16. T. D. Atkinson, *Local Style in English Architecture* (New York: Batsford, 1947). Atkinson gives the subject its most extensive treatment, but see also Darby, *A New Historical Geography*, 258–9; and Coones and Patten, *The Penguin Guide to the Landscape*, 223.
17. Atkinson, *Local Style*, 22. This was true not only in color and appearance, says Atkinson, but even things like ornament: 'The soft sandstones of the Midlands, the hard gritstones of the north demand a difference in architectural treatment and a smoother and rounder modeling of drapery, very different from the crisp treatment possible in the limestones' (30).
18. Charles Kightly, *The Customs and Ceremonies of Britain* (London: Thames & Hudson, 1986), 14.
19. The Abbots Bromley Horn Dance, which involves ancient reindeer horns and an elaborate twenty-mile dance, may have originated as a way to raise funds for the parish church. The Dunmow Flitch, mentioned by Chaucer's Wife of Bath, features the awarding of a side of bacon 'to married couples who can prove that they have never repented of their union during a period of at least a year and a day after the wedding.' The Burrator Reservoir Ceremony commemorates Sir Francis Drake's supplying Plymouth with a more reliable source of fresh water in 1591. Kightly, *Customs and Ceremonies*, 41–42, 103, 63.
20. For a contemporary (and critical) account of this practice, see Philip Stubbes, *The Anatomie of Abuses*, ed. Margaret Jane Kidnie (Tempe, AZ: Renaissance English Text Society, 2002), 213–215.
21. Kightly, *Customs and Ceremonies*, 113. This was despite a 1536 decree that attempted to make each parish 'hold its wake on the first Sunday in October, regardless of the date of the patronal festival' (113).
22. Ibid., 114.
23. Kightly's entries on each of these note regional variations.
24. David Cressy, 'The Protestant Calendar and the Vocabulary of Celebration in Early Modern England,' in *Society and Culture in Early Modern England* (Burlington, VT: Ashgate, 2003), 32. See also David Cressy, *Bonfires and Bells: National Memory and the Protestant Calendar in Elizabethan and Stuart England* (London: Weidenfeld & Nicolson, 1989).
25. Coones and Patten, *Penguin Guide to the Landscape*, 214.
26. Darby, *A New Historical Geography*, 259–272.
27. A. L. Rowse, *Tudor Cornwall* (London: Jonathan Cape, 1957), 22.
28. Nicholas Culpeper, *Culpeper's Complete Herbal* (Ware, Hertfordshire: Wordsworth, 1995), 1.
29. One early exception is John Ray's *South and East Country Words* (1674).
30. See Alexandra F. Johnston and Wim Hüsken (eds.), *English Parish Drama* (Atlanta: Rodopi, 1996). These collected essays discuss a number of local-sponsored dramatic activities in areas as diverse as Chester, West Yorkshire, and the Thames Valley.
31. Margaret Spufford, *Contrasting Communities: English Villages in the Sixteenth and Seventeenth Centuries*, 2nd edn. (Stroud: Sutton, 2000), xxii–xxiii.
32. Ibid., xxvii–xxviii.
33. Stephen Bending and Andrew McRae, *The Writing of Rural England, 1500–1800* (New York: Palgrave Macmillan, 2003), xiii. Even in 1801, this figure still stood at about 72 percent (xiii).

34. By 1650, some 350,000 people lived in London, but that was still only 7.2 percent of the total population of England. Roger Finlay and Beatrice Shearer, 'Population Growth and Suburban Expansion,' in *London 1500–1700: The Making of the Metropolis*, ed. A. L. Beier and Roger Finlay (New York: Longman, 1986), 37–59 (39).
35. Tristram Risdon, *Chorographical Description, or, Survey of the County of Devon* (London: E. Curll, 1714), 2. Subsequent citations of Risdon are from this edition; page numbers will be given in parentheses within the text.
36. Everitt, *Change in the Provinces: The Seventeenth Century*, 9.
37. Most hadn't seen a reproduced image of the monarch, much less seen him or her in person.
38. The full anecdote can be found in Everitt, *Change in the Provinces*, 9–10.
39. See John Morrill, *Revolt in the Provinces: The People of England and the Tragedies of War, 1630–1648*, 2nd edn. (New York: Longman, 1999), 132–151.
40. Alexandra Shepard and Phil Withington's influential *Communities in Early Modern England: Networks, Place, Rhetoric* (Manchester: Manchester University Press, 2000) embodies this trend and its Introduction provides a detailed summary of its key developments.
41. Clive Holmes, 'The County Community in Stuart Historiography,' *Journal of British Studies* 19: 2 (1980): 54–73.
42. Keith Wrightson, *English Society, 1580–1680* (New Brunswick, NJ: Rutgers University Press, 1982), 13.
43. Ibid., 224.
44. Coward, *Social Change and Continuity*, 7–9.
45. See Alastair Bellamy, *The Politics of Court Scandal in Early Modern England: News Culture and the Overbury Affair, 1603–1666* (Cambridge: Cambridge University Press, 2002); and Joad Raymond, *The Invention of the Newspaper: English Newsbooks, 1641–1649* (Oxford: Clarendon Press, 1996).
46. Margaret Spufford, 'The Pedlar, the Historian and the Folklorist: Seventeenth Century Communications,' *Folklore* 105 (1994): 13–24 (16).
47. For Spufford, the 1620s is the key decade; ibid., 21.
48. Beat Kumin, *The Shaping of a Community: The Rise and Reformation of the English Parish c. 1400–1560* (Brookfield, VT: Scolar Press, 1996), 247–249.
49. Ibid., 2, 257.
50. See Robert Tittler, 'The Emergence of Urban Policy, 1536–58,' in *The Mid-Tudor Polity, c. 1540–1560*, ed. Jennifer Loach and Robert Tittler (Basingstoke: Macmillan, 1980), 74–93; 'The End of the Middle Ages in the English Country Town,' *Sixteenth Century Journal* 18:4 (1987): 471–487; and *The Reformation and the Towns in England: Politics and Political Culture, c. 1540–1640* (Oxford: Clarendon Press, 1998).
51. See Robert Tittler, *Architecture and Power: The Town Hall and the English Urban Community, c. 1540–1640* (Oxford: Oxford University Press, 1991); and *The Face of the City: Civic Portraiture and Civic Identity in Early Modern England* (Manchester: Manchester University Press, 2007).
52. David Dean, 'Locality and Self in the Elizabethan Lottery of the 1560s,' in *Local Identities in Late Medieval and Early Modern England*, ed. Norman L. Jones and Daniel Woolf (Basingstoke: Palgrave Macmillan, 2007), 207–227 (208, 213). All examples of poesies later in the paragraph are from this article.

53. Some of the poesies that Dean mentions are: 'S. Maryes at the Toure, praye for me every hour' (a reference to the writer's parish church in Ipswich); 'God speede well, the auncient Towne of Arundell'; and 'Dunton upon the hill, would gayne with a good will' ('Locality and Self,' 213–214). Dean also reports, 'Several poesies celebrated their patron saint, St Laurence being the reference in more lots than any other, including that in Thanet' (214).

54. Dean, 'Locality and Self,' 207.

55. For example, Rafe Wilhouse's entry pleaded: 'Yarmouth haven god thee speed, the lorde he knoweth thy great need' (218) while John Michell of Devon wrote 'Topsham is buylded upon a red Rydge, I praye God sende a good lot to maintayne the Kay and Bridge' (215).

56. The numbers here and in the table above are compiled from the extensive list of geographical works provided by E. G. R. Taylor in the back of his *Tudor Geography, 1485–1583* (London: Methuen, 1930) and *Late Tudor and Early Stuart Geography, 1583–1650* (London: Methuen, 1934). The lists (and my calculations) include both manuscript and printed geographical works.

57. D. K. Smith, *The Cartographic Imagination in Early Modern England* (Burlington, VT: Ashgate, 2008), 6.

58. Rhonda Lemke Sanford, *Maps and Memory in Early Modern England: A Sense of Place* (Basingstoke: Palgrave Macmillan, 2002), 12.

59. In the two decades after Saxton, additional print and manuscript county maps appeared by John Norden for Middlesex, Surrey, Essex, and Hampshire; and by William Smith for Lancashire. In 1599, Peter Van Den Keer published *A collection of 28 Maps of the Counties of England and Wales.*

60. William Cunningham's *The Cosmological Glasse* (1559) was the first English work to describe the new continental triangulation methods that were bringing a new, mathematical exactness to surveys. According to Peter Eden, by 1598 estate surveys 'were a commonplace.' Eden, 'Three Elizabethan Estate Surveyors: Peter Kempe, Thomas Clerke, and Thomas Langdon,' in *English Map-Making, 1500–1650: Historical Essays*, ed. Sarah Tyacke (London: British Library, 1983), 68.

61. Taylor, *Late Tudor and Early Stuart Geography*, 42.

62. See also Richard Hasleton, *Strange and wonderful things happened to R.H. in his ten years' travels in foreign countries* (1595).

63. And indeed, a replica of Coryate's shoes are still on display in the Odcombe parish church.

64. Andrew McRae, *Literature and Domestic Travel in Early Modern England* (Cambridge: Cambridge University Press, 2009). McRae is especially interested in how travel contributed to new models of nationhood.

65. According to the *DNB*, King 'was apprenticed on 3 Sept. 1630 as [a] painter . . . After carrying on business for some years at Chester, he removed to London, where in 1656 he published The Vale Royall of England . . .' *Dictionary of National Biography*, Vol. 31 (London: Smith, Elder, & co., 1892), 126.

66. Daniel King, *The Vale-Royall of England. Or, The County Palatine of Chester Illustrated* (London: John Streater, 1656), iv, iii. Subsequent citations of King are from this edition; page numbers will be given in parentheses within the text. King's *Vale-Royall* is actually a combination of two earlier descriptions of the county by William Smith (c. 1584) and William Webb (1622), though King does add several pages of prefatory material and engravings of gentry arms.

67. For example, J. Hubrighe, *Almanack . . . with a rule to knowe the ebbes and fluddes . . . Also all the principal faires and martes etc.* (1568); Richard Grafton, *A little Treatise containing many proper tables and rules, &c.* (1571); John Richard Grafton, *Abridgement of the Chronicles of Englande* (1572); John Stow, *A Summarie of the Chronicles of England, &c.* (1575); and William Harrison's *Description of England* (1577).

68. Dunwich had once been the capital of Saxon East Anglia.

69. These reports were authored by Richard Tarleton and John Chapman, respectively.

70. William Averell and Thomas Marshe, respectively. The latter is actually a short ballad.

71. Perhaps in the same way that Midland, Texas became associated (and is still associated) in the American imagination with 'Baby Jessica' and her dramatic rescue from a well in 1987.

72. John Chandler, *Travels Through Stuart Britain: The Adventures of John Taylor the Water Poet* (Stroud: Sutton, 1999), ix.

73. *The praise of hemp-seed. With the voyage of Mr. Roger Bird and the writer hereof, in a boat of brown-paper, from London to Quinborough in Kent* (1619).

74. Taylor, for instance, includes an 'account of [Hull's] virtues, the quality of its government, its excellent water supply and defences,' 'a long description of a medicinal spring near Wallingford,' 'detailed descriptions of . . . Leicester's archaeological remains, Leeds parish church and the belvedere at Wharncliffe,' and 'historical descriptions . . . of Ipswich, Norwich, and King's Lynn' in his various journey descriptions. Chandler, *Travels Through Stuart Britain*, 63, 131, 153, 243.

75. Chandler, *Travels Through Stuart Britain*, 59.

76. Claire McEachern, *The Poetics of English Nationhood* (Cambridge: Cambridge University Press, 1996), 30. See also Andrew Hadfield, *Literature, Politics and National Identity: Reformation to Renaissance* (Cambridge: Cambridge University Press, 1994), 2. Krishan Kumar provides a similar articulation: 'It is common enough for nations, as for individuals, to develop a sense of themselves by a process of opposition and exclusion. What they are – French, German – is defined by what they are not – German, French. The content of national identity is more often than not a counter-image of what is seen as distinctive in the culture of the other nation or nations.' Krishan Kumar, *The Making of English National Identity* (Cambridge: Cambridge University Press, 2003), ix.

77. Taylor, *Tudor Geography*, 162.

78. John M. Adrian, 'Itineraries, Perambulations, and Surveys: The Intersections of Chorography and Cartography in the Sixteenth Century,' in *Images of Matter: Essays on British Literature of the Middle Ages and Renaissance*, ed. Yvonne Bruce (Newark: University of Delaware Press, 2005), 29–46 (29).

79. Philip Symonson's *New Description of Kent* appeared in 1596. John Norden published sections of his never-completed *Speculum Britanniae* on Middlesex (1593) and Hertfordshire (1598) while separate descriptions of Surrey, Essex, Sussex, and Hampshire remained in manuscript. Sampson Erdeswicke's *Certaine verie rare observations of Cumberlonde, Northumberlande . . .* (1574), Reginald Bainbrigg's *Collections relative to the Antiquities of Cumberland, Northumberland, Westmoreland, and Durham* (1602), and Thomas Beckham's *Collections for the County of Suffolk* (1602)

were completed but remained in manuscript. According to Jack Simmons, several other county chorographies generally associated with the first half of the seventeenth century – Reyce's *Suffolk* (1618), Burton's *Leicestershire* (1622), Risdon's *Devon* (1630), Smyth's *Berkeley* (1639) – were actually all begun around the turn of the century, and thus in my view more properly belong to this earlier phase. Jack Simmons, *English County Historians: First Series* (Wakefield: EP Publishing, 1978), 6–7.

80. John Hooker's *Description of the Cittie of Exeter*. Alexander Neville's *Description of Norwich* was originally written in Latin but translated in 1623. Lambarde's *Description of the City of Lincoln*, completed at the request of Lord Burleigh sometime in the latter half of the sixteenth century, remains in manuscript at the Bodleian Library. Henry Manship's *Great Yarmouth. A Book of the Foundation and Antiquity of the saide Towne* remained in manuscript until 1847. Thomas Nashe included a chorographical description of Great Yarmouth in his *Lenten Stuffe*.

81. William Burton, *The Description of Leicestershire* (London: John White, 1622). Subsequent citations of Burton are from this edition; page numbers will be given in parentheses within the text.

82. The *Breviary* was completed around 1618 but first published as *Suffolk in the XVIIth Century: The Breviary of Suffolk* (London: John Murray, 1902). Subsequent citations of Reyce are from this edition; page numbers will be given in parentheses within the text.

83. According to the *OED*, the only other contemporary secular meaning of the word 'breviary' was 'a brief summary' – which wouldn't seem to apply to an exhaustive work of this nature!

84. Thomas Gerard, *A Survey of Dorsetshire* (London: J. Wilcox, 1732), 8. Subsequent citations of Gerard are from this edition; page numbers will be given in parentheses within the text. The *Survey* was actually completed around 1633.

85. As its title implies, Sampson Erdeswicke's *Certaine verie rare observations of Cumberlonde, Northumberlande . . .* (1574) takes such rarities as its exclusive focus.

86. Richard Carew, *The Survey of Cornwall* (London: S.S. for John Jaggard, 1602), 54. Subsequent citations of Carew are from this edition; page numbers will be given in parentheses within the text.

87. Smyth notes 'the inbred delight, that both gentry, yeomanry, rascality, boyes, and children, doe take in a game called Stoball . . .' (10); Carew describes a game called 'Hurling,' different versions of which are 'played in the East of Cornwall than the West' (73 v.).

88. Smith's description was eventually published in Daniel King's *Vale-Royall of England*, 40. See n. 66.

89. Indeed, Smith himself had traveled extensively in Germany and throughout continental Europe.

90. Richard Helgerson, *Forms of Nationhood: The Elizabethan Writing of England* (Chicago: University of Chicago Press, 1992), 299.

91. Ibid., 138. Helgerson is referring to William Dugdale's voluminous *Antiquities of Warwickshire* (1656).

92. Jones and Woolf, 'Introduction,' in *Local Identities in Late Medieval and Early Modern England*, 2.

93. Lemster (or Leominster) is in Herefordshire while the Cotswolds lie mainly within Gloucestershire and Oxfordshire.

94. William Gray, *Chorographia: or, a Survey of Newcastle Upon Tine* (South Shields: George Nicholson, 1892), 20. Subsequent citations of Gray's 1649 work are from this edition; page numbers will be given in parentheses within the text.

95. William Lambarde, *The Description of the City of Lincoln*, Bodleian MS.Eng. hist.c.287. Lambarde adds begrudgingly that this is 'notwithstanding that the 3 several Bishopricks of Eli, Peterborow, and, Oxford, have since that time bene taken from it' (75).

96. The poem is probably by J. King, the author's cousin.

97. John Hooker, *The Description of the Citie of Ercester*, Vol. II (Devon and Cornwall Records Society, 1919–1947), 4.

98. William Lambarde, *A Perambulation of Kent*, ed. Richard Church (Bath: Adams and Dart, 1970), 226, 187.

99. Smyth reports that Berkeley hundred is comprised of 123 parcels ('hides') of 160 acres each, for a total of 19,680 acres (2).

100. The other 183 pages are devoted mostly to past inhabitants of the island (Celts, Romans, Picts, Saxons, Danes, and Normans) rather than to a cohesive description of the nation.

101. *England; a coloured facsimile of the maps and text from The theatre of the Empire of Great Britaine*, Vol. IV (London: Phoenix House, 1953–1954), 67.

102. The content of Derbyshire's boxes is pretty representative, though some of Speed's maps include variations like bird's eye views of two towns (Yorkshire includes views of both Richmond and Hull) or a thumbnail description of a key historical event associated with the county (Nottinghamshire gives an account of a battle from the reign of Henry VII).

103. Helgerson, *Forms of Nationhood*, 138.

104. These relics include 'a poor house' of uncertain founding date, a parish cross of uncertain origin, and an old hermitage. Bedwell is unable to shed any additional light on Tottenham High Cross's antiquities.

105. Wilhelm Bedwell, *A Briefe Description of the towne of Tottenham Highcrosse in Middlesex* (London: John Norton, 1631), E1. Subsequent citations of Bedwell are from this edition; page numbers will be given in parentheses within the text.

106. These annotations were found in Folger, STC 4503, copy 2 (1586); 4503, copy 3 (1586); 4507, copy 4 (1600); 4507, copy 5 (1600); 4509, copy 2 (1610); and 4510.3 (1637).

107. Folger, STC 4615, copy 4.

108. The particular copy that I discuss in this passage is in the Bodleian Library: Gough Dorset 5.

109. 1597 is the traditional date of publication, though Arden editor Giorgio Melchiori argues for the slightly later date of 1599. *The Arden Shakespeare Merry Wives of Windsor*, Third Series (Walton-on-Thames, Surrey: Thomas Nelson and Sons, 2000), 21–30. Subsequent quotations and line numbers of *Merry Wives* are from this edition.

110. Banbury (1.1.120) is in Oxfordshire, the next county over from Windsor's Berkshire. Brentford (4.2.72) is on the Thames, twelve miles east of Windsor. The Cotswolds (1.1.83) are further west, but also along the Thames.

111. Melchiori argues that the Garter Inn may not have actually existed (133), but it is at least imagined as a specific building in central Windsor. The famous episode where Falstaff is dumped out of the laundry basket and into a muddy ditch is firmly tied to a particular lane, mead, and river. Windsor Castle is mentioned twice (3.3.202; 5.5.56) while Windsor Forest is the setting for the final trick on Falstaff (4.4.27).

112. The whitsters (3.3.13) are 'whiteners, i.e. professional bleachers of clothes.' The poor knights of Windsor were a group of retired soldiers who lived in Windsor and received a pension from the Crown. Falstaff, the play implies, belongs to this group of knights. Melchiori, *Merry Wives*, 214, 21.

113. For instance, the word could be removed from the phrases 'The Windsor bell hath struck twelve' (5.5.1) and 'Cricket, to Windsor chimneys thou shalt leap' (5.5.43) without affecting their essential meaning.

114. According to Melchiori, 'The tale or legend seems to be of Shakespeare's own invention' (257). Even if he is a fabrication, Herne the Hunter is just the sort of legend that would flourish at the local level.

115. In fact, a much shorter quarto version of the play (published in 1602) actually eliminates most of the place details and introduces a more 'Italianate' flavor. Melchiori, *Merry Wives*, 10.

116. Shakespeare himself supplies considerable Midlands details for the Christopher Sly section of *Taming of the Shrew* (c. 1594). The anonymous *Arden of Feversham* (1592) dramatizes a notorious episode of Kentish history. London plays like Dekker's *Shoemaker's Holiday* (1599) are set within a richly detailed and recognizable London landscape.

117. After discussing the localized poesies created for the national lottery of 1567–1569, Dean situates them 'within the larger context of local knowledge [emerging] in this period.' 'Locality and Self,' 220.

118. Tusser is particularly concerned about variations among Essex, Norfolk, Suffolk, Leicestershire, Cambridgeshire, Lincolnshire, and Middlesex.

119. Heywood, p. 178, #5. Edgeware was then a small village outside London, while Rayleigh is located 30 miles to the east in Essex.

120. Which would seem to reflect Spenser's own experiences in the region as the personal secretary to the Bishop of Rochester.

121. Joan Grundy, *The Spenserian Poets* (New York: St. Martin's Press, 1969), 66.

122. James Turner, *The Politics of Landscape: Rural Scenery and Society in English Poetry, 1630–1660* (Cambridge, MA: Harvard University Press, 1979).

123. Both involved local opposition to national religious changes, and both were sponsored by powerful northern nobles.

124. Hotspur's father, Henry Percy, is referred to as 'Northumberland' throughout the play and 2.3 is presumably set in Warkworth Castle, the family estate. Mortimer's title is the Earl of March, though he cooperates with rather than resists the incursions of the Welsh Owen Glendower.

125. Neville Kirk (ed.), *Northern Identities: Historical Interpretations of 'The North' and 'Northernness'* (Brookfield, VT: Ashgate, 2000), 5.

126. Raymond Williams, *The Country and the City* (New York: Oxford University Press, 1973), 38. For more on increasing realism and native elements in English pastoral, see John Barrell and John Bull (eds.), *The Penguin Book of English Pastoral Verse* (London: Allen Lane, 1974), 141–145.

127. For Michelle O'Callaghan, the pastoral critiques of Drayton, Wither, Browne, and others amount not only to locally based critiques, but to an alternative 'shepherd's nation.' Michelle O'Callaghan, *The 'Shepheard's Nation': Jacobean Spenserians and Early Stuart Political Culture* (Oxford: Clarendon Press, 2000).

128. Encapsulated in lines 80–81: 'This maketh me at home to hunt and to hawk / And in foul weather at my book to sit.'

129. William Camden, *Britannia* (1610), 283.

130. *The Novels of Thomas Deloney*, ed. Merritt E. Lawlis (Bloomington: Indiana University Press, 1961), 68. Subsequent page numbers will be provided in the text.

131. At one point, Deloney even has the King say 'that no Trade in all the Land was so much to bee cherished and maintained as this, which . . . may well be called The life of the poor' (47). For an extended reading on the above episode as an instance of contemporary social protest on the part of Deloney, see Roze Hentschell, *The Culture of Cloth in Early Modern England: Textual Constructions of a National Identity* (Burlington, VT: Ashgate, 2008), 51–71.

132. Elsewhere Jack/Deloney actually calculates the total number of people maintained by the clothing industry at 'threescore thousand and six hundred persons' (57).

133. Cardinal Wolsey, the son of a butcher, was born in Ipswich, Suffolk in 1471. In opposing the clothier's complaint to the King, he is the emblem of someone who forgets where he comes from. When Jack quips that 'if my Lord Cardinals father had beene no hastier in killing of Calves then he is in dispatching of poore mens sutes, I doubt he had never worne a Myter' (59), Wolsey angrily has the clothiers thrown in prison.

134. The most probable date is 1612. There is also evidence that Dover 'improved or re-created' existing games rather than starting from scratch. See Christopher Whitfield, *Robert Dover and the Cotswold Games* (Evesham, Worcs.: The Journal Press, 1962), 13–15.

135. Ibid., 19.

136. All poem quotations and page numbers derive from the edition of *Annalia Dubrensia* published in E. R. Vyvyan, *Dover's Cotswold Games* (London: Tabard Press, 1970).

137. John Cole's poem says that Dover 'Makes the Games / Of Hide-parke common: as their Citie Dames' (66). Walton Poole asserts the superiority of the Cotswold Games to sports held in Royston, Newmarket, Brigants, Brackley, Bannsteed, and Sarum (71).

138. Though Drayton's account is probably of the version of the Games that existed before Dover revived them. Drayton's fanciful map of Gloucestershire includes a visual representation of the festivities.

139. Wrightson, *English Society*, 70.

140. Ronald Hutton, *The Rise and Fall of Merry England: The Ritual Year, 1400–1700* (Oxford: Oxford University Press, 1994), 194.

141. In the preceding lines, Trussell puts the Cotswold Games in the tradition of rushbearing, Whitsun ales, May games, and Hocktide pastimes.

142. Deloney goes even further back for the setting of *Thomas of Reading* (c. 1598) to the reign of Henry I, a time (Deloney says) when 'there was few or no beggars' and 'it was a rare thing to heare of a thiefe' (267).

143. John Stow, *Survey of London*, ed. H. B. Wheatley (London: J. M. Dent & Sons, 1960), 115.
144. See, for examples, Songs II, VII, and XXII.
145. The phrase is used by William Gray in his address 'To the Candid Reader' in *Chorographia: or, a Survey of Newcastle Upon Tine*.
146. As *A Homily Against Disobedience and Willful Rebellion* (1570) puts it: 'it is most evident that kings, queens, and other princes . . . are ordained of God, are to be obeyed and honoured of their subjects; that such subjects as are disobedient or rebellious against their princes disobey God and procure their owne damnation' (211). Ed. Ronald B. Bond (Toronto: University of Toronto Press, 1987).
147. Helgerson, *Forms of Nationhood*, 107–147. R. Malcolm Smuts, *Court Culture and the Origins of a Royalist Tradition in Early Stuart England* (Philadelphia: University of Pennsylvania Press, 1987).
148. McEachern, *Poetics of English Nationhood*, 5.
149. Shakespeare's *Henry VI, Part I*, written just two years after the defeat of Spain, is particularly rich in pro-unity speeches, for example: ' . . . when envy breeds unkind division. / There comes the ruin, there begins confusion' (4.1.193–194).
150. Coward, *Social Change and Continuity*, 30. Coward explains: 'it is possible that "growth" [of a sense of national community] implies too lineal a process . . . conscious of belonging to a national community may have reached peaks separated by troughs, the high points being the early years of the war against Spain in the 1580s, the period just before 1640 and during the next two decades, during the Exclusion Crisis of 1678–81, and again during the wars against France after 1689' (30).
151. Kumar, *The Making of English National Identity*, 39. The author, as she notes, is paraphrasing Hegel.
152. Eamon Duffy, *The Stripping of the Altars* (New Haven: Yale University Press, 1992), 502.
153. See Victor Harris, *All Coherence Gone: A Study of the Seventeenth Century Controversy Over Disorder and Decay in the Universe* (London: Cass, 1966).
154. Hiram Haydn, *The Counter-Renaissance* (New York: Grove Press, 1960), xv–xvi.
155. Ben Jonson, *Timber: or Discoveries Made upon Men and Matter*, in *Ben Jonson*, ed. C. H. Herford and P. Simpson, Vol. VIII (Oxford: Clarendon Press, 1970), 621.
156. Helgerson, *Forms of Nationhood*, 13.
157. J. D. Marshall, *The Tyranny of the Discrete: A Discussion of the Problems of Local History in England* (Aldershot: Scolar Press, 1997), 75.

2   William Lambarde and Tudor Centralization

1. The Pilgrimage of Grace (1536), the Western Rebellion (1547–1549), and Kett's Rebellion (1549), respectively. Lambarde was born in London in 1536 and died in 1601 at Westcombe Manor in East Greenwich, Kent.
2. Patricia Hyde and Michael Zell, 'Governing the County,' in *Early Modern Kent, 1540–1640*, ed. Michael Zell (Woodbridge, Suffolk: Boydell Press, 2000), 24.
3. David Loades, *Tudor Government* (Oxford: Blackwell, 1997), 131.

4. *The Oxford English Dictionary*, 2nd edn. (Oxford: Clarendon Press, 1989), Vol. XI, 518. Other contemporary definitions included 'a walk, a journey on foot' and a '[c]omprehensive relation or description.' Lambarde himself is credited with coining a new usage: '[t]he action of travelling through and inspecting a territory or region.' Nevertheless, it is clear from Lambarde's methodology of a circular progression around the dioceses of Kent that he also has in mind this more formal definition.

5. Perambulation was also an important ritual for the community of the parish church, yet it still served the same practical function of checking boundaries. See 'Beating the Bounds' in Charles Kightly's *The Customs and Ceremonies of Britain* (London: Thames & Hudson, 1986), 48–50. Survey maps were beginning to replace verbal property descriptions in the sixteenth century, but the latter were still much in use. For more on this trend, see Catherine Delano-Smith and Roger Kain, *English Maps: A History* (Toronto: University of Toronto Press, 1999), 114–118.

6. For example: 'I will not heere stande upon that matter, but forsaking the shore, betake me Northward to passe along the River Rother which divideth this Shire from Sussex: where, after that I shall have shewed you Apledore, Stone, and Newenden, I will pearce through the Wealde to Medway, and so labour to perfourme the rest of this purpose' (184).

7. William Lambarde, *A Perambulation of Kent*, ed. Richard Church (Bath, UK: Adams and Dart, 1970), 308. All citations of Lambarde are from this edition. Subsequent page numbers are given in parentheses within the text.

8. Even in Lambarde's day, 'order' was a complex word with many shades of meaning. The author's usage in the preceding examples seems to conform most to the *OED*'s third category of denotations for the word: 'sequence, disposition, arrangement . . . or regulated condition' (X.904). But 'order' as methodical arrangement need not preclude a political application. The oldest English forms of the word refer to 'orders of angels' and ranks of 'monastic order' (902) – concepts that effectively blend notions of orderly arrangement with notions of hierarchy and authority. Indeed, political order, it seems to me, is always derived from some form of orderly arrangement. In the fifteenth century, 'civil or public order' was coined as '[t]he condition in which the laws or usages regulating the public relations of individuals to the community, and the public conduct of members or sections of the community to each other, are maintained and observed' (905). In other words, it is no great leap to think about Lambarde's preoccupation with literary ordering as indirectly reflecting a concern about political order as well.

9. Such phrases also suggest an awareness of the precariousness of his enterprise, and the vigilance necessary to maintain order both in the *Perambulation* and in sixteenth-century Kent.

10. Tristram Risdon, *The Chorographical Description, or, Survey of the County of Devon* (London: E. Curll, 1714), 36. This work was completed in manuscript around 1630.

11. Daniel King, *The Vale-Royal of England. Or, The County Palatine of Chester Illustrated* (London: John Streater, 1656), 2.

12. Wotton's epistle 'To his Countriemen, the Gentlemen of the Countie of Kent' joins Lambarde's letter to Wotton in the prefatory material of the first printed edition of the *Perambulation* in 1576. The basic sentiment of this

quote – the importance of the gentry to the governing of the provinces – is a commonplace among modern historians.

13. Richard Helgerson supports such a political reading of the genre when he connects the 'shift in chorographical activity from the kingdom to the county' to emergent depictions of an 'oligarchic England' in the early seventeenth century. 'Nation or Estate? Ideological Conflict in the Early Modern Mapping of England,' *Cartographica* 30:1 (1993): 73–74. Helgerson explores the political implications of chorography in greater detail in the third chapter of *Forms of Nationhood: The Elizabethan Writing of England* (Chicago: University of Chicago Press, 1992).

14. Peter Clark, *English Provincial Society from the Reformation to the Revolution: Religion, Politics, and Society in Kent, 1500–1640* (Hassocks, Sussex: Harvester Press, 1977), 3.

15. In the chorographic works that follow Carew's *Survey of Cornwall* (1602), Richard Helgerson detects a 'much more exclusive focus on individual ownership of the land' that often took the form of detailed 'listing of genealogical and proprietary information.' Helgerson, 'Nation or Estate?' 73.

16. Retha Warnicke, *William Lambarde: Elizabethan Antiquary, 1536–1601* (Chichester, Sussex: Phillimore and Co., 1973), 4. I am indebted to Warnicke for the basic biographical information in this paragraph.

17. Warnicke suggests that Lambarde may also have moved his residence to Westcombe Manor as early as 1567. *William Lambarde*, 39–40. The Sewers Commission was authorized to oversee and maintain everything from drainage ditches to sea defenses.

18. In 'Governing the County,' Hyde and Zell say that 'Lambarde (himself the son of a Londoner) exaggerated the metropolitan input' (20) – an observation that supports the conclusion that I reach in the next sentence.

19. The ancient powers of the sheriff were curtailed, for instance.

20. A. L. Rowse, *The England of Elizabeth: The Structure of Society* (New York: Macmillan, 1951), 341.

21. Clark, *English Provincial Society*, 119.

22. Felicity Heal and Clive Holmes suggest that Tudor centralization relied heavily on voluntary compliance: 'the balance of power in the counties remained essentially traditional and the government sought to persuade gentlemen that they had a vested interest in the promotion of good order as defined by the centre.' *The Gentry in England and Wales, 1500–1700* (London: Macmillan, 1994), 184.

23. Loades, *Tudor Government*, 6. Though this articulation is a bit exaggerated, it is by no means singular. Heal and Holmes generally concur: 'In 1550 it was still possible to think of England as, in Dr Bernard's phrase, "a confederation of noble fiefdoms".' *The Gentry*, 196.

24. Loades says that minor liberties and other exemptions 'belonged to a distributive concept of authority, of which the feudal system itself had been the greatest example.' *Tudor Government*, 224.

25. Clark, *English Provincial Society*, 112–113.

26. For a detailed example of one local official's response to centralization, see Peter Fleming, 'Sir Thomas Cheyne, Lord Warden of the Cinque Ports, 1536–1558: Central Authority and the Defence of Local Privilege,' in *Regionalism and Revision: The Crown and its Provinces in England, 1200–1650*, ed. Peter Fleming,

Anthony Gross, and J. R. Lander (London: Hambledon Press, 1998), 123–144. Martin Elsky, on the other hand, depicts the complex negotiations (and greater compliance) of the Wroth family later in the century: 'Microhistory and Cultural Geography: Ben Jonson's "To Sir Robert Wroth" and the Absorption of Local Community in the Commonwealth,' *Renaissance Quarterly* 53:2 (Summer 2000): 500–528.

27. Hyde and Zell, 'Governing the County,' 19.
28. See Heal and Holmes on gentry motives of 'status' and 'local power' and the Crown's attempts to transform them into 'an ideology of public service.' *The Gentry*, 168–184.
29. It seems significant that the two major JP handbooks of the early modern period – Lambarde's *Eirenarcha* (1582) and Michael Dalton's *The Countrey Justice* (1618) – would both warn against JPs using too much discretion. The implication is that JPs continued to exercise private judgment and procedures that sometimes didn't square with the official line from Westminster.
30. Lambarde wrote *Archaionomia* (1568), a Latin translation of ancient Anglo-Saxon laws, as well as *Archeion, or A Discourse on the High Courts of Justice in England* (written in the 1580s, published in 1635).
31. Clark, *English Provincial Society*, 112.
32. Hyde and Zell, 'Governing the County,' 9–10. The authors derive some of their claims from J. Harris, *The History of Kent* (1719).
33. Clark, *English Provincial Society*, 118. Hyde and Zell ('Governing the County,' 14–16) do not point to a particular decade as crucial, but the developments they note in both the Assizes and the office of Lord Lieutenant are not inconsistent with Clark's basic assertion here.
34. In addition to serving on the local Commission of the Sewers, Lambarde also served as Collector for the Greenwich Marsh and was elected to an office on the Rochester Bridge Corporation.
35. Warnicke, *William Lambarde*, 70.
36. Constables have scope over a hundred or franchise, while borsholders and tithingmen serve a town or parish.
37. Usually five to fifteen parishes, in Kent. Warnicke says that after Lambarde 'gained personal insight into the role of a justice of the peace he realised that to be effective he had to have the co-operation of the lower Kentish officials, whose negligence sometimes increased the problems of law enforcement.' *William Lambarde*, 72.
38. Bernhard Klein, *Maps and the Writing of Space in Early Modern England and Ireland* (New York: Palgrave Macmillan, 2001), 139.
39. Though it is difficult to ascertain exactly what Lambarde means by the tag 'yeomanrie.' On the next page he uses it interchangeably with 'common people' – so it seems to extend to more than just small landowners.
40. That Lambarde is consciously projecting an ideal here, can be seen in the fractious reality of the JP case notebook that Lambarde kept from 1579–1587, the *Ephemeris*. It has been published by the Folger Shakespeare Library in *William Lambarde and Local Government: His 'Ephemeris' and twenty-nine charges to juries and commissions*, ed. Conyers Read (Ithaca, NY: Cornell University Press, 1962).
41. In addition to Lambarde's awareness of the sixteenth-century Kentish rebellions and disturbances that have already been noted in this chapter, he

writes more generally (and with perhaps more approval) of the natives' traditional defiance and independence: 'the communaltie of Kent was never vanquished by the Conquerour, but yeelded itself by composition, and besides that Gervasius affirmeth, that the forward in all battels belongeth to them (by a certein pre-eminence) in right of their manhood' (7).

42. Wyatt's Rebellion was raised in 1553–1554 to oppose Mary's intended marriage to Philip II of Spain.

43. Heal and Holmes, *The Gentry*, 359.

44. Hyde and Zell, 'Governing the County,' 9.

45. J. H. Gleason, *The Justices of the Peace in England: 1558 to 1640* (Oxford: Clarendon Press, 1969), 71.

46. Ibid. The religiously motivated Northern Rebellion began this year. This event provides the rationale for the Crown's new policy, and may also explain Lambarde's emphasis on the socio-political impact of religious division. Catholicism also played a role in at least two other sixteenth-century rebellions: the Pilgrimage of Grace (1536) and the Western Rebellion (1547–1549).

47. The author notes that Kent was the first part of England to be inhabited, it was the only county unvanquished by William the Conqueror (thereby securing its ancient privileges), its soldiers are traditionally on the front line of battles by 'auncient prerogative of manhood,' and it has long held a pre-eminence in ecclesiastical matters through the archbishopric of Canterbury (10, 19, 74).

48. Whether or not such an emphasis on Kent's distinctions from other counties constitutes a 'county community' or could potentially conflict with a larger vision of national uniformity, are questions that are outside the scope of this chapter. Much has been written on the presence of gentry county communities in early modern England. See, for instance, Alan Everitt, *The Local Community and the Great Rebellion* (London: Historical Association, 1969); John Morrill, *Revolt of the Provinces* (New York: Barnes and Noble, 1976); and Anthony Fletcher, *A County Community in Peace and War: Sussex, 1600–1660* (New York: Longman, 1975). Yet other historians have raised important objections to the county community 'school' of thought. For instance: Clive Holmes, 'The County Community in Stuart Historiography,' *Journal of British Studies* 19:2 (1980): 54–73; and Ann Hughes, *Politics, Society, and Civil War in Warwickshire, 1620–1660* (New York: Cambridge University Press, 1987). For an extensive treatment of this debate and fuller list of sources, see R. C. Richardson, *The Debate on the English Revolution Revisited*, 2nd edn. (New York: Routledge, 1988), 133–149.

49. Such a tendency goes against Michael Zell's characterization of the *Perambulation* as 'a model of Kent as a shire unified by its long history and common customs' in which '[t]he only differences or distinctions *within* Kent which were referred to by Lambarde was his insistence that north-west Kent, the region nearest London, was full of newcomers from the metropolis.' *Early Modern Kent*, 'Introduction,' 3.

50. It is a binary organizational model – the general followed by the particular – that Lambarde bequeathed to those chorographers that followed him. For example, the following chorographies make a clear distinction between relatively brief 'general' sections and longer 'particular' descriptions: Smith's

Vale Royal (1584), Carew's *Survey of Cornwall* (1602), Risdon's *Chorographical Description of Devon* (1630), and Gerard's *Survey of Dorsetshire* (1633).

51. The Saxon will is in Lambarde's *Perambulation*; the wells are in Wilhelm Bedwell's *A Briefe Description of the towne of Tottenham Highcrosse in Middlesex* (1631); and the proverbs are listed in John Smyth's *Description of the Hundred of Berkley* (c. 1639).

52. Richard Helgerson discusses particularization as the dominant mode of chorography in *Forms of Nationhood*, 131–139.

53. Jonathan Sawday, *The Body Emblazoned: Dissection and the Human Body in Renaissance Culture* (New York: Routledge, 1995), 2.

54. William Gray, *Chorographia: or, a Survey of Newcastle Upon Tine* (South Shields, Durham: George Nicholson, 1892), i.

55. The general narrowing of focus of English chorographic works from nation to counties, cities, and towns (though numerous exceptions hinder such a tidy chronology) seems to support this mindset.

56. Sawday, *The Body Emblazoned*, 3, 164.

57. A good illustration of both tendencies can be seen in Lambarde's one-page entry for Milton. He starts with the town's connection to King Alfred in the ninth century, skips ahead to its being ransacked in the eleventh century, and then closes with 'after which time, I have not read, neither is it likely, that the place was of any estimation . . . more than for the market only' (216).

58. Lambarde breaks his own rule when he gives a unified treatment of the Wars of the Roses in 'The Brent' section. Yet if anything, his acknowledgment that 'I will breake square for this once, and tell you out both the course and conclusion of all this tragicall historie' (420) only serves to highlight the cohesiveness that almost every other entry lacks.

59. Perhaps he is making some sort of epistemological claim, that one must understand place before one can understand the history that it has produced. If so, he does not end each entry with a peroration about why this place produced this type of historical event.

60. As Clive Holmes concludes in one of his arguments against the integrity of the county community: 'the bulk of the gentry's administrative experience was forged in smaller units than the county, and it could be argued that these smaller divisions became the cynosures of their loyalties.' Holmes, 'The County Community,' 62.

61. In *Forms of Nationhood*, Helgerson says that this emphasis on local privileges is a characteristic feature of the chorographies of the period, calling it: 'a sometimes jealous assertion of local prerogative or, when the prerogative was no longer in force, of a fond memory of former authority' (136). However, his eventual claim that focusing on local distinctions only serves to ratify the nation – 'the particularities . . . constantly remind us of the whole' and 'Nationalism is what ultimately justifies a project as particular as Dugdale's' (138) – seems a bit tidy. I would argue that chorography can articulate a genuine reverence for traditional and more organic structures.

62. For example, the privileges and unique government of the Cinque Ports 'being first granted by Edward the Conquerour, and William the Conquerour, and then confirmed and increased by William Rufus, Henrie the Second, Richard the First, Henrie the Third, and King Edward the First, be very great, considering either the honour and ease, or the freedome and exemption,

that the inhabitants have by reason of the same' (112–113). More recent monarchs had continued to endorse the arrangement 'in consideration of such service to bee done by them upon the Sea' (104).

63. William Lambarde, *Eirenarcha: or of The Office of the Justices of Peace* (London: Ra. Newbery and H. Bynneman, 1582), 7. Later, he restates this approach more pithily as 'not a uniting of minds but a restraining of hands' (9).

64. Clark, *English Provincial Society*, 125.

65. Lambarde, *Eirenarcha*, 63. He later explains that 'forasmuch as everie considerable circumstance can not be foreseene at the time of the making of the Lawe, they doe many times leave to be supplyed by the discreation of the Executioner of the Lawe' (64).

66. Quoted in Clark, *English Provincial Society*, 119.

67. See n. 40. For another example, see the manuscript letter of J. Stockwood (a Tonbridge schoolmaster) to Lambarde requesting informal legal advice for two of his parishioners. (BL.ms. Add. 70638, f. 17)

68. Warnicke, *William Lambarde*, 130–131.

3 Michael Drayton and Jacobean Court Culture

1. Helgerson places the first part of *Poly-Olbion* (1612) 'firmly . . . in the orbit of the Society of Antiquaries, many of whose members had been among Drayton's closest friends.' Richard Helgerson, *Forms of Nationhood: The Elizabethan Writing of England* (Chicago: University of Chicago Press, 1992), 128. See also Angus Vine, *In Defiance of Time: Antiquarian Writing in Early Modern England* (Oxford: Oxford University Press, 2010), 171–177.

2. Bart Van Es, '"The Streame and Currant of Time": Land, Myth, and History in the Works of Spenser,' *Spenser Studies* 18 (2003): 209–229 (224).

3. Ibid., 212. The rest of the article traces Spenser's engagement with chorography in the three works that appear in the next sentence.

4. William B. Hunter, Jr. (ed.), *The English Spenserians* (Salt Lake City: University of Utah, 1977), 1–2. For more on the poetic treatment of rivers in early modern literature, see Wyman H. Herendeen, *From Landscape to Literature: The River and the Myth of Geography* (Pittsburgh: Duquesne University Press, 1986).

5. Homer Nearing, *English Historical Poetry, 1599–1641* (Philadelphia: University of Pennsylvania Press, 1945), 24.

6. See S. Naqi Husain Jafri, *Aspects of Drayton's Poetry* (Delhi: Dobra House, 1988), 189.

7. Kathleen Tillotson, 'Michael Drayton as a "Historian" in the "Legend of Cromwell,"' *Modern Language Review* 34 (1939): 186.

8. Nearing, *English Historical Poetry*, 44.

9. Richard F. Hardin, *Michael Drayton and the Passing of Elizabethan England* (Lawrence: University Press of Kansas, 1973), 36.

10. Joan Grundy, *The Spenserian Poets* (New York: St. Martin's Press, 1969), 109.

11. Michael Drayton, *The Works of Michael Drayton*, 5 vols., ed. J. William Hebel (Oxford: Blackwell, 1931–1941). V:144. Subsequent citations are taken from this edition; volume and page numbers will be given in parentheses within the text. According to Hebel, these odes constituted a 'striking innovation'

because Drayton approaches the genre not just as 'a novel synonym for a song' but as a conventional classical form. As Hebel also notes, one John Soothern actually wrote some classical odes twenty years earlier, but his poems had very little effect on English poetry and went all but unnoticed (V:144).

12. George Parfitt, *English Poetry of the Seventeenth Century* (New York: Longman, 1985), 165–166. Alan Isler explains, 'For the sixteenth-century English, heroic poetry was a sufficiently broad and amorphous category.' Isler continues, 'Epic, romance, history, pseudo-biography, geography – examples of all of these and more might be listed indiscriminately under the single genre heading of "heroic poetry" by the eclectic Elizabethans.' 'Heroic Poetry and Sidney's Two "Arcadias",' *Modern Language Association Publications* 83:2 (1968): 368–379 (369, 373).

13. Grundy, *The Spenserian Poets*, 110.

14. Ibid., 115.

15. In many ways, such an approach seems to approximate classical notions of heroism more closely than contemporary Protestant ones.

16. Robert Devereux, *An Apologie of the Earle of Essex against those which falsly and maliciously taxe him to be the onely hinderer of the peace, and quiet of his countrey* (London: for J. Smethwick, 1600), B2v.

17. Ibid., B3.

18. *Ben Jonson*, ed. C. H. Herford and Percy Simpson, 11 vols. (Oxford: Clarendon Press, 1925–1963), VIII:398.

19. Such details, says Hebel, are a function of Drayton's realism: 'The illusion of actual letter-writing is maintained by description of the scene of writing.' Drayton, *Works*, V:98. But the thoroughness of description, I would argue, moves beyond mere realism. See, for instance, the prominence of Woodstock, Oxfordshire, in Rosamond's epistle to Henry II. Though the letter is less than 200 lines, the argument, epistle, and annotations that follow all describe her place of narration and anchor the letter in its physical surroundings (II:133–139).

20. Frances Yates, *The Art of Memory* (Chicago: University of Chicago Press, 1966), 274.

21. As the margin heading in Drayton's *Works* points out, 'the Plaine' is meant to indicate those areas bordering the Salisbury Plain, principally Hampshire and Wiltshire (II:19).

22. A similar passage in the *Battaile of Agincourt* (1627) is 111 lines long and catalogs the proclivities (via the military ensigns) of almost every English county (III.22–24).

23. Shortly after Elizabeth's death, Drayton penned *To the Majesty of King James. A gratulatorie Poem* (1603). Whether or not this poem's failure to properly mourn the death of Elizabeth before celebrating the ascension of James irreparably damaged Drayton's aspirations (as almost all of his biographers have alleged), his bid for patronage was not successful and he stopped trying after 1604.

24. In particular, see *The Owle* (1604) as well as Drayton's satirization of James as 'Olcon' in the pastoral *Shepherd's Sirena* (1627).

25. R. Malcolm Smuts, *Court Culture and the Origins of a Royalist Tradition in Early Stuart England* (Philadelphia: University of Pennsylvania Press, 1987), 24–25.

26. Hardin, *Passing of Elizabethan England*, 27.

27. See David B. Quinn, 'James I and the Beginnings of Empire in America,' *Journal of Imperial and Commonwealth History* 2:2 (January 1974): 135–152.

28. For numerical details on James I's selling of titles, see Lawrence Stone, *The Crisis of the Aristocracy, 1558–1641* (Oxford: Clarendon Press, 1965).

29. Jean Brink, *Michael Drayton Revisited* (Boston: Twayne, 1990), 66.

30. For general trends in historiography in the period, see F. Smith Fussner, *Tudor History and the Historians* (New York: Basic Books, 1970) and F. J. Levy, *Tudor Historical Thought* (San Marino, CA: Huntington Library, 1967).

31. For the complexity of this commentary, however, and Selden's own ambiguity towards myth, see Anne Lake Prescott, 'Drayton's Muse and Selden's "Story": The Interfacing of Poetry and History in *Poly-Olbion*,' *Studies in Philology* 87:1 (1990): 128–135; and Reid Barbour, *John Selden: Measures of the Holy Commonwealth in Seventeenth-Century England* (Toronto: University of Toronto Press, 2003), chapter 1.

32. Nearing, *English Historical Poetry*, 16.

33. Smuts, *Court Culture*, 16–18.

34. Ibid., 1.

35. Hardin, *Passing of Elizabethan England*, 102–103.

36. Drayton's disenchantment seems to partake of the larger rift that opened up between 'Court' and 'Country' in the early seventeenth century.

37. For instance, Helgerson (*Forms of Nationhood*, 139–145) argues that the poem offers an anti-monarchical form of nationhood centered on the county gentry, whereas Andrew McRae sees *Poly-Olbion* as asserting the centrality of the land itself and 'seek[ing] refuge in a conception of nationhood beyond the reach of "mans devouring hand".' *God Speed the Plough: The Representation of Agrarian England, 1500–1660* (New York: Cambridge University Press, 1996), 260.

38. 'Illustrations' written by the antiquarian John Selden accompany the first eighteen songs (published in 1612) but are absent from the last twelve (published in 1622).

39. Vine, *In Defiance of Time*, 169; Nearing, *English Historical Poetry*, 134.

40. Drayton also mentions the ancient British bards in his dedicatory ode to Sir Henry Goodere, asserting that the bards' musical compositions served 'To stirre their Youth to Warlike Rage, / Or their wyld Furie to asswage' (II:345).

41. The only exceptions I find are when the ancient dykes of Cambridgeshire (Song XXI) and Hadrian's Wall (Song XXIX) complain of their neglect.

42. The maps themselves were drawn by one William Hole.

43. Tradition held that Brutus first landed in England at the mouth of the River Dart (Devonshire) and that King Arthur died on the banks of the Camel River (Cornwall).

44. This basic difference can be seen by comparing *Poly-Olbion* to Spenser's most famous topographical passage: the marriage of the Thames and Medway (*FQ* IV.xi). Spenser catalogs the rivers that attend, but leaves out any sense of striving or competition. While Spenser emphasizes convergence (marriage), Drayton has his rivers boast, compete, and take part in mythological sub-plots.

45. Andrew Hadfield, 'Spenser, Drayton, and the Question of Britain,' *Review of English Studies*, 51:204 (2000): 582–599. The author employs this reading in arguing that *Poly-Olbion* seeks to problematize 'the question of Britain.'

46. Such an expectation may partially account for the bitter tone of the 1622 preface. In it, Drayton complains that Part I of *Poly-Olbion* has been largely

ignored despite the fact 'that there is scarcely any of the Nobilitie, or Gentry of this land, but that he is some way or other, by his Blood interressed therein' (IV:391). For more on the contemporary gentry interest in local history that Drayton seems keen to encourage, see Jan Broadway, *'No historie so meete': Gentry Culture and the Development of Local History in Elizabethan and Early Stuart England* (Manchester: Manchester University Press, 2006).

4 George Herbert and Caroline Religious Uniformity

1. Kevin Sharpe, *The Personal Rule of Charles I* (New Haven: Yale University Press, 1992), 331.
2. Such attempts, however, have yielded considerable variation. Izaak Walton, the poet's first biographer, claimed him rather nostalgically for the Laudians. Elizabeth Clarke, on the other hand, sees in Herbert 'The Character of a Non-Laudian Country Parson,' *Review of English Studies* 54:216 (2003): 479–496. Judith Maltby, in referring to Herbert as a 'model conformist parson,' comes down somewhere in between. '"By this Book": Parishioners, the Prayer Book and the Established Church,' in *The Early Stuart Church, 1603–1642*, ed. Kenneth Fincham (Stanford: Stanford University Press, 1993), 123.
3. Achsah Guibbory, *Ceremony and Community from Herbert to Milton* (Cambridge: Cambridge University Press, 1998), 44–78.
4. Annabel Patterson, *Censorship and Interpretation: The Conditions of Writing and Reading in Early Modern England* (Madison: University of Wisconsin Press, 1984), 33, 53.
5. Kenneth Fincham and Peter Lake, 'The Ecclesiastical Policies of James I and Charles I,' in *The Early Stuart Church*, ed. Fincham, 26.
6. These canons cover church membership, ordination, discipline, ritual, sacraments, visitations, courts, and other regulations related to the daily procedures of the English Church. For detailed analysis, see R. G. Usher, *The Reconstruction of the English Church*, 2 vols. (New York: D. Appleton, 1910), Vol. I, 385–390; Vol. II, 273–288.
7. On early Jacobean enforcement and its subsequent laxity, see Nicholas Tyacke, *Anti-Calvinists: The Rise of English Arminianism, c. 1590–1640* (Oxford: Clarendon Press, 1987), 185; also Kenneth Fincham, 'Clerical Conformity from Whitgift to Laud,' in *Conformity and Orthodoxy in the English Church, c. 1560–1660*, ed. Peter Lake and Michael Questier (Woodbridge, Suffolk: Boydell Press, 2000), 141. This does not mean, of course, that the Church stopped enforcement altogether and that local congregations were free to abandon both the Prayer Book and the 1604 Canons. It merely means that there was not a minute focus on following the letter of every canon. As a result, many ministers could get away with what Lake, Tyacke, and other Stuart church historians have called 'occasional conformity.' The Prayer Book was used and *most* canons were followed 'occasionally' rather than in every service. This might allow a more preaching-minded minister, for instance, to de-emphasize the role of church ritual in worship.
8. Peter Lake, 'Moving the Goal Posts? Modified Subscription and the Construction of Conformity in the Early Stuart Church,' in *Conformity and Orthodoxy*, ed. Lake and Questier, 202.

9. Patrick Collinson, *The Religion of Protestants: The Church in English Society, 1559–1625* (Oxford: Clarendon Press, 1982). Discussed by Fincham in his 'Introduction' to *The Early Stuart Church*, 5.
10. This shared Calvinist doctrine – centering on various notions of predestination – has been written about by Nicholas Tyacke, Julian Davies, Peter White, Peter Lake, and others.
11. Lake, 'Moving the Goal Posts,' 181. Lake argues that the practice was so widespread as to amount to a tacit assumption that was therefore hardly ever documented until some 'exceptional circumstances' brought it into the open (181–182, 203).
12. Fincham, 'Clerical Conformity,' 126.
13. Though it is also interesting to note that the impetus for conformity could sometimes originate at the local level. Maltby gives several examples of congregations presenting their own ministers. '"By this Book",' 119.
14. Fincham, *The Early Stuart Church*, 12.
15. Peter Lake, 'The Laudian Style: Order, Uniformity and the Pursuit of the Beauty of Holiness in the 1630s,' in *The Early Stuart Church*, ed. Fincham, 167–168.
16. See Sharpe, *Personal Rule*, 732.
17. Tom Webster, *Godly Clergy in Early Stuart England: The Caroline Puritan Movement, c. 1620–1643* (New York: Cambridge University Press, 1997), 191.
18. Julian Davies, *The Caroline Captivity of the Church: Charles I and the Remoulding of Anglicanism, 1625–1641* (Oxford: Clarendon Press, 1992), 62. In this passage, Davies is speaking of London Diocese prior to Laud's elevation to bishop in 1628.
19. Fincham, 'Clerical Conformity,' 127–129.
20. The growth of these practices is detailed in Collinson, *Religion of Protestants*, 242–283. According to Fincham, such a focus actually amounted to an alternative 'evangelical conformity.' 'Clerical Conformity,' 133.
21. Collinson, *Religion of Protestants*, 282.
22. Lake and Questier, *Conformity and Orthodoxy*, 123.
23. Ibid.
24. Judith Maltby, '"By this Book",' and John Fielding, 'Arminianism in the Localities: Peterborough Diocese, 1603–1642,' in *The Early Stuart Church*, ed. Fincham, 93–114.
25. Peter White, 'The *via media* in the Early Stuart Church,' in *The Early Stuart Church*, ed. Fincham, 212, 217. See also Sharpe, *Personal Rule*, 277.
26. And if the resulting consensus was still unsatisfactory, discontented parishioners could and did exercise other 'local options' of moving, patronizing lecturers, or going to church in other parishes.
27. Margaret Stieb, *Laud's Laboratory: The Diocese of Bath and Wells in the Early Seventeenth Century* (Lewisburg, PA: Bucknell University Press, 1982), 313.
28. On the tightening of conformity at the end of James's reign, see Davies, *Caroline Captivity*, 8, 63. Herbert was ordained as a deacon in 1626 and as a priest in 1630.
29. Lake, 'The Laudian Style,' 162.
30. Fincham and Lake, 'Ecclesiastical Policies,' 42.
31. Ibid., 24.
32. Sharpe, *Personal Rule*, 288.

33. Non-beneficed lecturers, Sharpe reminds us, tended to be more responsive to the wishes of their lay patrons than the church authorities. Ibid., 290.
34. Kenneth Fincham, 'Episcopal Government 1603–1640,' in *The Early Stuart Church*, ed. Fincham, 83.
35. Webster, *Godly Clergy*, 188, 202.
36. Sharpe, *Personal Rule*, 291.
37. Stieb, *Laud's Laboratory*, 284.
38. Ibid., 285–287, 305.
39. Ibid., 301.
40. Ibid., 302.
41. Webster, *Godly Clergy*, 250.
42. Tyacke, *Anti-Calvinists*, 224.
43. See Davies, *Caroline Captivity*, 80; Sharpe, *Personal Reign*, 348.
44. Davies, *Caroline Captivity*, 57.
45. Tyacke, *Anti-Calvinists*, 214.
46. Davies, *Caroline Captivity*, 20.
47. Quoted in Fincham and Lake, 'Ecclesiastical Policies,' 44.
48. Davies, *Caroline Captivity*, 21.
49. Sharpe, *Personal Rule*, 291.
50. *The Country Parson* was completed in 1632, but according to biographer Amy Charles, 'Herbert probably worked at *The Country Parson* during most of his time at Bemerton.' *A Life of George Herbert* (Ithaca, NY: Cornell University Press, 1977), 159.
51. Patterson, *Censorship and Interpretation*, 55.
52. That 1633 was the year of the new altar policy and the reissuance of the Book of Sports – two Laudian watershed events – has served to further cement this association.
53. Most historians now see the 1620s as the key decade for the rise of a formal Arminian party in England. Tyacke (*Anti-Calvinists*) specifically identifies the York House Conference in 1626 as a watershed moment. As Davies (*Caroline Captivity*, 24) points out, the 1641 Parliament also looked back on the mid-1620s (rather than 1629 or 1633) as the genesis of Arminian influence. Fincham and Lake ('Ecclesiastical Policies,' 38–40) view the King's religious preferences as 'ambiguous' from 1625–1629, but only because he was holding back to appease Parliament. For them, 1629 was the key year for Charles's emergent religious policies. Of course, the genesis of the Arminian movement can be dated much earlier. Tyacke refers to the Arminian disputes at Cambridge and Oxford in the 1590s (*Anti-Calvinists*, 29–86). For a detailed treatment of a local clash in the first decade of the seventeenth century, see Fielding, 'Arminianism in the Localities.'
54. Tyacke, *Anti-Calvinists*, 162. These debates were precipitated by Richard Montagu's publications of *A New Gagg for an Old Goose* (1624) and *Appello Caesarem* (1625). Herbert was actually an MP (for Montgomery borough) in the 1624 Parliament that petitioned *A New Gagg*, though Herbert's own viewpoint towards Arminianism at that time is difficult to ascertain.
55. Tyacke, *Anti-Calvinists*, 204–207.
56. Sharpe, *Personal Rule*, 143.
57. Kenneth Fincham (ed.), *Visitation Articles and Injunctions of the Early Stuart Church*, 2 vols. (Woodbridge, Suffolk: Boydell Press, 1998), Vol. II, 37. Davies

discusses the 1629 Instructions, though he is primarily interested in the question of their authorship. *Caroline Captivity*, 27.

58. Davies, *Caroline Captivity*, 27.
59. Webster, *Godly Clergy*, 187.
60. Tyacke, *Anti-Calvinists*, 181, 191.
61. Lake, 'Moving the Goal Posts,' 204.
62. Webster (*Godly Clergy*, 151–166) uses this prosecution as a case study of the new pressures to conform within the English Church. Thomas Hooker is also mentioned by Tyacke, *Anti-Calvinists*, 188.
63. Fincham, 'Episcopal Government,' 84.
64. Davies, *Caroline Captivity*, 295.
65. Ronald Cooley, '*Full Of All Knowledg*': George Herbert's Country Parson and Early Modern Social Discourse (Toronto: University of Toronto Press, 2004), 41.
66. Patterson, *Censorship and Interpretation*, 55–56.
67. Louis L. Martz (ed.), *George Herbert and Henry Vaughan: A Critical Edition of the Major Works* (New York: Oxford University Press, 1992), 190. All citations of *The Country Parson* are from this modernized-spelling edition. Subsequent page numbers are given in parentheses within the text.
68. Ibid., 479.
69. As they forestalled the initial attempt to publish *The Country Parson* in 1641, Laudian censors seemed to realize this as well. For their probable reasons – which don't seem to include Herbert's affinity for local variety – see Daniel Doerksen, '"Too Good for Those Times": Politics and the Publication of George Herbert's *The Country Parson*,' *Seventeenth-Century News* 49 (1991): 10–13. *The Country Parson* was finally published in 1652 by a Laudian apologist (of all people), Barnabas Oley.
70. In fact, Herbert frequently employs the words 'neighbour' and 'neighbourhood' when he is discussing parish socializing, evangelizing, charity, and perambulation.
71. Lake, 'The Laudian Style,' 166.
72. Ibid., 173, 167.
73. And for an early modern writer like Herbert, suggestiveness – or what Patterson calls 'inexactness' – is actually preferable to 'one-to-one correspondences' because it 'provid[ed] writers with an escape route if . . . "exceptions were taken".' *Censorship and Interpretation*, 55.
74. Herbert's approach may partially stem from issues of practicality and realism. That is, even if Herbert might have preferred elements of the Laudian program, he might balk at the practicality of the acceptance and effectiveness of a rigid uniformity (as he does with the parson's matrimonial state). But if so, Herbert doesn't seem to exhibit a sense of frustration that the Laudian ideal can't be adopted wholesale. On the contrary, there is a sense of artfulness and pleasure at making the appropriate choice throughout *The Country Parson*. Herbert seems to relish preaching and praying (for instance) as performative opportunities in which the parson carefully calculates his self-presentation (voice, gestures, etc.) to allure his audience and elicit a desired response.
75. The parson's handling of cases of conscience comes up in 'The Parson's Accessory Knowledges,' 'The Parson's Completeness,' 'The Parson's Eye,' 'The Parson in His House,' and 'The Parson's Library.'

76. For more on this fascination with 'circumstance' in the English Church of the 1620s and 1630s, see Reid Barbour's *Literature and Religious Culture in Seventeenth-Century England* (New York: Cambridge University Press, 2002), Introduction.

77. Gregory Kneidel's recent article probes the religious context of 'exactness' as part of Herbert's 'priestly vocabulary.' 'Herbert and Exactness,' *English Literary Renaissance* 36:2 (2006): 278–303. Local flexibility, I would argue, is a precondition for this parsonly aim to flourish.

78. Martz's endnote glosses 'country-duty' (Herbert's phrase) as 'national duty' (482). Such an interpretation, combined with the very next sentence's reference to bishops, suggests that Herbert has Church canons and other national religious directives in mind. The somewhat obsequious tone of the next sentence – '[the parson] carries himself very respectively, as to all the Fathers of the Church, so especially to his Diocesan, honouring him both in word and behavior' – suggests Herbert's awareness that he is walking a thin line.

79. Ramie Targoff, *Common Prayer: The Language of Public Devotion in Early Modern England* (Chicago: University of Chicago Press, 2001), 98.

80. Ronald Cooley has written incisively on this tricky passage, and my basic interpretation is indebted to him. Cooley also observes that the ambiguity of Herbert's formulation serves his own need to appeal to multiple audiences within the parish. 'John Davenant, *The Country Parson*, and Herbert's Calvinist Conformity,' *George Herbert Journal* 23:1–2 (1999/2000), 1–13 (9–10).

81. Other adjustments that Herbert leaves up to his parson include the frequency with which Communion is given (219) and the age at which children take their first Communion (218). The preponderance of such instances in *The Country Parson* (though most of them would, strictly speaking, be allowed by the higher authorities) suggests an approach to parish religion that affirms the value of local variation. Though Herbert doesn't directly challenge any major Laudian injunctions – this would have been extremely difficult in the religious climate of the 1630s – it is the consistency of Herbert's mindset and methodology of adaptation that presents a tacit challenge to the new conformity. It is not really that Herbert wants to be subversive; it is simply that Herbert's religious vision does not depend on uniformity in the same way that the Laudians' does.

82. Brian Vickers, *Francis Bacon and Renaissance Prose* (Cambridge: Cambridge University Press, 1968), 77.

83. *Outlandish Proverbs* are reprinted in *The Works of George Herbert*, ed. F. E. Hutchinson (Oxford: Clarendon Press, 1978), 321–355. Those mentioned in the text are (in order of occurrence) # 643, #181, and #168.

84. Diana Benet, 'Herbert's Proverbs: The Magic Shoe,' in *Like Season'd Timber: New Essays on George Herbert* ed. Edmund Miller and Robert DiYanni (New York: Peter Lang, 1987), 149.

85. Quoted in Vickers, *Francis Bacon*, 72.

86. Targoff, *Common Prayer*, 85–117.

87. Debora Shuger, *Habits of Thought in the English Renaissance* (Berkeley: University of California Press, 1990), 91–119.

88. For instance, Herbert dutifully stipulates in 'The Parson's Church' that 'all the books appointed by authority be there' but he is otherwise silent on their effective use (208).

89. While at Cambridge, Herbert also composed some Latin verse to defend the English Church from Puritan criticism. The *Musae Responsoriae*, Herbert's response to some of Andrew Melville's verses, does praise as well as defend specific rituals of the Church. However, it is difficult to evaluate their relationship to the argument that I am launching here. Since said rituals were somewhat loosely enforced when Herbert was writing (between 1620 and 1622) such praise does not necessarily equate with Herbert's full endorsement. In fact, differences between the *Musae* and *The Country Parson* may even reflect a shift in Herbert's attitude towards Church ritual (from specific praise to ambiguous moderation) once enforcement begins to tighten.

90. Unfortunately, the poem's composition cannot be dated with any certainty. 'The British Church' is one of those poems that Amy Charles judges 'would be hazardous to venture further in assigning specific dates to.' *A Life of George Herbert*, 87.

91. Martz, *George Herbert and Henry Vaughan*, 458–459.

5   Izaak Walton, Lucy Hutchinson, and the Experience of Civil War

1. This characterization is from Andrew Marvell's 'An Horatian Ode upon Cromwell's Return from Ireland,' line 30.

2. For more on Parliamentary retreat during the 1650s – particularly amongst the Presbyterian gentry – see J. T. Cliffe, *Puritans in Conflict: The Puritan Gentry During and After the Civil Wars* (New York: Routledge, 1988), 180–183.

3. Izaak Walton, *The Compleat Angler* (New York: Modern Library, 1937), 38. All citations of Walton are from this edition, with subsequent page numbers provided parenthetically within the text. The *Angler* was originally published in 1653, but was expanded significantly for a second edition in 1655. The third (1661) and fourth (1668) editions contain only minor alterations, but the fifth and final edition (1676) published in Walton's lifetime has substantial changes. Since the first three editions are not readily accessible to modern readers, I have chosen the Modern Library (4th) edition rather than the more commonly reprinted 5th edition because the former is basically a 1650s text while the latter is more of a Restoration text. For a complete textual history of these seventeenth-century editions, see John R. Cooper, *The Art of The Compleat Angler* (Durham: Duke University Press, 1968), 166–184.

4. *The Compleat Angler*'s generic variety has fueled a critical search to identify and explain the literary predecessors for these extra-fishing components. Cooper, for example, has separate chapters on the pastoral, georgic, and dialogue components of the work in *The Art of The Compleat Angler*. Meanwhile, Joe Snader argues that it is this very blend of 'didactic narrative' and 'scenes of pleasure and mirth' that has made the *Angler* so appealing to readers. 'The Compleat Angler and the Problems of Scientific Methodology,' *John Donne Journal* 12:1–2 (1993), 182.

5. Jonquil Bevan, *Izaak Walton's The Compleat Angler: The Art of Recreation* (Brighton: Harvester Press, 1988), 21. Steven Zwicker makes a similar claim that the book is 'an act of self-definition and consolation for the exiled and sequestered community of Stuart loyalists.' 'Hunting and Angling: *The Compleat*

Angler and *The First Anniversary*,' in *Lines of Authority: Politics and English Literary Culture, 1649–1689* (Ithaca: Cornell University Press, 1993), 64.

6. Thomas Weaver, Edward Powell, and Gilbert Sheldon, for example. By 1653, Walton had already written the biographies of two exemplary Anglican clergymen (Donne in 1640 and Wotton in 1651) and would go on to compose three others (for Herbert, Hooker, and Sanderson).

7. B. D. Greenslade, '*The Compleat Angler* and the Sequestered Clergy,' *Review of English Studies* 5:20 (Oct. 1954): 361–366.

8. Earl Miner, *The Cavalier Mode from Jonson to Cotton* (Princeton, NJ: Princeton University Press, 1971), 44–45, 304–305.

9. Zwicker, 'Hunting and Angling,' 68–74.

10. Cooper, *The Art of The Compleat Angler*, 47.

11. Ibid., 69. Bevan argues that the gypsies and beggars in the text 'call to mind the activities of the "Diggers" or "True Levellers".' *The Art of Recreation*, 110.

12. Theobalds was built by Lord Burghley in the sixteenth century, came into royal possession in 1607, and was eventually demolished during the Commonwealth.

13. Bevan, *The Art of Recreation*, 59.

14. Izaak Walton, *The Compleat Angler*, ed. John Buxton (Oxford: Oxford University Press, 2008), 342.

15. Marjorie Swann, '*The Compleat Angler* and the Early Modern Culture of Collecting,' *English Literary Renaissance* 37:1 (Winter 2007), 100.

16. Walton moved to London in 1611 at the age of 18 and maintained a residence there throughout the Civil War and Interregnum.

17. Piscator and Venator may be Latinized abstractions, but the vast number of other people who inhabit the text – including Thomas Wotton, Gilbert Sheldon, George Herbert, Thomas Wharton, John Donne, and Alexander Nowell – are real enough.

18. Walton always maintained close connections with Stafford. In the 1650s he bought farmland there and by 1655 was 'probably dividing his time between Clerkenwell and Staffordshire.' Bevan, *The Art of Recreation*, 17. One of the poems in *The Compleat Angler* actually mentions 'Shawford-brooke,' a branch of the River Sow that runs through land owned by Walton. Buxton (ed.), *The Compleat Angler*, 350.

19. P. G. Stanwood, *Izaak Walton* (New York: Twayne, 1998), 64–65.

20. Cooper, *The Art of the Compleat Angler*, 62–64.

21. Although all of Walton's five biographies – Donne (1640), Wotton (1651), Hooker (1665), Herbert (1670), and Sanderson (1678) – are useful in assessing *The Compleat Angler*, I will refer most frequently to the *Life of Wotton*. It is the only one published during the Civil War and Interregnum years and, as such, the one that most fully partakes of the historical milieu in which I am attempting to place *The Compleat Angler*.

22. Allan Pritchard, *English Biography in the Seventeenth Century: A Critical Survey* (Toronto: University of Toronto Press, 2005), 80–81. Walton's biography of Donne is the exception since 'Donne was entirely urban in his tastes and had refused rural preferments when they were offered him' (86).

23. Ibid., 81.

24. For instance, 21 of the 55 pages of the *Life of Wotton* are devoted to his Eton retirement, whereas only 13 pages describe his twenty years of diplomatic

service in Venice. Sanderson eventually became Bishop of Lincoln, while Hooker was appointed rector of the Temple Church and spent a lot of time in London.

25. Pritchard, *English Biography*, 83.
26. Ibid., 79.
27. Izaak Walton, *The Lives of John Donne, Sir Henry Wotton, Richard Hooker, George Herbert, & Robert Sanderson*, ed. S. B. Carter (London: Falcon, 1951). In subsequent citations, page numbers are provided in the text.
28. Pritchard, *English Biography*, 82.
29. Henley Bridge spans the Thames west of London, connecting Oxfordshire to Berkshire.
30. As many of the place references in the paragraph also reveal, Walton tends to follow chorographers in imagining counties as distinctive local units.
31. Walton even mentions 'Cambden' by name. See, for instance, pp. 193, 210. The verses from Drayton are taken from a sonnet in *Idea's Mirrour* (1594).
32. On the importance of practical experience in completing one's angling education, see also pp. 20, 130, 171, 190, and 206.
33. This argument also helps address the perceived disconnect between the piscatory and non-piscatory parts of the work that critics have long lamented. Cooper articulated 'the critical problem' in *The Art of the Compleat Angler* as a lack of artistic unity between the 'wholly practical and informative handbook' and 'those passages of narration, of pastoral description, and of moral and religious meditation wherein the charm of the book and its value as literature are felt to lie' (5). Marjorie Swann has recently suggested that forty years later little has changed: 'scholars who analyze *The Compleat Angler* as a conservative political work pay little attention to Walton's plethora of fish.' '*The Compleat Angler* and the Early Modern Culture of Collecting,' 100.
34. David Hill Radcliffe, '"Study to be quiet": Genre and Politics in Izaak Walton's *Compleat Angler*,' *English Literary Renaissance* 22:1 (1992), 97.
35. Zwicker, 'Hunting and Angling,' 89.
36. Radcliffe, '"Study to be quiet",' 110.
37. Cooper, *The Art of The Compleat Angler*, 74. Here, Cooper reads the *Angler* primarily through a pastoral lens in which the two main characters 'get their identity from the city' and move 'from city to country and back again.'
38. N. H. Keeble, 'Introduction' to *Memoirs of the Life of Colonel Hutchinson* (Rutland, VT: Charles E. Tuttle, 1995), xx. All citations of Hutchinson are from this Everyman's Library edition that is based on the original manuscript held in the Brewhouse Yard Museum in Nottingham. Subsequent page numbers are given in parentheses within the text.
39. Keeble, 'Introduction,' 2.
40. In considering the narrative content of the *Memoirs* in its own right, my analysis will supplement the recent critical focus on Hutchinson's status as a woman writer. See, for instance: David Norbrook, '"But a Copie": Textual Authority and Gender in Editions of *The Life of John Hutchinson*,' in *New Ways of Looking at Old Texts, III*, ed. W. Speed Hill (Tempe, AZ: Arizona Center for Medieval and Renaissance Studies, 2004), 109–130; Susan Wiseman, *Conspiracy and Virtue: Women, Writing, and Politics in Seventeenth-Century England* (New York: Oxford University Press, 2006), 179–233; Paul Salzman, *Reading Early Modern Women's Writing* (New York: Oxford University Press,

2006), 135–175; Sharon Cadman Seelig, *Autobiography and Gender in Early Modern Literature: Reading Women's Lives, 1600–1680* (New York: Cambridge University Press, 2006), 73–89.

41. According to the *Memoirs*, Thomas Hutchinson was arrested when Charles I 'had broken up a Parliament . . . and durst not trust those gentlemen . . . to return for some time to their own counties, for which they served' (40).

42. The contemporary title by which the work is known – *Memoirs of the Life of Colonel Hutchinson* – was only appended in 1806 by Julius Hutchinson, the first editor of the work.

43. This accident occurred just after the death of Margaret Hutchinson, John's mother. He was subsequently raised by her sister, Lady Ratcliffe, who 'had such a motherly tenderness toward him that he grew and prospered in her care' (38).

44. The Hutchinson estate of Owthorpe was located in the Vale of Belvoir, approximately 12 miles southeast of Nottingham (Keeble, *Memoirs*, 359). Bulwell was then a small town some 4 miles northwest of Nottingham.

45. In fact, before finally accompanying her husband into Nottinghamshire, Lucy Hutchinson, rather 'than to leave at once her mother and all the rest of her dear relations, had propounded to him to buy an office, which he was not of himself very inclinable to' (56).

46. Such evidence, even allowing for Lucy Hutchinson's subjectivity in labeling the Parliamentary side as the party of peace, seems to lend support to John Morrill's claim that many people across England were hesitant to get involved on either side. *Revolt in the Provinces: The People of England and the Tragedies of War, 1630–1648*, 2nd edn. (New York: Longman, 1999), 132–151.

47. For a sampling of Lucy Hutchinson's vituperative complaints against such people, see pp. 113, 115, 173, 183–184, and 192.

48. For other Royalist attempts to bribe John Hutchinson, see pp. 134, 142.

49. Lucy Hutchinson also begins the *Memoirs* with a long view of the political and religious developments that led to the English Civil War (pp. 57–75).

50. Robert Mayer sees these dilations as helping to establish Lucy Hutchinson's narrative authority and setting a 'pattern that she follows throughout the text, alternating between the narrative of her husband's life and an account of the larger events of which his (and her) life formed a part.' 'Lucy Hutchinson: A Life in Writing,' *Seventeenth Century* 22 (2007), 320, 314. But the space that she devotes to them as well as the qualifiers with which she introduces them seem to support Susan Cook's assertion that 'Lucy's intentions for these interludes, though, are always to explain them in terms of footnotes to her husband's history.' '"The Story I Most Particularly Intend": The Narrative Style of Lucy Hutchinson,' *Critical Survey* 5:3 (1993), 274.

51. For instance, she describes the groundswell of support for restoring the monarch thus: 'the town of Nottingham, as almost all the rest of the island, began to grow mad and declare themselves so in the desires of the King. And the boys, set on by their fathers and masters, got drums and colours and marched up and down the town, and trained themselves in a military posture, and offered many affronts to the soldiers of the army that quartered in the town' (275). She then goes on to describe a violent incident between the two parties.

52. '[T]he godly of those days,' Lucy Hutchinson complains, '. . . would not allow him to be religious because his hair was not in their cut nor his words in their phrase, nor such little formalities altogether fitted to their humour; who were, many of them, so weak as to esteem rather for such insignificant circumstances than for solid wisdom, piety, and courage' (87). Again, the author asserts the superiority of inner virtue over the external markers of party affiliation.
53. Cliffe, *Puritans in Conflict*, 197–201. Cliffe's appendix, 'A Catalogue of Leading Puritan Gentry Families,' lists the families who had estate revenue of £1,000 or more prior to the outbreak of the Civil War.
54. Ibid., 65.
55. Much of this timeline is drawn from the excellent 'Chronology' in the front of Keeble's edition, as Lucy Hutchinson hardly ever includes exact years.
56. Including the foresight to burn two houses near the fort at the edge of the bridge 'into which if the Cavaliers had put any men, they might have done much mischief to the assailants' (132).
57. On the morning of the assault, Hutchinson plants additional 'colours' and townsmen among the troops 'to make the better show' (131); later the Nottingham troops 'call[ed] to the Cavaliers in the fort, and [kept] them in abusive replies' while a small group of soldiers quietly crept in and disabled some of their defenses (132).
58. In fact, Lucy Hutchinson does begin her manuscript by writing an address 'To My Children,' a section of which is devoted to the abstract description of 'His Virtues.' This section breaks off abruptly – 'All this and more is true, but I so much dislike the manner of relating it that I will make another essay' (30) – implying a preference for the concrete examples of her husband's activities (that follow) rather than an abstract catalogue of his virtues.
59. For further analysis on these factors, see Keeble's note on p. 361. For more on the antagonism between rural gentry (the Hutchinsons) and urban elites (the Committee) that may have contributed to the Colonel's difficulties, see David Norbrook, '"Words more than civil": Republican Civility in Lucy Hutchinson's "The Life of John Hutchinson"', in *Early Modern Civil Discourses*, ed. Jennifer Richards (Basingstoke: Palgrave Macmillan, 2003), 68–84.
60. See, for instance, pp. 175, 182, 187, and 197.
61. For similar passages, see pp. 246, 300, and 303.
62. When the short-lived Second Civil War was about to break out in the spring of 1648, John Hutchinson turned down a second commission to resume his duties as Governor of Nottingham Castle. As it turned out, Nottingham did not play an important role in this conflict, though Oliver Cromwell did stop at the town (and was visited by John Hutchinson) on his way north to a victory at Preston.
63. This conclusion would certainly be supported by John Hutchinson's vexed experience with local office during the First Civil War.
64. According to Keeble, Lucy Hutchinson's emphasis on these pursuits is also part of her argument that her husband exceeds the Royalist gentlemen 'in precisely those accomplishments upon which Royalists prided themselves, which, indeed, they supposed distinguished their Cavalier culture from the vulgarity of all rebels and fanatics' (xxii). For more on John Hutchinson's art collecting – including his purchase of paintings from Charles I's dispersed

royal collection – see Linda Levy Peck, *Consuming Splendor: Society and Culture in Seventeenth-Century England* (New York: Cambridge University Press, 2005), 268–269.

65. Occasional conformity (described in the previous chapter) aided this goal, as when parts of the Prayer Book service were shortened to leave more time for preaching.

66. Keeble, *Memoirs*, 364.

67. Lucy Hutchinson reports that her husband 'had a great intimacy with many of these' and 'owned and protected them as far as he had power' (222).

68. The *Memoirs* makes a similar assertion when the Colonel's authority is later extended to the town of Nottingham: since 'the Parliament and generals had, at such a distance, been moved to put it unsought for upon it, it was a work which God called him to' (138).

69. For instance, when advised to quit his post at Nottingham and join the Parliamentary army (since the latter might later prove much more pardonable than to 'keep a castle against your King'), John Hutchinson 'was resolved to persist in the same place in which it had pleased God to call him to the defense of it' (122).

70. Although the religious claim that God calls people to specific tasks is not strictly a Puritan one, William Haller shows how it galvanized the Puritan movement and 'gave . . . to the general doctrine of God's calling a definite application.' *The Rise of Puritanism* (New York: Harper Torchbooks, 1957), 124.

71. Alexandra Walsham, 'The Godly and Popular Culture,' in *The Cambridge Companion to Puritanism*, ed. John Coffey and Paul C. H. Lim (New York: Cambridge University Press, 2008), 282.

72. Ibid., 282.

73. Hutchinson's characterization is typical of the seventeenth-century Puritan autobiographer, who is 'likely to be exclusively focused on those aspects of life which he takes to be directly relevatory of God's mercies.' Joan Webber, *The Eloquent 'I': Style and Self in Seventeenth-Century Prose* (Madison: University of Wisconsin Press, 1968), 13. The *Autobiography*, or 'The Life of Mrs. Lucy Hutchinson, Written by Herself,' is a manuscript fragment that was included in the first published edition of the *Memoirs* (1806) but is no longer extant. In Keeble's edition, it only runs to about thirteen pages.

74. Lucy Hutchinson's preoccupation with the relevance of 'little things' can also be seen in her engagement with Lucretian philosophy – she translated the entire *De rerum natura* in the 1640s and 1650s – and its commitment to the materiality of even those things we cannot see. See Jonathan Goldberg, 'Lucy Hutchinson Writing Matter,' *English Literary History* 73 (2006): 275–301.

75. As when, for instance, Waller's plot to deliver London to the King was brought to light just in time (105) and when the members of the disbanded Rump Parliament chose to 'submit to this providence of God' and take a wait-and-see approach (254).

76. N. H. Keeble, 'Puritanism and Literature,' in *The Cambridge Companion to Puritanism*, ed. Coffey and Lim, 313. On self-examination as a basic feature of Puritan religion, see Owen C. Watkins, *The Puritan Experience* (London: Routledge & Kegan Paul, 1972), 9–12. On the formative role of

conscience in the life and ministry of John Bunyan, a famed Puritan contemporary of the Hutchinsons, see Richard Greaves, *John Bunyan and English Non-conformity* (London: Hambledon Press, 1992), 70.

77. John Hutchinson entreats the 'double dealing' Mr. Millington 'to declare himself ingenuously as his conscience led him, though it should be against him' (171).

78. Hutchinson released some of the Parliamentary cannoniers who had been imprisoned for 'separating from the public worship and keeping little conventicles in their own chamber,' declaring that he 'was not satisfied in keeping men prisoners for their consciences so long as they lived honestly and inoffensively' (159, 167).

79. The most dramatic example is the Colonel's decision to assent to the King's execution (235), though, as we have already seen, he felt an internal prompting to join the Parliamentary side at one time but not another.

80. Lucy Hutchinson's approach to contingency may also owe something to her engagement with the 'mitigated skepticism' of Lucretian philosophy, as 'the Epicureans were considered preeminent exemplars of a careful and irenic method.' Reid Barbour, 'Between Atoms and the Spirit: Lucy Hutchinson's Translation of Lucretius,' *Renaissance Papers* (1994), 8.

81. In addition to instances where John Hutchinson uses his conscience with regards to the larger Puritan cause and his duties in Parliament, the *Memoirs* also mentions the consciences of Presbyterians, Royalists, the King, and those Parliamentarians who recanted their beliefs at the Restoration.

82. The entire episode (as well as the quoted material in this paragraph) can be found on p. 123.

83. Keeble includes this poem as an appendix in his edition of the *Memoirs* with the title: 'Verses: Written by Mrs. Hutchinson in the small book containing her own life, and most probably composed by her during her husband's retirement from public business to his seat at Owthorpe' (339–340).

84. Keeble translates this inscription: 'Away, keep far off, you profane people (Virgil, *Aeneid* VI.258),' *Memoirs*, 375.

85. Keeble, *Memoirs*, 375.

6   The Country House Poem and the Localization of Empire

1. At Haddon Hall in Derbyshire, for instance, the estate chapel also functioned as a parish church.

2. See, for example, William A. McClung, *The Country House in English Renaissance Poetry* (Berkeley: University of California Press, 1977), 28–45, 123–131; Malcolm Kelsall, *The Great Good Place: The Country House and English Literature* (New York: Columbia University Press, 1993), 32–48; James Turner, *The Politics of Landscape: Rural Scenery and Society in English Poetry, 1630–1660* (Cambridge, MA: Harvard University Press, 1979), 142–146; and Kari Boyd McBride, *Country House Discourse in Early Modern England* (Brookfield, VT: Ashgate, 2001).

3. A conventional critical reading of the genre. See, for example, Hugh Jenkins, *Feigned Commonwealths: The Country-House Poem and the Fashioning of the Ideal Community* (Pittsburgh: Duquesne University Press, 1998).

4. Alastair Fowler lists 'To Richard Cotton, Esq.' first in his book *The Country House Poem: A Cabinet of Seventeenth-Century Estate Poems and Related Items* (Edinburgh: Edinburgh University Press, 1994). Rather than use the standard editions for dozens of authors, all quotations, line numbers, page numbers, and dates will come from this book which conveniently combines these important poems into a single scholarly edition.
5. 'To Richard Cotton, Esq.' was first published in Whitney's *Choice of Emblemes* (1586). The modern facsimile reprint is *A Choice of Emblemes*, introduced by John Manning (Brookfield, VT: Scolar Press, 1989), and it is from this edition that the Latin motto translation is taken.
6. Kathryn Hunter, 'Geoffrey Whitney's "To Richard Cotton, Esq.": An Early English Country House Poem,' *The Review of English Studies* 28:112 (1977): 439–440.
7. William Smith's 1584 chorographical description of Cheshire observes: 'Likewise, doth every man keep certain Hives of Bees; but no greater store, commonly, than to serve their own turn; yet some do bring to the Market both Wax and Honey.' Daniel King, *The Vale Royale of England* (Little S. Bartholomews: John Streater, 1656), 18.
8. Hunter, 'Geoffrey Whitney,' 439.
9. Heather Dubrow, 'The Country-House Poem: A Study in Generic Development,' *Genre* 12 (1979), 162. The particularized landscapes of the country house poem probably originate with Virgil's *Georgics*. In fact, H. M. Richmond makes the *Georgics* the origin of a seventeenth-century 'rural lyricism' that often features particular places. '"Rural Lyricism": A Renaissance Mutation of the Pastoral,' *Comparative Literature* 16:3 (1964), 193–196. Alastair Fowler argues persuasively that the georgic mode is the key to unifying the otherwise irreconcilable variety found among English country house poem representatives. 'Country House Poems: The Politics of a Genre,' *The Seventeenth Century* 1:1 (1986): 1–14. Other classical models for the English country house poem include Martial's Epigram III.lviii and Horace's Second Epode. For a more complete discussion of these and other models, refer to Kelsall, *The Great Good Place*, 10–24.
10. Ever since Richard Harris set up a cherry orchard in Teynham in the 1530s, Kent had become famed for its fruit-growing. Drayton mentions cherries specifically when 'Saluting the deare soyle' of Kent in Song XVIII of *Poly-Olbion* (1612). Penshurst's 'walls . . . of the country stone' assert the estate's architectural continuity with the surrounding natural landscape and human dwellings. For more on country house architecture, see McClung, *The Country House*.
11. Richmond, 'Rural Lyricism,' 204.
12. For an alternate interpretation of the winter weather's significance, see Mary Ann C. McGuire, 'The Cavalier Country-House Poem: Mutations on a Jonsonian Tradition,' *Studies in English Literature, 1500–1900* 19:1 (1979), 99.
13. This aesthetic, as we shall later see, includes a delight in the importation and composite arrangement of foreign objects.
14. For a fuller treatment, see Dubrow, 'The Country-House Poem,' 176–177.
15. R. H. Tawney, 'The Rise of the Gentry, 1558–1640,' *Economic History Review* 11 (1941). The emerging money economy is also seen by Don

Wayne (*Penshurst: The Semiotics of Place and the Poetics of History* [Madison: University of Wisconsin Press, 1984]) as a tension in 'Penshurst'; by Charles Molesworth ('Property and Virtue: The Genre of the Country House Poem in the Seventeenth Century,' *Genre* 1 [1968], 141–157) as a factor in the Civil War, and by Marjorie Swann (*Curiosities and Texts: The Culture of Collecting in Early Modern England* [Philadelphia: University of Pennsylvania Press, 2001]) as an informing tenet of the Restoration country house poem.

16. Fowler, 'Country House Poems,' 12.

17. Felicity Heal and Clive Holmes, *The Gentry in England and Wales, 1500–1700* (London: Macmillan, 1994), 282–286.

18. See, for example, Herrick's 'The Hock Cart' (1648) and Marvell's 'Upon Appleton House' (c. 1654).

19. For a detailed explanation of this dynamic, see Molesworth, 'Property and Virtue,' 146.

20. Swann's *Curiosities and Texts* is particularly useful in demonstrating 'how collecting practices were used to imagine – and sometimes to realize – new forms of selfhood and social identity in seventeenth-century England' (12). See also Linda Levy Peck, *Consuming Splendor: Society and Culture in Seventeenth-Century England* (New York: Cambridge University Press, 2005), 186; Lorna Weatherill, *Consumer Behavior and Material Culture in Britain, 1660–1760*, 2nd edn. (New York: Routledge, 1996), 191; and Walter E. Houghton, Jr., 'The English Virtuoso in the Seventeenth Century,' *Journal of the History of Ideas* 3:1 (Jan. 1942), 63.

21. Nicholas Cooper, *Houses of the Gentry, 1480–1680* (New Haven: Yale University Press, 1999), 15.

22. McGuire, 'The Cavalier Country-House Poem,' 97.

23. Jyotsna G. Singh (ed.), *A Companion to the Global Renaissance: English Literature and Culture in the Era of Expansion* (Malden, MA: Wiley-Blackwell, 2009), 5.

24. Ibid., 2.

25. Ibid., 12.

26. C. G. A. Clay, *Economic Expansion and Social Change: England, 1500–1700*, 2 vols. (New York: Cambridge University Press, 1984), Vol. II, 138–139.

27. Peck, *Consuming Splendor*, 129, 135.

28. Alison Games, *The Web of Empire: English Cosmopolitans in an Age of Expansion, 1560–1660* (New York: Oxford University Press, 2008), 46.

29. Peck, *Consuming Splendor*, 151.

30. Ibid., 14.

31. Barbara Sebek, 'Global Traffic: An Introduction,' in *Global Traffic: Discourses and Practices of Trade in English Literature and Culture from 1550 to 1700*, ed. Barbara Sebek and Stephen Deng (Basingstoke: Palgrave Macmillan, 2008), 1.

32. Clay (*Economic Expansion*, 141) says that in 1602 London drew two-thirds of its imports from northwest Europe but by 1650 this number had shrunk to only one-third (140). Trade with Spain and the Levant was initially responsible for this decline, but 'it was the extra-European trades which were to make the running in the latter part of the century.'

33. Peck, *Consuming Splendor*, 3. The author also demonstrates that luxury consumption increased over the course of this period, despite the interruption of the Civil War (230–276).

34. Ibid., 216–217.

35. Ibid., 179–182.
36. The borrowings in these areas were 'not new' but 'gained momentum.' Ibid., 228.
37. Amy L. Tigner, 'The Flowers of Paradise: Botanical Trade in Sixteenth- and Seventeenth-Century England,' in *Global Traffic*, ed. Sebek and Deng, 138.
38. Peck, *Consuming Splendor*, 153.
39. Ibid., 358.
40. Singh, *A Companion to the Global Renaissance*, 2.
41. Blair Hoxby, *Mammon's Music: Literature and Economics in the Age of Milton* (New Haven: Yale University Press, 2002), 5–8.
42. Ibid., 1.
43. See Daniel Vitkus, 'The New Globalism: Transcultural Commerce, Global Systems Theory, and Spenser's Mammon,' in *A Companion to the Global Renaissance*, ed. Singh, 31–49; and Richard Kroll, *Restoration Drama and 'The Circle of Commerce': Tragicomedy, Politics, and Trade in the Seventeenth Century* (New York: Cambridge University Press, 2007).
44. Games, *The Web of Empire*, 9.
45. Peck, *Consuming Splendor*, 18.
46. Anna Neill, *British Discovery Literature and the Rise of Global Commerce* (New York: Palgrave Macmillan, 2002), 23. This was not a purely theoretical hope, as Anna Bryson has shown how the shift from 'courtesy' to 'civility' in English manners looked to continental – and especially Italian – models. *From Courtesy to Civility: Changing Codes of Conduct in Early Modern England* (New York: Oxford University Press, 1998).
47. Sebek, 'Global Traffic,' 10.
48. Hoxby, *Mammon's Music*, 2–3.
49. The first and third treatises were written by Thomas Munn; the second by Lewes Roberts. These and similar documents are available in J. R. McCulloch (ed.), *Early English Tracts on Commerce* (Cambridge: Economic History Society, 1952).
50. Sebek, 'Global Traffic,' 2.
51. See Bruce McLeod, *The Geography of Empire in English Literature, 1580–1745* (New York: Cambridge University Press, 1999), 90; Andrew Hadfield, 'The Benefits of a Warm Study: The Resistance to Travel Before Empire,' in *A Companion to the Global Renaissance*, ed. Singh, 102–103; and Sebek, 'Global Traffic,' 10.
52. See Peck, *Consuming Splendor*, 183; Gitanjali Shahani, '"A Foreigner by Birth": The Life of Indian Cloth in the Early Modern English Marketplace,' in *Global Traffic*, ed. Sebek and Deng, 180, 186.
53. Alison Games, 'England's Global Transition and the Cosmopolitans who made it Possible,' *Shakespeare Studies* 35 (2007): 24–31 (25).
54. Hadfield, 'The Benefits of a Warm Study,' 101.
55. Ibid., 103. Joyce Appleby draws a similar conclusion – 'Luxury was not a personal indulgence; it was a national calamity' – in 'Consumption in Early Modern Social Thought,' in *Consumption and the World of Goods*, ed. John Brewer and Roy Porter (London: Routledge, 1993), 166.
56. Sebek, 'Global Traffic,' 10.
57. Games, *The Web of Empire*, 8.
58. According to Clay, 'Never before had a war been fought so exclusively for economic reasons.' *Economic Expansion*, 189.

59. Games, *The Web of Empire*, 290–293, 298–299.
60. Linda Colley, *Britons: Forging the Nation, 1707–1837* (New Haven: Yale University Press, 1992), 56.
61. Hadfield, 'The Benefits of a Warm Study,' 103–104.
62. Lea Knudsen Allen, '"Not every man has the luck to go to Corinth": Accruing Exotic Capital in *The Jew of Malta* and *Volpone*,' in *Global Traffic*, ed. Sebek and Deng, 95–114.
63. Ibid., 107.
64. Tigner, 'The Flowers of Paradise,' 138.
65. McLeod, *The Geography of Empire*, 82. In this chapter, the author also discusses the country house as an emblem of colonization that involves similar strategies for taming, controlling, and ordering unruly forces.
66. Simon Schama, 'Perishable Commodities: Dutch Still-Life Painting and the "Empire of Things",' in *Consumption and the World of Goods*, ed. Brewer and Porter, 478.
67. Schama attributes this mindset to Barthes in 'Perishable Commodities,' 479. Although Schama goes on to critique this view and argue that such paintings also encode a critique of the vanity of worldly goods, his analysis – like Barthes's – arises from a careful reading of the symbolism and compositional arrangement of the particular objects in the painting.
68. Appleby, 'Consumption in Early Modern Social Thought,' 162.
69. Hoxby, *Mammon's Music*, 3.
70. 'By the time of the Civil War,' reports R. L. Greenall, 'it has been estimated that there were as many as 350 families of gentry in Northamptonshire, and the county had become famous for its country houses, which ranged from great Elizabethan "prodigy houses" down to the modest manor houses of the squires.' *A History of Northamptonshire* (London: Phillimore, 1979), 60. As Earl of Westmorland, Mildmay Fane's estate at Apethorpe was somewhere between these two extremes.
71. For a detailed biography, see Gerald Morton, *A Biography of Mildmay Fane, Second Earl of Westmorland, 1601–1666* (Lewiston, NY: Edwin Mellen Press, 1990).
72. In a similar passage in 'A Peppercorn or Small Rent,' Fane characterizes Campden House as a place 'Wherein I may survey at ease / What travellers by land and seas / With toil and trouble seek to gain, / Although at home I still remain' (lines 7–10). Later, he observes that the variety of this estate constitutes a 'sampler of the Creation' (line 161).
73. J. T. Cliffe, *The World of the Country House in Seventeenth-Century England* (New Haven: Yale University Press, 1999), 61.
74. Lucia Impelluso, *Gardens in Art*, trans. Stephen Sartarelli (Los Angeles: J. Paul Getty, 2005), 58.
75. Cliffe, *The World of the Country House*, 61.
76. Fowler, *The Country House Poem*, 231.
77. Ibid., 232.
78. Ibid., 231.
79. For the basic features of landscape sketched out in this paragraph, I am indebted to Henry V. S. Ogden and Margaret S. Ogden, *English Taste in Landscape in the Seventeenth Century* (Ann Arbor: University of Michigan Press, 1955).

80. Cooper, *Houses of the Gentry*, 324.
81. Turner, *Politics of Landscape*, 18.
82. Ibid., 5.
83. Fowler, *The Country House Poem*, 242.
84. For a more detailed technical description, see Ogden and Ogden, *English Taste in Landscape*, 37–40; and Turner, *Politics of Landscape*, ch. 1.
85. Ogden and Ogden, *English Taste in Landscape*, 40. H. V. S. Ogden, 'The Principles of Variety and Contrast in Seventeenth Century Aesthetics, and Milton's Poetry,' *Journal of the History of Ideas* 10:2 (Apr. 1949), 171.
86. Turner, *Politics of Landscape*, 14–15.
87. In the seventeenth century, 'enameling' was already a specialized decorative – and painterly – term. According to the *OED*, the term was applied to 'the process of entirely covering metals with enamel, to form a ground for painting in vitrifiable colours, or for any ornamental or economic purpose.' *OED online*, 'Enamel, v.' Entry 1.a.
88. Fowler, *The Country House Poem*, 248.
89. Heal and Holmes, *The Gentry in England and Wales*, 301.
90. Cliffe, *The World of the Country House*, 45. Cliffe lists the Dutch artist Jan Siberechts as an early practitioner of the former.
91. Ogden and Ogden, *English Taste in Landscape*, 160.
92. Ibid., 72.
93. Turner, *Politics of Landscape*, 10.
94. On this trend, see Olive Cook, *The English Country House: An Art and a Way of Life* (New York: Putnam, 1974), 58, 112. See also McClung on the role of professional architects in building country houses that '[bear] little or no relationship to the community around it.' *The Country House in English Renaissance Poetry*, 89–90.
95. Oliver Hill and John Cornforth, *English Country Houses: Caroline, 1625–1685* (Woodbridge, Suffolk: Antique Collectors' Club, 1985), 26. For a description of the basic features of Pratt's 'centrally planned house,' see Heal and Holmes, *The Gentry in England and Wales*, 301.
96. Thomas Fuller, *History of the Worthies of England* (London: T. Tegg, 1840), Vol. I, 6. Subsequent volume and page numbers included in the text.

Conclusion

1. Folger, STC 4503, copy 2.
2. Alexander Pope, 'Windsor Forest,' *The Poems of Alexander Pope*, gen. ed. John Butt, Vol. I (ed. E. Audra and Aubrey Williams, London: Methuen, 1961), pp. 149–150, lines 14–16.
3. Pope, 'Epistle to Burlington,' *The Poems of Alexander Pope*, gen. ed. John Butt, Vol. III-ii (ed. F. W. Bateson, 1951), p. 142, line 57.
4. Richard Helgerson, *Forms of Nationhood: The Elizabethan Writing of England* (Chicago: University of Chicago Press, 1992), 136, 146.

Select Bibliography

Adrian, John M., 'Itineraries, Perambulations, and Surveys: The Intersections of Chorography and Cartography in the Sixteenth Century,' in Yvonne Bruce (ed.), *Images of Matter: Essays on British Literature of the Middle Ages and Renaissance* (Newark: University of Delaware Press, 2005), 29–46.

Allen, Lea Knudsen, '"Not every man has the luck to go to Corinth": Accruing Exotic Capital in *The Jew of Malta* and *Volpone*,' in Barbara Sebek and Stephen Deng (eds.), *Global Traffic: Discourses and Practices of Trade in English Literature and Culture from 1550 to 1700* (Basingstoke: Palgrave Macmillan, 2008), 95–114.

Appleby, Joyce, 'Consumption in Early Modern Social Thought,' in John Brewer and Roy Porter (eds.), *Consumption and the World of Goods* (London: Routledge, 1993), 162–173.

Atkinson, T. D., *Local Style in English Architecture* (New York: Batsford, 1947).

Barbour, Reid, 'Between Atoms and the Spirit: Lucy Hutchinson's Translation of Lucretius,' *Renaissance Papers* (1994): 1–16.

— *John Selden: Measures of the Holy Commonwealth in Seventeenth-Century England* (Toronto: University of Toronto Press, 2003).

— *Literature and Religious Culture in Seventeenth-Century England* (New York: Cambridge University Press, 2002).

Bending, Stephen and McRae, Andrew, *The Writing of Rural England, 1500–1800* (New York: Palgrave Macmillan, 2003).

Benet, Diana, 'Herbert's Proverbs: The Magic Shoe,' in Edmund Miller and Robert DiYanni (eds.), *Like Season'd Timber: New Essays on George Herbert* (New York: Peter Lang, 1987), 139–150.

Bevan, Jonquil, *Izaak Walton's The Compleat Angler: The Art of Recreation* (Brighton: Harvester Press, 1988).

Brennan, Gillian, *Patriotism, Power, and Print* (Cambridge: James Clarke, 2003).

Brink, Jean, *Michael Drayton Revisited* (Boston: Twayne, 1990).

Broadway, Jan, *'No historie so meete': Gentry Culture and the Development of Local History in Elizabethan and Early Stuart England* (Manchester: Manchester University Press, 2006).

Bryson, Anna, *From Courtesy to Civility: Changing Codes of Conduct in Early Modern England* (New York: Oxford University Press, 1998).

Charles, Amy, *A Life of George Herbert* (Ithaca, NY: Cornell University Press, 1977).

Clark, Peter, *English Provincial Society from the Reformation to the Revolution: Religion, Politics, and Society in Kent, 1500–1640* (Hassocks, Sussex: Harvester Press, 1977).

Clarke, Elizabeth, 'The Character of a Non-Laudian Country Parson,' *Review of English Studies* 54:216 (2003): 479–496.

Clay, C. G. A., *Economic Expansion and Social Change: England, 1500–1700*, 2 vols. (New York: Cambridge University Press, 1984).

Cliffe, J. T., *Puritans in Conflict: The Puritan Gentry During and After the Civil Wars* (New York: Routledge, 1988).

— *The World of the Country House in Seventeenth-Century England* (New Haven: Yale University Press, 1999).

Colley, Linda, *Britons: Forging the Nation, 1707–1837* (New Haven: Yale University Press, 1992).

Collinson, Patrick, 'Biblical Rhetoric: The English Nation and National Sentiment in the Prophetic Mode,' in Claire McEachern and Debora Shuger (eds.), *Religion and Culture in Renaissance England* (Cambridge: Cambridge University Press, 1997), 15–45.

— *The Religion of Protestants: The Church in English Society, 1559–1625* (Oxford: Clarendon Press, 1982).

Cook, Olive, *The English Country House: An Art and a Way of Life* (New York: Putnam, 1974).

Cook, Susan, '"The Story I Most Particularly Intend": The Narrative Style of Lucy Hutchinson,' *Critical Survey* 5:3 (1993): 271–277.

Cooley, Ronald, *'Full Of All Knowledg': George Herbert's Country Parson and Early Modern Social Discourse* (Toronto: University of Toronto Press, 2004).

— 'John Davenant, *The Country Parson*, and Herbert's Calvinist Conformity,' *George Herbert Journal* 23:1–2 (Fall 1999/Spring 2000): 1–13.

Coones, Paul and Patten, John, *The Penguin Guide to the Landscape of England and Wales* (New York: Penguin, 1986).

Cooper, John R., *The Art of The Compleat Angler* (Durham: Duke University Press, 1968).

Cooper, Nicholas, *Houses of the Gentry, 1480–1680* (New Haven: Yale University Press, 1999).

Coward, Barry, *Social Change and Continuity: England, 1550–1750* (New York: Addison Wesley Longman, 1997).

Cressy, David, *Bonfires and Bells: National Memory and the Protestant Calendar in Elizabethan and Stuart England* (London: Weidenfeld & Nicolson, 1989).

Darby, H. C., *A New Historical Geography of England* (Cambridge: Cambridge University Press, 1973).

Davies, Julian, *The Caroline Captivity of the Church: Charles I and the Remoulding of Anglicanism, 1625–1641* (Oxford: Clarendon Press, 1992).

Dean, David, 'Locality and Self in the Elizabethan Lottery of the 1560s,' in Norman L. Jones and Daniel Woolf (eds.), *Local Identities in Late Medieval and Early Modern England* (Basingstoke: Palgrave Macmillan, 2007), 207–227.

Delano-Smith, Catherine and Kain, Roger, *English Maps: A History* (Toronto: University of Toronto Press, 1999).

Doerksen, Daniel, '"Too Good for Those Times": Politics and the Publication of George Herbert's *The Country Parson*,' *Seventeenth-Century News* 49 (1991): 10–13.

Drayton, Michael, *The Works of Michael Drayton*, 5 vols., ed. J. William Hebel (Oxford: Blackwell, 1931–1941).

Dubrow, Heather, 'The Country-House Poem: A Study in Generic Development,' *Genre* 12 (1979): 153–179.

Duffy, Eamon, *The Stripping of the Altars* (New Haven: Yale University Press, 1992).

— *The Voices of Morebath: Reformation and Rebellion in an English Village* (New Haven: Yale University Press, 2001).

Elsky, Martin, 'Microhistory and Cultural Geography: Ben Jonson's "To Sir Robert Wroth" and the Absorption of Local Community in the Commonwealth,' *Renaissance Quarterly* 53:2 (Summer 2000): 500–528.

Escobedo, Andrew, *Nationalism and Historical Loss in Renaissance England: Foxe, Dee, Spenser, Milton* (Ithaca: Cornell University Press, 2004).

Everitt, Alan, *Change in the Provinces: the Seventeenth Century* (Leicester: Leicester University Press, 1969).

— *Landscape and Community in England* (London: Hambledon Press, 1985).

— *The Local Community and the Great Rebellion* (London: Historical Association, 1969).

Finberg, H. P. R., *The local historian and his theme; an introductory lecture delivered at the University College of Leicester, 6 November 1952* (University College of Leicester, 1954).

Fincham, Kenneth (ed.), *The Early Stuart Church, 1603–1642* (Stanford: Stanford University Press, 1993).

— *Visitation Articles and Injunctions of the Early Stuart Church*, 2 vols. (Woodbridge, Suffolk: Boydell Press, 1998).

Fleming, Peter, 'Sir Thomas Cheyne, Lord Warden of the Cinque Ports, 1536–1558: Central Authority and the Defence of Local Privilege,' in Peter Fleming, Anthony Gross, and J. R. Lander (eds.), *Regionalism and Revision: The Crown and its Provinces in England, 1200–1650* (London: Hambledon Press, 1998), 123–144.

Fletcher, Anthony, *A County Community in Peace and War: Sussex, 1600–1660* (New York: Longman, 1975).

Fowler, Alastair, 'Country House Poems: The Politics of a Genre,' *The Seventeenth Century* 1:1 (1986): 1–14.

— (ed.), *The Country House Poem: A Cabinet of Seventeenth-Century Estate Poems and Related Items* (Edinburgh: Edinburgh University Press, 1994).

Fussner, F. Smith, *Tudor History and the Historians* (New York: Basic Books, 1970).

Games, Alison, *The Web of Empire: English Cosmopolitans in an Age of Expansion, 1560–1660* (New York: Oxford University Press, 2008).

Gleason, J. H., *The Justices of the Peace in England: 1558 to 1640* (Oxford: Clarendon Press, 1969).

Goldberg, Jonathan, 'Lucy Hutchinson Writing Matter,' *English Literary History* 73 (2006): 275–301.

Greaves, Richard, *John Bunyan and English Non-conformity* (London: Hambledon Press, 1992).

Greenslade, B. D., '*The Compleat Angler* and the Sequestered Clergy,' *Review of English Studies* 5:20 (Oct. 1954): 361–366.

Grundy, Joan, *The Spenserian Poets* (New York: St. Martin's Press, 1969).

Guibbory, Achsah, *Ceremony and Community from Herbert to Milton* (Cambridge: Cambridge University Press, 1998).

Hadfield, Andrew, 'The Benefits of a Warm Study: The Resistance to Travel Before Empire,' in Jyotsna G. Singh (ed.), *A Companion to the Global Renaissance: English Literature and Culture in the Era of Expansion* (Maiden, MA: Wiley-Blackwell, 2009), 101–113.

— *Literature, Politics and National Identity: Reformation to Renaissance* (Cambridge: Cambridge University Press, 1994).

— *Shakespeare, Spenser, and the Matter of Britain* (Basingstoke: Palgrave Macmillan, 2004).

— 'Spenser, Drayton, and the Question of Britain,' *Review of English Studies* 51:204 (2000): 582–599.

Haller, William, *The Rise of Puritanism* (New York: Harper Torchbooks, 1957).

Hardin, Richard F., *Michael Drayton and the Passing of Elizabethan England* (Lawrence: University Press of Kansas, 1973).

Harris, Victor, *All Coherence Gone: A Study of the Seventeenth Century Controversy Over Disorder and Decay in the Universe* (London: Cass, 1966).

Haydn, Hiram, *The Counter-Renaissance* (New York: Grove Press, 1960).

Heal, Felicity and Holmes, Clive, *The Gentry in England and Wales, 1500–1700* (London: Macmillan, 1994).

Helgerson, Richard, *Forms of Nationhood: The Elizabethan Writing of England* (Chicago: University of Chicago Press, 1992).

Hentschell, Roze, *The Culture of Cloth in Early Modern England: Textual Constructions of a National Identity* (Burlington, VT: Ashgate, 2008).

Herbert, George, *The Works of George Herbert*, ed. F. E. Hutchinson (Oxford: Clarendon Press, 1978).

Herendeen, Wyman H., *From Landscape to Literature: The River and the Myth of Geography* (Pittsburgh: Duquesne University Press, 1986).

Holmes, Clive, 'The County Community in Stuart Historiography,' *Journal of British Studies* 19:2 (1980): 54–73.

Horn, James, *Adapting to a New World: English Society in the Seventeenth-Century Chesapeake* (Chapel Hill, NC: University of North Carolina Press, 1994).

Houghton, Jr., Walter E., 'The English Virtuoso in the Seventeenth Century,' *Journal of the History of Ideas* 3:1 (Jan. 1942): 51–73, 190–219.

Hoxby, Blair, *Mammon's Music: Literature and Economics in the Age of Milton* (New Haven: Yale University Press, 2002).

Hughes, Ann, *Politics, Society, and Civil War in Warwickshire, 1620–1660* (Cambridge: Cambridge University Press, 1987).

Hutchinson, Lucy, *Memoirs of the Life of Colonel Hutchinson*, ed. N. H. Keeble (Rutland, VT: Charles E. Tuttle, 1995).

Hutton, Ronald, *The Rise and Fall of Merry England: The Ritual Year, 1400–1700* (Oxford: Oxford University Press, 1994).

Hyde, Patricia and Zell, Michael, 'Governing the County,' in Michael Zell (ed.), *Early Modern Kent, 1540–1640* (Woodbridge, Suffolk: Boydell Press, 2000), 7–38.

Impelluso, Lucia, *Gardens in Art*, trans. Stephen Sartarelli (Los Angeles: J. Paul Getty, 2005).

Jafri, S. Naqi Husain, *Aspects of Drayton's Poetry* (Delhi: Dobra House, 1988).

Jenkins, Hugh, *Feigned Commonwealths: The Country-House Poem and the Fashioning of the Ideal Community* (Pittsburgh: Duquesne University Press, 1998).

Johnston, Alexandra F. and Hüsken, Wim (eds.), *English Parish Drama* (Atlanta: Rodopi, 1996).

Jones, Norman L. and Woolf, Daniel (eds.), *Local Identities in Late Medieval and Early Modern England* (Basingstoke: Palgrave Macmillan, 2007).

Keeble, N. H., 'Puritanism and Literature,' in John Coffey and Paul C. H. Lim (eds.), *The Cambridge Companion to Puritanism* (New York: Cambridge University Press, 2008), 309–324.

Kelsall, Malcolm, *The Great Good Place: The Country House and English Literature* (New York: Columbia University Press, 1993).

Kightly, Charles, *The Customs and Ceremonies of Britain* (London: Thames & Hudson, 1986).

Kirk, Neville (ed.), *Northern Identities: Historical Interpretations of 'The North' and 'Northernness'* (Brookfield, VT: Ashgate, 2000).

Klein, Bernhard, *Maps and the Writing of Space in Early Modern England and Ireland* (New York: Palgrave Macmillan, 2001).

Kneidel, Gregory, 'Herbert and Exactness,' *English Literary Renaissance* 36:2 (2006): 278–303.

Kroll, Richard, *Restoration Drama and 'The Circle of Commerce': Tragicomedy, Politics, and Trade in the Seventeenth Century* (New York: Cambridge University Press, 2007).

Kumar, Krishan, *The Making of English National Identity* (Cambridge: Cambridge University Press, 2003).

Kumin, Beat, *The Shaping of a Community: The Rise and Reformation of the English Parish, c. 1400–1560* (Brookfield, VT: Scolar Press, 1996).

Lake, Peter and Questier, Michael (eds.), *Conformity and Orthodoxy in the English Church, c. 1560–1660* (Woodbridge, Suffolk: Boydell Press, 2000).

Lambarde, William, *A Perambulation of Kent*, ed. Richard Church (Bath: Adams and Dart, 1970).

— *William Lambarde and local government: his 'Ephemeris' and twenty-nine charges to juries and commissions*, ed. Conyers Read (Ithaca: Cornell University Press, 1962).

Levy, F. J., *Tudor Historical Thought* (San Marino, CA: Huntington Library, 1967).

Lewis, Christopher, *Particular Places: An Introduction to English Local History* (London: British Library, 1989).

Loach, Jennifer and Tittler, Robert (eds.), *The Mid-Tudor Polity, c. 1540–1560* (Basingstoke: Macmillan, 1980).

Loades, David, *Tudor Government* (Oxford: Blackwell, 1997).

Maley, Willy, *Nation, State, and Empire in English Renaissance Literature* (Basingstoke: Palgrave Macmillan, 2003).

Marshall, J. D., *The Tyranny of the Discrete: A Discussion of the Problems of Local History in England* (Aldershot: Scolar Press, 1997).

Mayer, Robert, 'Lucy Hutchinson: A Life in Writing,' *Seventeenth Century* 22 (2007): 305–335.

McBride, Kari Boyd, *Country House Discourse in Early Modern England* (Brookfield, VT: Ashgate, 2001).

McClung, William A., *The Country House in English Renaissance Poetry* (Berkeley: University of California Press, 1977).

McEachern, Claire, *The Poetics of English Nationhood* (Cambridge: Cambridge University Press, 1996).

McGuire, Mary Ann C., 'The Cavalier Country-House Poem: Mutations on a Jonsonian Tradition,' *Studies in English Literature, 1500–1900* 19:1 (1979): 93–108.

McLeod, Bruce, *The Geography of Empire in English Literature, 1580–1745* (New York: Cambridge University Press, 1999).

McRae, Andrew, *God Speed the Plough: The Representation of Agrarian England, 1500–1660* (Cambridge: Cambridge University Press, 1996).

— *Literature and Domestic Travel in Early Modern England* (Cambridge: Cambridge University Press, 2009).

Miner, Earl, *The Cavalier Mode from Jonson to Cotton* (Princeton: Princeton University Press, 1971).

Molesworth, Charles, 'Property and Virtue: The Genre of the Country House Poem in the Seventeenth Century,' *Genre* 1 (1968): 141–157.

Morrill, John, *Revolt in the Provinces: The People of England and the Tragedies of War, 1630–1648*, 2nd edn. (New York: Longman, 1999).

Morton, Gerald, *A Biography of Mildmay Fane, Second Earl of Westmorland, 1601–1666* (Lewiston, NY: Edwin Mellen Press, 1990).

Mottram, Stewart, *Empire and Nation in Early English Renaissance Literature* (Rochester, NY: D. S. Brewer, 2008).

Nearing, Homer, *English Historical Poetry, 1599–1641* (Philadelphia: University of Pennsylvania Press, 1945).

Neill, Anna, *British Discovery Literature and the Rise of Global Commerce* (New York: Palgrave Macmillan, 2002).

Norbrook, David, '"Words more than civil": Republican Civility in Lucy Hutchinson's "The Life of John Hutchinson",' in Jennifer Richards (ed.), *Early Modern Civil Discourses* (Basingstoke: Palgrave Macmillan, 2003), 68–84.

O'Callaghan, Michelle, *The 'Shepheard's Nation': Jacobean Spenserians and Early Stuart Political Culture* (Oxford: Clarendon Press, 2000).

Ogden, H. V. S., 'The Principles of Variety and Contrast in Seventeenth Century Aesthetics, and Milton's Poetry,' *Journal of the History of Ideas* 10:2 (Apr. 1949): 159–182.

Ogden, H. V. S. and Ogden, Margaret S., *English Taste in Landscape in the Seventeenth Century* (Ann Arbor: University of Michigan Press, 1955).

Patterson, Annabel, *Censorship and Interpretation: The Conditions of Writing and Reading in Early Modern England* (Madison: University of Wisconsin Press, 1984).

Peck, Linda Levy, *Consuming Splendor: Society and Culture in Seventeenth-Century England* (New York: Cambridge University Press, 2005).

Phythian-Adams, Charles, *Re-thinking English Local History* (Leicester: Leicester University Press, 1987).

Prescott, Anne Lake, 'Drayton's Muse and Selden's "Story": The Interfacing of Poetry and History in *Poly-Olbion*,' *Studies in Philology* 87:1 (1990): 128–135.

Prichard, Alan, *English Biography in the Seventeenth Century: A Critical Survey* (Toronto: University of Toronto Press, 2005).

Quinn, David B., 'James I and the Beginnings of Empire in America,' *Journal of Imperial and Commonwealth History* 2:2 (January 1974): 135–152.

Radcliffe, David Hill, '"Study to be quiet": Genre and Politics in Izaak Walton's *Compleat Angler*,' *English Literary Renaissance* 22:1 (Winter 1992): 95–111.

Raymond, Joad, *The Invention of the Newspaper: English Newsbooks, 1641–1649* (Oxford: Clarendon Press, 1996).

Richardson, R. C., *The Debate on the English Revolution Revisited*, 2nd edn. (New York: Routledge, 1988).

Richmond, H. M., '"Rural Lyricism": A Renaissance Mutation of the Pastoral,' *Comparative Literature* 16:3 (Summer 1964): 193–210.

Rowse, A. L., *The England of Elizabeth: The Structure of Society* (New York: Macmillan, 1951).

Sanford, Rhonda Lemke, *Maps and Memory in Early Modern England: A Sense of Place* (Basingstoke: Palgrave Macmillan, 2002).

Sawday, Jonathan, *The Body Emblazoned: Dissection and the Human Body in Renaissance Culture* (New York: Routledge, 1995).

Schama, Simon, 'Perishable Commodities: Dutch Still-Life Painting and the "Empire of Things",' in John Brewer and Roy Porter (eds.), *Consumption and the World of Goods* (London: Routledge, 1993), 478–506.

Schwyzer, Philip, *Literature, Nationalism, and Memory in Early Modern England and Wales* (Cambridge: Cambridge University Press, 2004).

Sebek, Barbara and Deng, Stephen (eds.), *Global Traffic: Discourses and Practices of Trade in English Literature and Culture from 1550 to 1700* (Basingstoke: Palgrave Macmillan, 2008).

Shahani, Gitanjali, '"A Foreigner by Birth": The Life of Indian Cloth in the Early Modern English Marketplace,' in Barbara Sebek and Stephen Deng (eds.), *Global Traffic: Discourses and Practices of Trade in English Literature and Culture from 1550 to 1700* (Basingstoke: Palgrave Macmillan, 2008), 179–200.

Sharpe, Kevin, *The Personal Rule of Charles I* (New Haven: Yale University Press, 1992).

Shepard, Alexandra and Withington, Phil (eds.), *Communities in Early Modern England: Networks, Place, Rhetoric* (Manchester: Manchester University Press, 2000).

Shuger, Debora, *Habits of Thought in the English Renaissance* (Berkeley: University of California Press, 1990).

Simmons, Jack, *English County Historians: First Series* (Wakefield: EP Publishing, 1978).

Singh, Jyotsna G. (ed.), *A Companion to the Global Renaissance: English Literature and Culture in the Era of Expansion* (Malden, MA: Wiley-Blackwell, 2009).

Smith, D. K., *The Cartographic Imagination in Early Modern England* (Burlington, VT: Ashgate, 2008).

Smuts, R. Malcolm, *Court Culture and the Origins of a Royalist Tradition in Early Stuart England* (Philadelphia: University of Pennsylvania Press, 1987).

Snader, Joe, '*The Compleat Angler* and the Problems of Scientific Methodology,' *John Donne Journal* 12:1–2 (1993): 169–189.

Spufford, Margaret, *Contrasting Communities: English Villages in the Sixteenth and Seventeenth Centuries*, 2nd edn. (Stroud: Sutton, 2000).

Stanwood, P. G., *Izaak Walton* (New York: Twayne, 1998).

Stieb, Margaret, *Laud's Laboratory: The Diocese of Bath and Wells in the Early Seventeenth Century* (Lewisburg, PA: Bucknell University Press, 1982).

Swann, Marjorie, '*The Compleat Angler* and the Early Modern Culture of Collecting,' *English Literary Renaissance* 37:1 (Winter 2007): 100–117.

— *Curiosities and Texts: The Culture of Collecting in Early Modern England* (Philadelphia: University of Pennsylvania Press, 2001).

Targoff, Ramie, *Common Prayer: The Language of Public Devotion in Early Modern England* (Chicago: University of Chicago Press, 2001).

Taylor, E. G. R., *Late Tudor and Early Stuart Geography, 1583–1650* (London: Methuen, 1934).

— *Tudor Geography, 1485–1583* (London: Methuen, 1930).

Thirsk, Joan, *Agricultural Regions and Agrarian History in England, 1500–1750* (Basingstoke: Macmillan, 1987).

Tigner, Amy L., 'The Flowers of Paradise: Botanical Trade in Sixteenth- and Seventeenth-Century England,' in Barbara Sebek and Stephen Deng (eds.), *Global Traffic: Discourses and Practices of Trade in English Literature and Culture from 1550 to 1700* (Basingstoke: Palgrave Macmillan, 2008), 137–156.

Tittler, Robert, *Architecture and Power: The Town Hall and the English Urban Community, c. 1540–1640* (Oxford: Oxford University Press, 1991).

— *The Face of the City: Civic Portraiture and Civic Identity in Early Modern England* (Manchester: Manchester University Press, 2007).

— *The Reformation and the Towns in England: Politics and Political Culture, c. 1540–1640* (Oxford: Clarendon Press, 1998).

Turner, James, *The Politics of Landscape: Rural Scenery and Society in English Poetry, 1630–1660* (Cambridge, MA: Harvard University Press, 1979).

Tyacke, Nicholas, *Anti-Calvinists: The Rise of English Arminianism, c. 1590–1640* (Oxford: Clarendon Press, 1987).

Tyacke, Sarah (ed.), *English Map-Making, 1500–1650: Historical Essays* (London: British Library, 1983).

Underdown, David, *Fire From Heaven: Life in an English Town in the Seventeenth Century* (New Haven: Yale University Press, 1992).

Usher, R. G., *The Reconstruction of the English Church*, 2 vols. (New York: D. Appleton, 1910).

Van Es, Bart, '"The Streame and Currant of Time": Land, Myth, and History in the Works of Spenser,' *Spenser Studies* 18 (2003): 209–229.

Vickers, Brian, *Francis Bacon and Renaissance Prose* (Cambridge: Cambridge University Press, 1968).

Vine, Angus, *In Defiance of Time: Antiquarian Writing in Early Modern England* (Oxford: Oxford University Press, 2010).

Walsham, Alexandra, 'The Godly and Popular Culture,' in John Coffey and Paul C. H. Lim (eds.), *The Cambridge Companion to Puritanism* (New York: Cambridge University Press, 2008), 277–293.

Walton, Izaak, *The Compleat Angler*, ed. John Buxton (Oxford: Oxford University Press, 2008).

Warnicke, Retha, *William Lambarde: Elizabethan Antiquary, 1536–1601* (Chichester, Sussex: Phillimore and Co., 1973).

Watkins, Owen C., *The Puritan Experience* (London: Routledge & Kegan Paul, 1972).

Wayne, Don, *Penshurst: The Semiotics of Place and the Poetics of History* (Madison: University of Wisconsin Press, 1984).

Weatherill, Lorna, *Consumer Behavior and Material Culture in Britain 1660–1760*, 2nd edn. (New York: Routledge, 1996).

Webber, Joan, *The Eloquent 'I': Style and Self in Seventeenth-Century Prose* (Madison: University of Wisconsin Press, 1968).

Webster, Tom, *Godly Clergy in Early Stuart England: The Caroline Puritan Movement, c. 1620–1643* (New York: Cambridge University Press, 1997).

Whitfield, Christopher, *Robert Dover and the Cotswold Games* (Evesham, Worcs.: The Journal Press, 1962).

Williams, Raymond, *The Country and the City* (New York: Oxford University Press, 1973).

Wrightson, Keith, *English Society, 1580–1680* (New Brunswick, NJ: Rutgers University Press, 1982).

Yates, Frances, *The Art of Memory* (Chicago: University of Chicago Press, 1966).

Zwicker, Steven, *Lines of Authority: Politics and English Literary Culture, 1649–1689* (Ithaca: Cornell University Press, 1993).

Index

New World, 2, 13, 77, 85, 161–2, 165, 166
  see also global expansion
Norfolk, 7, 83, 127
North of England, the, 34–5, 51, 83, 90, 135
  see also individual county entries
  see also Great Yarmouth; Norwich
Northamptonshire, 8, 45, 94, 141, 167, 177
Northumberland, 15, 19, 23, 35, 127, 128
  see also Newcastle
Norwich, 17, 20
nostalgia, 41–2, 70
Nottingham, 133–53
  chief object of Hutchinson's loyalty, 136–7
  in the First Civil War, 139–42
  in the Interregnum, 142–3
  Nottingham Castle, 134, 140–2
  reactions to the onset of war, 135–7
  in the Second Civil War, 142
  town magazine, 136, 140
  Trent bridge, 140–1, 153
  other references, 46, 49, 78, 173–4
Nottinghamshire, 1, 6, 176
  in the Civil War, 141
  and the Hutchinson family, 134–5
  reactions to Civil War, 135–7
  see also Nottingham

Odcombe, Somerset, 14
Ogden, Henry V. S. and Margaret S., 170–1, 174, 176, 216 n. 79, 217 nn. 84, 85, 91, 92
order
  in the Caroline church, 102, 108–9, 112–13
  as a gentry concern, 51–3
  and narrative method, 52, 57
  see also Perambulation of Kent; social harmony
Ortelius, Abraham, 12
Outlandish Proverbs (Herbert), 114
Owthorpe, Nottinghamshire, 134, 135, 137, 142
  contrasted with the national sphere, 143

as a local sphere of influence, 142–3
and the private conscience, 150–3
Oxford, 94, 120
Oxfordshire *see* Oxford; Woodstock

parish, 37, 44, 144
  and distinctive literary traditions, 8
  in Herbert's *Country Parson*, 96–119
  and local customs, 6
  and local government, 56, 57
  as a unit of local identity, 3, 4, 5, 10, 18, 45, 107–8, 110, 116
Parliament, 39, 169, 181
Parliamentarians *see* Civil War;
    Memoirs of the Life of Colonel Hutchinson; Puritans
particularization, 20, 63–9, 155
pastoral, 35–6, 125, 126, 131, 199 n. 24, 206 n. 4, 208 nn. 33, 37
Patterson, Annabel, 97, 104, 105
Peak district, 26, 34, 90–1, 94
Peck, Linda Levy, 162–3, 211 n. 64, 214 nn. 20, 27, 29, 30, 33, 34, 215 nn. 38, 39, 45, 52
Peirs, William, 101
'Penshurst, To' (Jonson), 154, 156, 158, 160
'Peppercorn or Small Rent, A' (Fane), 170
perambulation, 51–2, 59, 108
  see also Perambulation of Kent
Perambulation of Kent (Lambarde), 51–73
  anatomizing tendencies, 64–6
  basic organizational features, 57–8
  as a bid for social status, 54
  and the Church, 62
  and the county unit, 63
  gavelkind, 69
  historical lessons in, 60–1
  local distinctions, 63–4
  local government structures, 67–8
  particularization and decentralization, 57, 63–9, 70
  rebellions, 61
  the social order, 60
  treatment of history, 66–7
  uniformity and centralization, 57, 58–63, 70
  other references, 19, 74